MANAGING PEOPLE IN EDUCATION

Edited by
Tony Bush and David Middlewood

P·C·P
Paul Chapman
Publishing Ltd

Selection and editorial material, chapters 1, 4, 10, 12 and 13 Copyright © 1997,
Tony Bush and David Middlewood. Chapters 3, 9, 11 and 14 © as credited.
All other material © Paul Chapman Publishing.

Paul Chapman Publishing Ltd
144 Liverpool Road
London
N1 1LA

British Library Cataloguing in Publication Data

Managing people in education
1.Education – Personnel management
I.Bush, Tony, 1943– II.Middlewood, David
371.2'01

ISBN 1 85396 336 4

Typeset by Palimpsest Book Production Limited,
Polmont, Stirlingshire
Printed and bound in Great Britain

ABCDEFGH 987

CONTENTS

Series Editor's foreword   vii
Tony Bush
Preface   viii
Tony Bush and David Middlewood
Notes on contributors   xiii
Glossary of terms   xvi

Section A: Setting the scene
  1 The changing context of management in education   3
     Tony Bush
  2 Managing for people and performance   15
     Colin Riches
  3 The learning organisation   31
     Jacky Lumby

Section B: Organisational issues
  4 Management structures   45
     Tony Bush
  5 Management roles in education   61
     Valerie Hall
  6 Managing through teams   76
     John O'Neill

Section C: Individual issues
  7 Managing teachers' time under systemic reform   93
     Jim Campbell and Sean R. St J. Neill
  8 Managing stress in education   113
     Megan Crawford
  9 Managing for equal opportunities: the gender issue   123
     Marianne Coleman

Section D: The management of key processes

10 Managing recruitment and selection   139
    David Middlewood
11 Managing induction and mentoring   155
    Marianne Coleman
12 Managing appraisal   169
    David Middlewood
13 Managing staff development   186
    David Middlewood
14 Managing individual performance   203
    Keith Foreman

Author index   220
Subject index   223

SERIES EDITOR'S FOREWORD

The 1980s and 1990s have been decades of rapid and multiple change in the management of education. The international trend towards self-managing schools and colleges has greatly increased the demands on managers. Teachers well versed in curricular and pedagogic skills are having to exercise management functions for which they are often inadequately prepared.

The development of effective managers in education requires the support of literature which presents the major issues in clear, intelligible language while drawing on the best of theory and research. While there has been a big increase in books about aspects of school management in the 1990s, the literature is often characterised by description and prescription. The purpose of this series is to examine the impact of the many changes in the management of schools and colleges, drawing on empirical evidence. The approach is analytical rather than descriptive and generates conclusions about the most effective ways of managing schools and colleges on the basis of research evidence.

The aim of the series, and of this volume, is to develop a body of literature with the following characteristics:

- Directly relevant to school and college management.
- Prepared by authors with national and international reputations.
- An analytical approach based on empirical evidence but couched in intelligible language.
- Integrating the best of theory, research and practice.

Managing People in Education is the first volume in the series and it is underpinned by the philosophy that the effective management of all the people who work in schools and colleges is essential if the challenges of self-management are to be met and overcome. Effective managers are able to deliver high-quality education for children and students while providing both challenge and support for teachers and associate staff. The purpose of this book, and the series, is to provide guidance for teachers and managers seeking to develop their skills for the benefit of these pupils and students.

Tony Bush
University of Leicester
July 1996

PREFACE

People are the most important resource in any organisation. They provide the knowledge, skill and energy which are essential ingredients of success. Even in an era increasingly dominated by technology, what differentiates effective and ineffective organisations are the quality and commitment of the people who work there.

In education, the focus on people is particularly significant. Schools, colleges and universities have the demanding and vital role of developing the potential of children and young people. To do this successfully requires more than a firm grasp of subject knowledge and pedagogy. It also needs a sensitive understanding of the individual circumstances, foibles and potential of each pupil or student. Successful teachers invariably develop good relationships with their charges because they know that effective learning depends on mutual respect.

Education provides a unique management challenge because it is geared to the development of human potential. The aims or 'mission statements' of most schools and colleges stress the need to value children and students as individuals to help them to develop intellectually and socially. Educational institutions are 'people centred' because young people are at the heart of their business.

The development of a climate geared to effective learning and teaching cannot be achieved without sensitive management of the people who work in schools and colleges. Valuing children and young people as individuals is a necessary, but insufficient, condition for success. Consideration for the adults who work in the institution is essential if the emphasis on care for students is not to be exposed as meaningless, or hypocritical, rhetoric.

The management of people is an established element in the curriculum of most advanced courses in educational management as it is in general management programmes. However, there is a surprising dearth of literature on this topic as it applies to education. In particular, there are few books which deal with human resource management in self-managing schools and colleges. The introduction of local management of schools

(LMS), grant-maintained status (GMS) and incorporation of colleges, and their international equivalents, locates the responsibility for staff management firmly with the principal, senior staff and governors. This volume examines the management of people within this context of self-management.

The title of this book has been chosen to reflect the editors' view that people are at the centre of quality schools and colleges. The fashionable term 'human resource management' depersonalises teachers and associate staff, appearing to regard them as inputs little different from material resources. Sensitive management of people as individuals with different personalities, backgrounds and personal and professional needs is a vital dimension in the development of successful organisations.

The shift to self-management is a significant element of a constantly changing educational landscape. School and college staff have had to absorb substantial and continual change in curriculum, assessment, finance, governance and evaluation. In the overtly political climate which has spawned these innovations, the frequent pleas for a period of stability are likely to fall on deaf ears. Managers need to accept change as the norm and to develop strategies to harness the best features of imposed change for the benefit of children and students. This, in turn, requires high-order management of staff so that they are stimulated rather than demoralised by the frequent shifts in educational policy.

The chapters in this book examine the implications of educational change for the management of all the people who work in schools and colleges. Teachers have traditionally been regarded as the key resource in education but the role of associate staff has become increasingly important in the 1990s. This is partly because schools and colleges have employed more staff in a variety of roles as they have taken on many management responsibilities formerly exercised on their behalf by local or central government. The previous rigid distinctions between teaching and non-teaching staff have been replaced in many institutions by a more flexible approach. Associate staff are assuming some of the tasks, inside and outside the classroom, previously regarded as the preserve of teachers. The editors welcome many of these changes and the specific topics featured in this book apply to both education professionals and para-professionals. Indeed, distinguishing between the two groups would negate the principle, inherent in the title, that *all* people are entitled to effective and sensitive management.

An important overarching theme in the management of people is that of equal opportunities. Despite the legal position in many countries, this issue remains problematic in education as elsewhere. The ostensible commitment to equality, manifested in mission statements and in job advertisements, has not been matched by a significant improvement in the proportion of women, or black people, or the disabled, in the management of schools or colleges. The editors' view is that the aspiration for equal opportunities needs to be matched by appropriate management strategies if disadvantage is to be overcome.

The philosophy of this book is to harness relevant research and theory in order to enhance management practice in education. There is a body of literature which prescribes 'best practice' for managers but provides little empirical support for such prescriptions. There are also books describing practice but lacking analysis or synthesis. The editors' intention is to articulate good practice on the basis of evidence in educational settings. The ideas presented in this volume are derived from international research and practice and apply to all phases of education. The emphasis is on applying research findings to improve practice in schools and colleges. All fourteen chapters have been specifically commissioned for this volume.

The book is organised in four sections which each address broad aspects of the management of people. Section A, 'Setting the scene', deals with the context for human resource management. In Chapter 1, Tony Bush discusses the changing context of management in education. The radical shift in the nature of employment in many countries has profound implications for the educational process. While there are continuing pressures to link education to the world of work, a focus on specific skills linked to a single industry leads to a serious risk of obsolescence. The author examines the implications for the management of people of the international trend towards self-managing schools and colleges. Governors and senior managers now take full responsibility for the management of staff. Effective management of people requires an active approach to equal opportunities and a recognition that associate staff have the same entitlements as teachers and lecturers. He concludes by asserting that a genuine concern for staff welfare is just as important as organisational effectiveness.

In Chapter 2, Colin Riches revisits the debate about whether to give primacy to performance or the needs of staff. The pressure to produce results has intensified as governments seek educational improvement to underpin economic growth. He argues that motivating and developing staff are essential elements in the achievement of effective performance in education.

Jacky Lumby, in Chapter 3, describes the learning organisation, a concept which acknowledges that the effective performance of any organisation is achieved through a commitment to the personal development of all staff. She argues that a commitment to learning for staff is wholly consistent with a focus on learning and teaching for pupils and students.

Section B, 'Organisational issues', focuses on those organisational devices which facilitate the effective management of organisations. In Chapter 4, Tony Bush examines the purpose and relevance of structures in education. He shows that most institutions adopt bureaucratic structures but argues that the more flexible structures now prevalent in further education, and the 'flatter' structures of many primary schools, indicate a recognition that hierarchy may not be the most appropriate way to structure educational organisations.

In Chapter 5, Valerie Hall discusses the concept of role and its application to education. She argues that many of the current assumptions about management roles lead to conflict and ambiguity but suggests that a greater emphasis on self-development provides the potential for individuals to shape their own roles regardless of the organisational structure.

John O'Neill, in Chapter 6, challenges the conventional approach to working in teams, arguing that these models underestimate the potential and reality of conflict in organisations. Differences of view are inevitable and should be regarded as a healthy element in effective teamwork. A nominal team approach may be ineffective in schools and colleges where the central professional task involves individual work with young people.

In Section C, the focus is on the main 'Individual issues' affecting the management of people. The pressure for improved performance with static or diminishing resources has led to increased demands on staff time in many countries. The research carried out by Jim Campbell and Sean Neill is reported in Chapter 7. They demonstrate that school teachers in England and Wales spend far more time on professional work than their contract requires. This 'overwork' arises primarily from teacher conscientiousness, reflecting commitment to children and young people.

Working long hours in a people-centred occupation provides an obvious potential for stress. As Megan Crawford demonstrates in Chapter 8, stress and its effective management are significant issues in many schools and colleges. The rapid and multiple policy changes of the 1980s and 1990s have increased levels of stress and many more teachers and managers have been unable to cope with these pressures. She concludes by arguing that managers need to adopt positive strategies for minimising and handling severe stress.

In Chapter 9, Marianne Coleman refers to the importance of equal opportunities in education and illustrates the main issues with respect to gender. She demonstrates that women are relatively weakly represented in management positions in education and analyses the main causes of disadvantage. She argues that managers have a responsibility to adopt an active approach to the promotion of equal opportunities in education.

The final section of the book, 'The management of key processes', addresses five of the central issues in the management of people. In Chapter 10, David Middlewood examines the management of recruitment and selection. He argues that the enhanced emphasis on performance increases the importance of effective recruitment and selection. He points to the research evidence showing that selection procedures are ineffective in many countries and sets out a strategy for the management of recruitment and selection.

Marianne Coleman, in Chapter 11, demonstrates the value of effective induction and mentoring as a dimension of staff management in education. She argues that induction is essential not only for new entrants to the teaching profession but for all staff new to organisations. She notes the increasing importance of mentoring in many countries and concludes that a mentoring culture often develops in successful organisations.

Appraisal has become an important process in many countries and has the potential to link the performance and people dimensions of management. David Middlewood, in Chapter 12, shows that appraisal relates to improving individual performance and to greater organisational effectiveness. He argues that effective management of appraisal in education includes setting an appropriate climate, ensuring links with development plans and effective monitoring and evaluation of the process.

In Chapter 13, David Middlewood examines the management of staff development in education. He argues the need for an inclusive approach which involves all staff in the development process. He examines the purposes of staff development and considers the tensions inherent in trying to meet a range of needs in the organisation.

The final chapter, by Keith Foreman, examines the critical issue of the management of individual performance. Government pressures to improve standards in many countries have clear implications for the performance of individual teachers and raise critical issues about the assessment, management and motivation of performance. Underperformance is a significant preoccupation of government agencies in England and Wales and elsewhere and the author examines the pressure for firm action and the implications for incompetent performers. He also examines the case for performance-related pay and assesses its efficacy in raising standards.

The final paragraphs of the book stress the need for managers to recognise that teachers and associate staff are individuals with emotions as well as rational minds. This reinforces the editors' view that *Managing People* is the appropriate title for this book because human beings are more than 'resources' to be managed.

The editors are grateful for the co-operation of the authors whose work is featured in this book. We also wish to thank Christopher Bowring-Carr for preparing the Index. We are also grateful to Joyce Palmer and other colleagues in EMDU for their work in producing the manuscript of this book.

Tony Bush and David Middlewood
July 1996

NOTES ON CONTRIBUTORS

Tony Bush is Professor of Educational Management and Director of the Educational Management Development Unit at the University of Leicester. He was formerly a teacher in secondary schools and colleges and a professional officer with a local education authority. He was senior lecturer in educational policy and management at the Open University before joining Leicester in January 1992. He has published extensively on several aspects of educational management. His main recent books are *Managing Autonomous Schools: The Grant Maintained Experience* (1993; with M. Coleman and D. Glover; Paul Chapman), *The Principles of Educational Management* (1994; with J. West-Burnham; Longman) and *Theories of Educational Management* (second edition, 1995; Paul Chapman).

Jim Campbell is Professor of Education and Director of the Institute of Education at the University of Warwick. He has taught in primary and secondary schools, and is the editor of *Education 3–13*. His publications include *Developing the Primary School Curriculum* (Cassell; 1985), *Humanities in the Primary School* (Falmer; 1989) and *Breadth and Balance in the Primary Curriculum* (Falmer; 1993).

With his colleague Sean Neill he conducted the Teaching as Work project, the findings of which were published in four volumes: *Primary Teachers at Work* (Routledge; 1994), *Secondary Teachers at Work* (Routledge; 1994), *The Meaning of Infant Teachers' Work* (Routledge; 1994) and *Curriculum Reform at Key Stage 1: Teacher Commitment and Policy Failure* (Longman; 1994). He is National President of the Education Section of the British Association for the Advancement of Science (1996) and was National Chair (1991–4) of the Association for the Study of Primary Education.

Marianne Coleman is a lecturer in educational management and Director of Distance Learning at the Educational Management Development Unit of the School of Education of the University of Leicester.

She has had extensive experience in secondary education including working for the advisory service of a large LEA. Her main research interests include women in educational management and the mentoring of headteachers. She is co-author with Tony Bush and Derek Glover of *Managing Autonomous Schools: The Grant Maintained Experience* (Paul Chapman; 1993).

Megan Crawford worked as a teacher and deputy headteacher in primary schools both in London and the south east for eleven years. She joined the Open University in 1990, and currently works as a lecturer in the Centre for Educational Policy and Management. Her research interests include all aspects of human resource management, and in particular stress management, non-teaching staff and managing change.

Keith Foreman was the principal of two community colleges in Cambridgeshire and Leicestershire before joining the Educational Management Development Unit of Leicester University in 1994 as Senior Tutor. He is a consultant to schools and LEAs, and was a member of the DES School Management Task Force from 1989 to 1992. His research interests lie in the broad field of school leadership.

Valerie Hall is a senior lecturer in human resource management at the National Development Centre for Educational Management and Policy at the University of Bristol. She currently manages the taught doctor of education programme at the University of Bristol, the first of its kind in Europe. She has taught in schools, colleges and universities for over thirty years. During the past twenty years she has been involved in a number of research projects, including the POST project looking at the selection of secondary heads, the CROSH project (changing role of the secondary head) and the SMT project (senior management teams in secondary schools). Her latest book *Dancing on the Ceiling: A Study of Women Managers in Education* (Paul Chapman; 1996) describes her study of education management from a gender perspective.

Jacky Lumby is a Lecturer in educational management in the Educational Management Development Unit at the University of Leicester. She has wide experience of education having taught and held a variety of responsibilities in secondary schools, adult and community education, and most recently in further education. She has also worked within the field of management development in a Training and Enterprise Council. Her special interests are the management of the vocational education and competence-based approaches to education and training.

David Middlewood is Senior Tutor in Educational Management, responsible for school and college-based programmes at the Educational Management Development Unit of the University of Leicester. He taught in schools and community colleges for twenty-five years, including nine years as a headteacher, before joining Leicester University in 1990. His special interests are appraisal (in which he has extensive research experience), staff development and management structures. His publications include work on appraisal, human resources and development planning.

Sean R. St J. Neill is a senior lecturer at the University of Warwick. In addition to studies of teachers' workloads, he has recently been involved with colleagues in the Policy Analysis Unit at Warwick in two studies of grant-maintained schools and a study of the effect of the introduction of the Code of Practice for special educational needs. He is the author of *Classroom Nonverbal Communication* (Routledge, 1991) and (with Chris Caswell) of *Body Language for Competent Teachers* (Routledge, 1993).

John O'Neill teaches educational management at Massey University in New Zealand. Previously he held a similar post with Leicester University. He is currently engaged in doctoral research on the role of the secondary school head of department. His publications include *Effective Curriculum Management, Co-ordinating Learning in the Primary School* (edited with Neil Kitson; Routledge; 1996). He was also co-author (with David Middlewood and Derek Glover) of *Managing Human Resources in Schools and Colleges* (Longman; 1994).

Colin Riches is a lecturer in educational management in the Centre for Education Policy and Management at the Open University. He has a wide experience of teaching, having taught in special schools, a secondary school, colleges of FE and education and a polytechnic, prior to joining the Open University. He has written extensively on human resource management issues and skills for educational management courses and has special interest in leadership, interviewing and support staff in education. Among other publications he has edited (jointly with C. Morgan; Open University Press; 1989) *Human Resource Management in Education*.

GLOSSARY OF TERMS

DES	Department of Education and Science
DfEE	Department for Education and Employment
ERA	Education Reform Act 1988
FEDA	Further Education Development Agency
FEFC	Further Education Funding Council
GM	Grant maintained
Headlamp	Headteacher Leadership and Management Programme
HEI	Higher education institution
HMCI	Her Majesty's Chief Inspector of Schools
HMI	Her Majesty's Inspectorate
HRM	Human resource management
INSET	In-service education and training (of teachers)
ITE	Initial teacher education
LEA	Local education authority
LMS	Local management of schools
MCI	Management Charter Initiative
NC	National Curriculum
NCE	National Commission for Education
NFER	National Foundation for Educational Research
NPQH	National Professional Qualification for Headship
NQT	Newly qualified teacher
NVQ	National Vocational Qualification
OECD	Organisation for Economic Co-operation and Development
Ofsted	Office for Standards in Education
PI	Performance indicator
PIT	Pool of inactive teachers
PRP	Performance-related pay
SMT	Senior management team
SMTF	School Management Task Force
TTA	Teacher Training Agency
TQM	Total quality management

Section A: setting the scene

The three chapters in this section each acknowledge the need for continual reappraisal and awareness of the wider context within which managers of people operate. In Chapter 1, Tony Bush describes some of the issues affecting this context and how they impinge on the work of managers. As schools and colleges take responsibility for their own management, there have been new pressures and challenges. Many of these have strong personal implications, including pay and promotion, security, stress and motivation, for the people who work in them.

Colin Riches, in Chapter 2, revisits the debate about the tension between the dual demands upon managers – to support people and to do so in a way which produces effective results. He argues that genuine HRM concepts and principles can provide the means by which managers sustain support for people to achieve effective performance in their organisation. In Chapter 3, Jacky Lumby describes and debates the learning organisation, a concept which acknowledges that effective performance of an organisation is achieved through a commitment to the constant self-development of all the people who work in it. This concept, as she points out, should be particularly apt for organisations where the key purpose is learning itself.

1

THE CHANGING CONTEXT OF MANAGEMENT IN EDUCATION

Tony Bush

INTRODUCTION: THE CHANGING CONTEXT OF WORK

As we approach the new millennium there are few certainties in the world of work. The global nature of the economy, and the rapid pace of technological development, force changes in the workplace that would have been unimaginable just a few decades ago. 'Jobs for life' are as rare now as they were commonplace in the 1950s and this means a radical reappraisal of the nature of work and its place in people's lives.

Handy (1994) draws attention to the contrast between those who have 'proper' jobs and those who are on the fringe, with poorly paid, often part-time, employment; 'bits and pieces of pocket-money work'. He points to the dilemma of economic growth being increasingly underpinned by this low-wage philosophy: 'America, in the years from 1973 to 1989, managed to create 32 million net new jobs . . . but it was mostly hamburger work for hamburger pay' (Handy, 1994, p. 8). In contrast with this economic underclass is the remaining group of people in full-time employment who continue to enjoy good pay and conditions but in a climate of high pressure to perform. The 'shakeout' of employees means that those remaining must work harder, to sustain output and to demonstrate the commitment necessary to provide a (partial) guarantee that their heads will not be the next on the block.

Handy (1994) points out that such 'totally consuming' jobs are not for everyone. They tend to exclude other aspects of life, including family and hobbies, and may create other problems for society. There is also the very real risk of 'burnout' as the stress of the long hours, high pressure and insecurity begin to affect performance. Megan Crawford examines some of the dysfunctional consequences of stress in Chapter 8 but the wider issue is the problem of society fragmenting into the 'haves' with good, well paid but insecure jobs, and the 'have-nots' who are unemployed, underemployed or working for low wages.

The impact of these changes on education have been limited but seem certain to become more profound in the future. Preparation for the world of work is a powerful imperative for education, with a significant impact on both the aims and content of the curriculum. Lofthouse (1994, p. 144) refers to this vocational approach with its

> emphasis placed on instrumental values where the needs of the individual are subordinated to the requirements of society. Employment and enterprise are perceived as vital to the growth of a free-enterprise society. With over-riding weight placed on individual survival through employment, vocational definitions of the curriculum stress the transmission of useful knowledge.

A fundamental problem with this approach is that the precise nature of a work-related curriculum is difficult to define in the context of such rapidly changing work patterns. Flexibility and transferable skills may be more important than specific knowledge focused on a single industry. This has particular salience for further education but is relevant for all sectors. The decline of the coal, shipbuilding and textile industries, for example, exposes graphically the limitations of a specific vocational curriculum and the human consequences of non-transferable skills.

Schools have been relatively sheltered from the impact of employee 'shakeout' and unemployment. In the 1990s, however, there are signs of growing insecurity and of increasing stress and 'burnout' with stress-related retirements at a record level (Williams, 1996). The research by Campbell and Neill (1994a; 1994b) shows that there is significant overload in schools in England and Wales arising from what they describe as 'teacher conscientious'.

Staff in further education colleges have been expected to adjust to rapid, and often painful, change since incorporation in 1993. Funding is increasingly linked to recruitment of students and successful completion of courses. Business values have become prominent, conditions of service have been 'eroded', more part-time staff have been employed and senior managers are increasingly drawn from the business sector. Elliott and Hall (1994, p. 9) point to the dysfunctional consequences of 'the cultural transformation from education to business' in further education:

> While such foundations may prove adequate for the survival of colleges as financially viable institutions, they are inadequate for their survival as providers of high quality post-school educational experiences . . . The danger is an obvious one. Starved of adequate staffing, courses are reduced to minimum contact time, staff are overworked, overstressed and overtired,

conflict between teaching and management staff becomes systemic, morale falls, staff goodwill is withdrawn.

O'Neill (1994) refers to the potential for self-managing schools and colleges to determine the precise nature of their staffing on the basis of their specific needs rather than have a staffing structure imposed by the LEA. He argues that educational institutions need to be able to exercise maximum discretion in three aspects of staffing:

- The type and length of employment contract offered.
- The linkage between pay and market forces.
- The range of additional benefits which form part of a complete retention and development package.

This increasing flexibility is already evident in further education where almost half the total staff are part time and 52 per cent of teaching staff are on part-time contracts (FEDA, 1995, p. 11). It is also beginning to impact on schools where local management of schools (LMS) forces senior managers and governors to prepare a cost-benefit analysis, explicitly or implicitly, when selecting new teachers or associate staff. The perceived quality of current and potential staff, once the decisive factor, has to be considered alongside the budgetary implications of recruitment or retention. This change in stance has led to an increase in the early retirements of experienced, and more expensive, staff, and the replacement of departing staff with newly qualified teachers. There is also evidence of greater use of part-time staff, a significant increase in temporary contracts to provide flexibility and the employment of classroom assistants as an inexpensive alternative to teachers (Levacic, 1995).

SELF-MANAGING SCHOOLS AND COLLEGES

The pressure for developed and developing economies to become more efficient in order to compete effectively on the world stage has led to a heightened awareness of the links between educational capability and economic performance (Dearing, 1996). A skilled workforce depends largely on the achievements and outputs of schools, colleges and universities. This has led to a plethora of legislation as governments have sought to raise educational standards.

A major thrust in the legislation has been the development of self-managing schools and colleges in many countries. The Australian writers Caldwell and Spinks (1992, p. 4) define this concept:

A self-managing school is a school in a system of education where there has been significant and consistent decentralisation to the school level of authority to make decisions related to the allocation of resources . . . The school remains accountable to a central authority for the manner in which resources are allocated.

Self-management in England and Wales takes one of three forms:

- *LMS* which devolves funding and resource management to governing bodies and limits the powers of LEAs. This is the dominant mode of self-management which applies to some 23,000 primary, secondary and special schools.
- *Grant-maintained status* which applies when schools choose to 'opt out' of LEA control and receive their budgets direct from the Funding Agency for Schools (FAS). This applies to about 1,100 schools.
- *Incorporation* of further education colleges, independent of LEAs, which receive their budgets mainly from the Further Education Funding Council (FEFC).

The shift to self-management is underpinned by the assumption that management is likely to be more effective if it happens 'close to the action' rather than at a distance from the institution. School and college managers are able to determine their own priorities on the basis of an assessment of their specific needs rather than simply responding to priorities set by national or local governments. Caldwell and Spinks (1992, p. 14) argue the case for self-management:

> It is simply more efficient and effective in the late twentieth century to restructure systems of education so that central bureaucracies are relatively small and schools are empowered to manage their own affairs within a centrally determined framework of direction and support. Two arguments have usually been offered, one is concerned with responsiveness, the other with priorities for resource allocation in times of economic restraint or budgetary crisis.

The emphasis on self-management has been welcomed by many principals in schools and colleges (Bush *et al.*, 1993) because it facilitates greater institutional control of policies and resources. However, it poses problems for small primary schools whose heads often have a full-time class teaching role. The extra management demands have to be accommodated during evenings and weekends, adding to the stress referred to earlier.

The shift to self-management has been accompanied by a new accent on accountability to parents as surrogate 'consumers' rather than to teachers, the 'producers' of education. The concept of 'open enrolment' in England and Wales allows parents to express a preference for the school their children will attend, although that preference may not be met if the school is oversubscribed. This limitation diminishes parental choice but the concept remains a powerful component of government ideology in the UK and elsewhere.

The emphasis on consumer power also applies in further education where responsiveness is to the needs of employers as well as to those of students. These developments in both sectors mean that managers have to give heightened attention to the attitudes and preferences of those who 'consume' educational services, directly or indirectly. Inevitably, this means that market accountability has become more significant: 'The notion of market accountability has been reinforced by the legislation and this model is probably the most relevant for schools and colleges in the 1990s. Satisfying customers and potential customers is now the most important indicator of success' (Bush, 1994, p. 323). The pressure for schools to compete for clients is sharpened by the publication of 'league tables' of performance in public examinations and tests. A low placing in these lists is likely to lead to a fall in demand for places with knock-on effects for pupil numbers, budgets, staff levels and the quality of teaching and learning. Adherence to national educational norms is sought through the imposition of a National Curriculum for schools and through a national inspection regime for both schools and further education.

The shift to self-management, and the inspection regime, are intended to raise standards. In further education, funding is linked closely to student retention and completion rates. For schools, there is intense pressure on headteachers and staff to improve their position in the league tables. The weakness of such a powerful competitive environment is that it is bound to lead to 'winners' and 'losers'. Only one school can top the table but this does not mean that children and staff in the other schools should be valued less.

The presence of a National Curriculum, and state-sponsored inspection, means that self-managing schools have limited scope to develop on an individual basis. All schools offer a standard 'product' and competition is confined to the perceived quality of the educational process, as evidenced by inspection reports and examination and test results, and to the 'image' presented to prospective clients.

MANAGING PEOPLE IN A NEW CLIMATE

The shift to self-management, and the pressure on resources, have led to two major developments in the management of people:

- traditional staffing structures and historical divisions between professional and non-professional work are increasingly being called into question;
- organisations are less tolerant of 'organisational slack' or of suboptimal performance by teachers and other staff. Schools and colleges are under pressure to ensure competent performance from all staff (O'Neill *et al.*, 1994, p. 29).

The change to self-management means that governors and senior managers need to take full responsibility for the management of staff. It is no longer possible to hide behind national or local government officers and inspectors or to blame them for shortcomings. Human resource management, in all its aspects, has to be handled within the organisation. In particular, schools and colleges have to operate in accordance with both legislation and changing societal expectations.

Equal opportunities

One significant area influenced by the law and by changing attitudes is that of equal opportunities. As David Middlewood indicates in Chapter 10, recruitment and selection procedures must have regard to legislation on equal opportunities. Applicants should not be disadvantaged because of race, religion, disability or gender but, in practice, it can be difficult to ensure equality of opportunity.

In Chapter 9, Marianne Coleman points out that there are several barriers to career progress for women despite the legislation enshrining equal opportunities. These obstacles may be summarised as

- women make fewer applications for promoted posts;
- women are more likely to experience conflict between their professional and family roles;
- women are more likely to take career breaks;
- educational culture is male-centred;
- there is overt and covert discrimination against women; and
- there is a limited number of suitable female role models.

Some of these barriers also apply to other areas of disadvantage, including race. There is a dearth of black teachers in British schools despite the legislation outlawing discrimination. As long ago as 1986, the Commission for Racial Equality (CRE, 1986) drew attention to the shortage of black teachers and the need for strategies to increase their numbers. Research in eight LEAs with a significant proportion of people from ethnic minorities found that only 2 per cent of teachers were black. The proportion of black teachers in promoted posts was even lower. There was little improvement by the end of the 1980s. Clay *et al.* (1995) report that in 1989 only 2.4 per cent of students on BEd courses were from black ethnic groups.

It appears logical to assume that the following barriers, adapted from the Coleman analysis, operate to limit the appointment and advancement of black people in education:

- Black people make fewer applications for promoted posts.
- Educational culture is Eurocentric.
- There is overt and covert discrimination against black people.
- There are few suitable black role models.

The CRE (1986) research presents evidence of perceived discrimination and also implies that cultural factors and the absence of suitable role models may apply to black teachers and aspirants. Singh's (1988) survey of Asian sixth-formers indicates that well qualified pupils were deterred from becoming teachers because of their personal experiences of racism from other pupils and staff. McLaughlin (1993) also refers to racism as a disincentive for prospective teachers: 'Bigotry is probably another factor reducing the number of black and Asian teachers . . . Many [people] believe minority teachers get a raw deal – and that pupils know it' (quoted in Clay *et al.*, 1995, p. 22). There may be a double disadvantage for black women seeking to enter, or advance within, the teaching profession. The stereotype of the white male manager in education is a significant barrier for aspiring black women, as one headteacher suggests: 'I had to work hard – doubly hard to prove I was a good head, a good black headteacher, a good, black, female headteacher. I felt I was in a glass cage. I felt very lonely' (Mortimore and Mortimore, 1991, p. 81). The under-representation of women and black people in senior posts in education is unfair. An even more significant consequence may be the underutilisation of human capital and the lost potential for more effective teaching and leadership in schools and colleges. If women and black students are deterred from pursuing careers in education because of the lack of suitable role models, and/or through perceived discrimination, the effect is to limit the overall quality of the teaching force with inevitable implications for the quality of teaching and learning.

Associate staff

Another potential area of disadvantage in education relates to associate staff. Teachers are invariably regarded as the prime resource in schools and colleges because of their central role in the teaching and learning process. They are also usually paid significantly more than associate staff, although the differential has narrowed to some extent since the introduction of LMS. There may be a double disadvantage for the high proportion of associate staff who are women.

The increasing emphasis on managerial effectiveness in education has led to a reappraisal of the role of associate staff. Mortimore *et al.*'s (1992, p. 19) research shows that flexible deployment of associate staff can enhance the cost-effectiveness of schools:

> If two schools which are comparable in every respect are equally effective in terms of performance, the one that uses the smaller amount of resources is the more cost-effective . . . Cost-effectiveness, in this sense of the term, is highly desirable. A school that uses its resources more cost-effectively releases resources which it can use to promote further development.

There is increasing evidence of schools using the flexibility provided by LMS to deploy associate staff in imaginative ways. Wallace and Hall's (1994) research shows that some schools now include a bursar in their senior management teams. In many schools, associate staff are undertaking administrative tasks formerly performed by highly paid senior staff (Mortimore *et al.*, 1992). Research by Levacic (1995) shows that many schools have increased the use of classroom assistants, technicians and librarians during the 1990s. 'Local management has stimulated the growth of a para-teaching force in schools' (Levacic, 1995, p. 155).

There are similar trends in further education. Kedney and Brownlow (1994) refer to the introduction of new para-professional roles such as workshop supervision, student guidance and support, and course design which would have been regarded as lecturers' work until the early 1990s. There has also been an increase in the number of senior managers appointed from the business sector (Elliott and Hall, 1994). There has been a reduction in the proportion of time spent by students in formal classroom programmes and an increase in learning supervised by associate staff. Kedney and Brownlow (1994, pp. 11–12) spell out the financial pressures driving these changes:

> The imperatives to reduce unit costs in the drive for efficiency set by the funding mechanisms will mean more than reducing taught hours for students and expecting lecturers to teach longer and more flexibly . . . The future points to the potential removal of the institutionalised distinction between academic and support staff and the development of a new and more flexible model.

Schools and colleges make their own judgements about the balance of staffing in the light of their specific requirements but making the best use of the talents of all staff makes good sense. The effective management of associate and teaching staff is an essential element in education as O'Neill *et al.* (1994, p. 7) suggest:

> A broader definition of the term people is inclusive rather than exclusive. It suggests that each adult employed within the school or college plays a critical role in its success. Acknowledging the unique contribution of individuals engenders their commitment.

PEOPLE AND PERFORMANCE

The management of staff in self-managing schools and colleges is located with governing bodies, principals and senior staff. The link between the leading professionals and lay governors is vital for the health of the organisation and requires 'managing' just as much as other relationships. Where governors and staff work together constructively and harmoniously, it provides a powerful basis for success (Bush *et al.*, 1993) but conflict, or separation, between professionals and lay governors, may serve to inhibit development.

People are the most significant resource available to school and college managers. Their selection, induction, deployment, development and appraisal are the responsibility of principals and senior managers, reporting to the governing body. The quality of their work, and their motivation to perform well, are related directly to the nature of the human resource management process. Where staff management is skilled and sympathetic, a successful organisation is likely to result. Where it is clumsy and inadequate, poor performance may occur. The fundamental issue of managing for people or performance is examined by Colin Riches in Chapter 2.

The pressure for schools and colleges to compete for clients reinforces the need for high performance which is necessarily related to the quality and commitment of all staff. Teachers and associate staff often work significantly more than their contracted hours in order to deliver the performance needed to meet the requirements of internal managers and external assessors.

The contract of employment introduced in 1987 requires school teachers in England and Wales to work for 1,265 hours of 'directed time'. This time includes five days of compulsory in-service training. During these hours, headteachers are able to specify the activities of teachers:

> Under the contract teachers have to perform such duties as may be reasonably assigned to them by their head teacher. For example, head teachers could ensure, by the allocation of directed time, that teachers attend parents' evenings, curriculum planning sessions, and other school meetings.
>
> (Busher and Saran, 1992, p. 23)

Teachers are also required to work beyond their contracted hours to perform their duties satisfactorily. Preparation for teaching and marking pupils' work, for example, are expected to be undertaken during this additional time. As a result, the 1,265 hours constitute a minimum rather than a maximum figure, as research by Busher and Saran (*ibid.*, p. 39) demonstrates:

> Some heads pointed out that teachers in their schools . . . worked far more than 1265 hours . . . By 1990 most heads commented that their staff were working incredibly long hours, that there was sickness and work-related stress, that they were having to protect their staff and in some cases 'tell them to work less'.

The problem of 'overcommitment' also emerges from the research of Campbell and Neill (1994a; 1994b) in primary and secondary schools. Teachers were working for 54 hours a week, well beyond their contractual commitments. The researchers explain this 'overcommitment' and point to some of its dysfunctional consequences:

> The teachers were primarily motivated by a sense of vocation or obligation to their pupils . . . The occupational culture of the school remained stubbornly at odds with the assumptions of central government's legislation on working conditions . . . It is unlikely . . . that anyone other than the teachers themselves will take steps to reduce work overload, since most of the overload is in the teachers' own time.
>
> (Campbell and Neill, 1994a, pp. 223–4)

The partly self-induced heavy workload of teachers suggests that most staff fulfil O'Neill *et al.*'s (1994) assumption that commitment is an essential component of successful organisations. However, long working hours may serve to diminish effectiveness and reduce the quality of work performance. In this context, senior managers have a responsibility to limit overload in order to promote the quality of teaching and learning:

> A major function for heads and other managers in the post-ERA period might be to find ways to limit teacher workloads by identifying priorities for their schools, and filtering out demands which make the most conscientious teachers' workloads unreasonable . . . There is no evidence that very long hours lead to better quality of teaching.
>
> (Campbell and Neill, 1994a, p. 224)

The evidence of overcommitment suggests that teachers and associate staff are highly motivated but may be risking 'burnout' through working long hours over extended periods. In this context, managers need refined motivational skills to build high morale, sustain good performance and avoid dysfunctional overload. Riches (1994, p. 239) refers to the link between motivation and the 'high performance cycle':

- There should be high expectations of staff. Low expectations are demotivating.
- Managers should ensure a sense of satisfaction in return for effort.
- Satisfaction will derive from personally meaningful work which members are capable of and in part from managers taking pains to reward performance.
- Managers should encourage staff to set specific, challenging but realistic goals for high performance.
- Feedback on performance helps staff to effective task strategies and to be motivated.

This approach is reinforced by Torrington and Weightman (1989, p. 52) who stress the importance of valuing staff. They identify four types of esteem on the basis of their research in secondary schools:

- Consideration and praise.
- Feedback.
- Delegation.
- Consultation and participation.

Another dimension of motivation relates to staff development. Taking a proactive stance towards individual professional development provides tangible evidence of managers' appreciation of staff commitment. Elliott and Hall (1994, p. 8), however, caution that staff development in further education may be directed towards organisational rather than personal objectives and form part of a response to changes imposed by external bodies:

> Staff development is likely to be highlighted to greater prominence, but as

a means of widening staff competence in order better to meet institutional needs. It is further likely that multiskilling will be privileged in order to maximise 'output'. Retraining and redeploying staff provides one alternative to declaring staff redundant.

While individual staff development may serve to increase motivation, there is an emerging view that high performance may also be linked to pay. In England and Wales, this is specifically encouraged by the formal pay and conditions policies and in rhetoric from ministers (Tomlinson, 1992a). Performance related pay (PRP) is discussed in detail by Keith Foreman in Chapter 14.

The rationale for PRP is that people work more effectively with financial incentives (Tomlinson, 1992b), but the evidence of Campbell and Neill (1994a; 1994b) shows that teacher conscientiousness is widespread and arises from commitment to pupils rather than financial reward. The argument that financial incentives promote improved performance in vocational employment remains unproven.

CONCLUSION: MANAGING THE CONTEXT

The context for human resource management in education provides a searching text of management capability. High unemployment, and an increase in short-term, low-paid jobs, raise important questions about the purpose of education. While governments urge schools and colleges to prepare young people for the world of work, specific skills are subject to obsolescence as a consequence of industrial change.

The international trend towards local management means that senior managers, and lay governors, are increasingly responsible for handling the human consequences of multiple change. The emphasis on consumers rather than producers, by governments in the UK and elsewhere, requires responsiveness to the needs of students, parents and employers. However, effective education can be achieved only by motivating teachers and associate staff to 'deliver' high quality.

Campbell and Neill's research, discussed in Chapter 7, shows that teachers demonstrate their commitment to their students by working long hours. As Riches (1994) and Torrington and Weightman (1989) stress, praise for teachers and associate staff is essential if this overcommitment is not to lead to dysfunctional stress or 'burnout'. A genuine concern for staff welfare should not be subordinated to the need for organisational efficiency.

REFERENCES

Bush, T. (1994), Accountability in education, in Bush, T. and West-Burnham, J. (eds) *The Principles of Educational Management*, Harlow, Longman.
Bush, T., Coleman, M. and Glover, D. (1993) *Managing Autonomous Schools: The Grant-Maintained Experience*, London, Paul Chapman.

Busher, H. and Saran, R. (1992) *Teachers' Conditions of Employment*, London, Kogan Page.

Caldwell, B. and Spinks, J. (1992) *Leading the Self-Managing School*, London, Falmer.

Campbell, R. and Neill, S. (1994a) *Primary Teachers at Work*, London, Routledge.

Campbell, R. and Neill, S. (1994b) *Secondary Teachers at Work*, London, Routledge.

Clay, J., Cole, M. and George, R. (1995) Visible minority ethnic representation in teaching and teacher education in Britain and The Netherlands: some observations, *Journal of Further and Higher Education*, Vol. 19, No. 2, Summer, pp. 9–27.

Commission for Racial Equality (1986), *Black Teachers: The Challenge of Increasing Supply*, London, CRE.

Dearing, R. (1996) *Review of Qualifications for 16–19 Year Olds*, Hayes, Schools Curriculum and Assessment Agency.

Elliott, G. and Hall, V. (1994) FE Inc. – Business orientation in further education and the introduction of human resource management, *School Organisation*, Vol. 14, No. 4, pp. 3–10.

Further Education Development Agency (1995) *Managing the FE Sector*, FEDA, Blaydon.

Handy, C. (1994) *The Empty Raincoat*, London, Hutchinson.

Kedney, B. and Brownlow, S. (1994) *Funding Flexibility*, Mendip Paper 0062, Bristol, The Staff College.

Levacic, R. (1995) *Local Management of Schools: Analysis and Practice*, Buckingham, Open University Press.

Lofthouse, M. (1994) Managing the curriculum, in Bush, T. and West-Burnham, J. (eds) *The Principles of Educational Management*, Harlow, Longman.

Mortimore, P., Mortimore, J., Thomas, H. and Cairns, R. (1992) *The Innovative Uses of Non-Teaching Staff in Primary and Secondary Schools Project, Final Report*, London, Institute of Education, University of London.

O'Neill, J. (1994) Managing human resources, in Bush, T. and West-Burnham, J. (eds) *The Principles of Educational Management*, Harlow, Longman.

O'Neill, J., Middlewood, D. and Glover, D. (1994), *Managing Human Resources in Schools and Colleges*, Harlow, Longman.

Riches, C. (1994) Motivation, in Bush, T. and West-Burnham, J. (eds) *The Principles of Educational Management*, Harlow, Longman.

Singh, R. (1988) *Asian and White Perceptions of the Teaching Profession*, Bradford, Bradford and Ilkley Community College.

Tomlinson, H. (1992a) Performance-related pay for teachers in the 1990s, in Tomlinson, H. (ed.) *Performance Related Pay in Education*, London, Routledge.

Tomlinson, H. (1992b) Performance-related pay in the 1980s: the changing climate, in Tomlinson, H. (ed.) *Performance Related Pay in Education*, London, Routledge.

Torrington, D. and Weightman, J. (1989) *The Reality of School Management*, Oxford, Blackwell.

Wallace, M. and Hall, V. (1994) *Inside the SMT: Teamwork in Secondary School Management*, London, Paul Chapman.

Williams, E. (1996) Stepping down on doctor's orders, *The Times Educational Supplement*, 15 March.

2

MANAGING FOR PEOPLE AND PERFORMANCE

Colin Riches

INTRODUCTION: SOME DILEMMAS

'Performance', with its associated concepts of competences and effectiveness, has become a driving influence in education today. A climate has gradually developed in many countries in which performance has dominated educational debates of all kinds. Performance ranges wide, from that of young children to college governors (Graystone, 1996). It is interesting to observe that when Drucker (1974) wrote his seminal book, *Management: Tasks, Responsibilities, Practices* he drew marked distinctions between the way business and service organisations perform. He argued that service institutions, such as government agencies, the armed services, the education service and health-care institutions, often perform badly because, unlike businesses, where income is dependent upon results arising out of customer satisfaction, service organisations are not paid by performance but receive a budget which is unrelated to their success. In British education today the ideology of the marketplace has made this distinction invalid. If schools or colleges do not perform in the sense of achieving results which satisfy their customers they eventually close like bankrupt businesses!

Any discussion of this topic poses questions about the relationship between individuals, with their own needs and drives, and the way they perform in any institutional context. There are inevitable tensions between organisational demands for performance and the individual needs of people within an organisation. In all aspects of people management, ranging from handling a mini-crisis to dealing with long-term problems of motivation, there are dilemmas between seeing people as a resource for organisational advancement and effectiveness and considering their own demands and sensitivities. The problem emerges on a day-to-day basis but also when a person's whole career is in conflict with the expectations of managers. At the root of the issue might be quite profound ethical divergences between directive behaviour by managers and the freedom required by individual members to act autonomously as they deem best. Some commentators, e.g. Hoyle and Jones (1995, p. 74, emphasis added), have argued that this has become a question of who *controls* education.

> The last decade and a half has seen the education system undergo a radical transformation, particularly in terms of administration and policy . . . Control over the teaching profession has become more overt, a process helped by the rise of *managerialism* as a significant force at the school level. Here heads and deputies have become the hierarchical agents of both control and implementation.

Managers have found themselves called to greater accountability (i.e. being called to account for performance) to an ever-widening constituency, including parents and students, for *results* which are difficult to deliver, given the limitations on resources and the widespread demoralisation of members of the teaching profession.

'Managerialism' has as its central focus the notion that 'value for money is only achieved through the production of measurable outcomes' (Kydd, 1996). Its most important characteristic within education is that it adopts the ideology of 'business' in which the curriculum is the input, students are the throughput and success is designated by measurable outcomes. In such a model 'managed' institutions seem to be set against the notion of schools, colleges and universities as communities of professionals. The concept of the autonomous professional is marginalised. While there are dilemmas in the relationship between individuals as autonomous agents, and the pressure to perform, as quantified in supposed measurable ways, people generally achieve most if their personal dispositions are understood, valued and taken into account when considering ways of maximising performance.

However this view is not to devalue and debase performance. Indeed, to conceive of organisations apart from the way they perform would be very strange. Staff are appointed to a given organisation to perform certain tasks to some assumed standard. In what Drucker (1989) liberally defines as 'the spirit of performance', the first requirement is 'high performance standards, for the group as well as for each individual. The organisation must cultivate in itself the habit of achievement' (p. 156). This performance has to be *managed*, i.e. people need to be led towards improving their standards in explicit and systematic ways to produce more favourable outcomes than would be achieved in *ad hoc* ways. However, a truly managed approach is not direction by edict but guidance by example and through a valuing of the development needs of members of the organisation and their involvement in policy-making and the allocation of resources. This is the liberal spirit of performance. The overall view taken in this chapter is that all attempts made to improve should be conducted in that same spirit, which values employees as human beings and enables them to do extraordinary things. This is management which makes improved outcomes possible by empowering people to aspire and achieve new heights of performance.

EVALUATION OF PERFORMANCE

'Performance' may be simply defined as the accomplishment of a task or activity. Performance *effectiveness* is the extent to which a particular measurable target is achieved, and performance *efficiency* is the cost for a given level of achievement. Efficiency and effectiveness have become favourite words in management literature, but the meaning of the terms is sometimes confused. 'Efficiency', in this context, is the relationship between actual inputs and actual outputs (the performance); whereas 'effectiveness' is the degree to which planned achievement is realised. The problem may arise as to how one is to know *if* what has been done is *the* accomplishment of something (performance) and what is the expected *standard*.

Before human performance can be studied and better understood there are four basic problems to consider:

1) The reliability of performance or consistency or stability over time. Are the best (or worst) performers at time 1 the best or (worst) performers at time 2? Psychological evidence indicates that this is not necessarily so because people are inconsistent in their performances or conditions in which the performances take place may vary (Cascio, 1991).
2) The reliability of job performance *observations* in which different methods may result in markedly different conclusions about performance.
3) The dimensionality of job performance: a great variety of predictors can be used but most empirical studies and people in practice use only a global measure or criterion and that is unrealistic (Ronan and Prien, 1971).
4) In performance the moderating effects of situational variables, such as organisational characteristics or leadership influences, invariably come into play.

These general points are made to demonstrate that there is a good deal of subjectivity surrounding the evaluation of performance. Nevertheless performance indicators (PIs), i.e. 'precise, often measurable descriptions of outcomes which one aims to achieve' (Oldroyd *et al.*, 1996 p. 50), do exist although their precision and value can be called into question. In evaluating the aims, objectives, strategies and development plan of a school or college, and how they relate to one another, we need to know what are the 'signals of success' to indicate if the objectives have been achieved. Rogers and Badham (1994, p. 107) have pointed out that PIs are not an absolute or general measure of performance. They should be viewed alongside other evaluation evidence; 'they should be capable of collection over a period of time on a constant basis', should be relevant to the objective and can be quantitative or qualitative.

In England and Wales, the work of the Office for Standards in Education (Ofsted) is predicated on the notion that PIs do exist for schools and that whether they have been achieved or not can be measured by looking at evidence obtained chiefly at the time of inspection. Its evaluation criteria seem to confuse efficiency and effectiveness measures in that 'The *efficiency* of the school is to be judged by (among other things) the efficiency and effectiveness with which staff, learning resources and accommodation are deployed to attain the school's aims and objectives and to match its priorities' (Ofsted, 1993, p. 14, emphasis added). In a stringent critique of these inspections, Fitz-Gibbon (1996a) claims that there is no checking of evidence gained by inspectors for internal consistency and, so-called, 'quantitive' data are obtained and used in a rough and ready way. She concludes (*ibid.* p. 21) that while 'Schools must be accountable for outcomes . . . those outcomes must be credibly, reliably, efficiently, validly and fairly assessed' and infers that this is not happening in the work of Ofsted.

The 'snapshot' method of inspecting schools raises the issue of the extent to which their performance can be indicated and judged during the limited period in which evidence is obtained. The philosophy here is that outcome criteria take precedence over process criteria. Even if the raw data of league tables of students' examination performance can be tempered by value-added data so that the progress made by students is taken into account (Fitz-Gibbon, 1996b), the emphasis is still on arrival rather than what has been learned of educational value during the journey. A consistent trend is for teachers and managers to be judged almost entirely on measurable end results rather than on their less quantifiable performances along the way. In this context, it is unsurprising that a system of evaluating the performance of individual teachers involves the use of a simple 1–7 grading scale. 'The perspective is clearly one of external accountability in which priority is given to educational attainments or outcomes, rather than the process of teaching and learning in its own right' (O'Neill *et al.*, 1994, p. 23). This is not to devalue the importance of performance but to question the limited range of judgements employed. The spirit of performance embraces wider parameters.

A wide-ranging but limiting way of measuring *managerial* performance is by looking at competences. The competency-based movement starts from the premise of measuring what is *done* rather than what is *thought*; it is all about the ability to perform given acts, however widely or narrowly defined. The Management Charter Initiative (MCI) was established by the National Council for Vocational Qualifications to accredit generic management qualifications. A functional analysis takes place in which the key purposes of a job are determined, as are the key roles in carrying it out and the key units and elements of those roles. For example, one key role, 'managing people', has four elements including contributing to the recruitment and selection of personnel, which in turn has two elements – 'define future personnel requirements' and 'contribute to the assessment and selection of candidates against team and organisational requirements'. To each of the latter are attached performance criteria and a range of indicators that performance has been achieved (MCI, 1991). These 'standards' relate to what has been done and not to its quality; to satisfactory performance and not to whether it is superior or not. This atomistic approach examines the parts of job performance but not the ability to integrate the various elements. In response to this criticism MCI identified clusters of personal competences required of a manager, i.e. planning, managing others, managing oneself and using intellect to optimise the achievement of results, but these are not integrated into the skill competency statements. One is left with a picture of performance competences as many discrete parts which leave one wondering what a competent quality manager in general and in education in particular would look like!

Some other models of competences are more holistic such as the Boyatzis (1982) model, which does define competence in terms of superior performance, distinguishing threshold competences from superior management performance, relating them to the person in the job, seeing them as possessed so that they inform behaviour unconsciously (as traits or motives) or consciously (as self-image or social role) or demonstrated as skills. His approach comes near to the definition of competence by Pollard and Tann (1994, p. 64) as 'a combination of knowledge, understanding and skill as well as the ability to apply them in particular situations. This includes motives, traits, attitudes and aspects of a teacher's self-image and role'. Effective performance as a manager, and also obtaining effective performance, in the broadest sense, from those being managed, is more than the sum of discrete parts which contribute to the total performance – there is a certain internal synergy taking place which strengthens and adds value to that performance.

A continuing theme for the remainder of this chapter is that performance matters – although there are problems of definition, measurement and characteristics – but so do people; that organisational performance matters but so does individual performance; that there are tensions between meeting organisational and individual performance needs; and that effective HRM is vital in establishing a true spirit of performance in an organisation.

EFFECTIVE HRM: MANAGING PEOPLE AND THE ORGANISATION – A SCHEMA

In discussing performance, the significance of *people* in an organisation may be given insufficient emphasis:

Managing is about dealing with people and things. Things are comparatively easy to manage . . . People are different! They do not obey any known laws of behaviour and do not accept organisation and arrangement without comment, possibly protest – or even refusal. Each person has all the rights, moral and legal, that our society accepts as fair and proper.

(Preston, 1989, p. 2)

People then are employees and performers with legal and moral rights; they are to be treated as ends and not only as means to an organisational end. There are conflicts inherent in the view that people are semi-mechanical human resources to be assessed in quantitive, calculative terms as assets in an organisation – a 'hard' variant of HRM – rather than as valued human beings required to fulfil tasks given effective communication, motivation and leadership – a 'soft' variant. 'There is always the fear in HRM that hard business values come to rule both managers and teaching staff alike, with managers more willing adapters of the new ethic than lecturers' (Elliott and Hall, 1994, p. 4). A middle view, which eschews hard or soft variants, is that HRM is all about the improvement of performance or productivity – however problematical these may be to define – through the effective use of human resources; always acknowledging that humans in an organisation are the most important part of getting things done. People need to be managed to optimise their own and institutional performance and value being managed. No one gains from an *ad hoc* approach to managing people; to ignore them, to treat them as pawns on an institutional chess board is neither ethical nor liberal nor any assistance towards performance.

The context or environment in which HRM operates is highly significant. Here we refer to all the external environmental influences on educational institutions in general and HRM in particular, which are affected by ideologies – often enshrined in legislation – views, expectations and preferences. The impact of consumerism, giving consumers greater rights and obliging professionals to take these into account (Dennison, 1993), and managerialism, which questions the judgements of professionals in their own institutions, has been quite profound.

HRM may be usefully conceptualised as set out in Figure 2.1. The model is a linear input–output model from mission, goals, strategies, policies, plans and programmes to processes concerned with managing people to outcomes in terms of improved performance. 'Evaluation is the process of systematically collecting and analysing information in order to form value judgements based on firm evidence. These judgements are concerned with the extent to which particular targets are being achieved' (Rogers and Badham, 1994). This applies to the functional area of HRM as to every other sphere of management. There is always room for improvement in the management cycle.

HRM is about human resource *management*. The management of people does not involve processes which are different in kind from those of management in general. It embraces all the core activities of management:

THE CONTEXT (GENERAL)
Governors, clients, competitors, technology, local government, professional associations, etc.

Functional tasks	*Key concepts*	*General actions*	*specific actions*	IMPROVEMENT OF PERFORMANCE
Staff selection	Validity and reliability of various measures of future performance in selection; the assessment centre	Questioning of existing procedures of selection; the importance of using a battery of tests for selection	Analysing and evaluating selection procedures in specific schools and colleges on the evidence of existing research	Effective and efficient outcomes
Leadership of staff	Leadership as awareness of self, task, situation and group; mission; creating an organisational culture	Developing skills of self-awareness, observation and practice; establishing clear goals and creating attitudes and actions which are motivational	Examining leadership in practice in schools and colleges at all levels	Learning and action by:
Motivation of staff	Nature and theories of motivation; stress; creating motivation	Analyse factors of motivation, demotivation and stress; strategies for enhancing and motivation	Motivating the teacher; managing teacher stress; coping by the teacher	• organisation
Staff appraisal and development	The nature and methods of appraisal; identifying development needs; development programmes	Diagnosis of needs; training for appraisal; developing INSET programmes for all types of staff in various contexts	Individual appraisal of senior, support staff, etc.; evaluation of INSET needs in a particular educational organisation	• group
Interpersonal relationships	Types of communication; the process-decoding, interpreting, encoding; types; barriers; contexts	Learning to analyse the process, to identify barriers and to operate in a variety of interpersonel contexts	Managing communication for interpersonal relationships in a school and between educational agencies	• individual

GENERAL MANAGEMENT CONCEPTS
- Planning
- Organising
- Controlling/leading
- Co-ordinating
- Evaluating

ESTABLISHING
Mission
Goals
Strategies
Policies
Plans
Programmes

THE CONTEXT (SPECIFIC)
Governors, catchment area, models of organisation/management, culture, etc.

Figure 2.1 Conceptualisation of HRM

planning or working out how aims are to be achieved;
organising by analysing the activities to be carried out and making decisions
to meet objectives;
commanding through *leading*; . . .
co-ordinating activities so that targets are achieved;
evaluating the effectiveness of all these managerial activities.

                                              (Riches and Morgan, 1989)

Within the major functional area of HRM are the so-called operative
functions which are outlined in the central section of Figure 2.1 – such as
selection, leading and appraisal (which will be elaborated upon below). The
scope of HRM, as we have seen, is even wider than this in that it is involved
in the whole process of helping to improve human performance and to
shape the long-term planning and development of human resources.

In Figure 2.1, each operative function (the list is not exclusive) within
HRM has key concepts or general notions associated with it, out of which
theories may develop, some general actions which may be taken on the
basis of these concepts and more specific actions related to the context
of application which derive from these. We have chosen only to introduce
the following operative functions in this chapter, conscious that many of
them will be developed in later chapters: 1) staff selection; 2) leadership;
3) motivation; 4) staff appraisal and development; and 5) interpersonal
relationships. The correct order for presenting these themes is arguable;
for example, the *sine qua non* of all HRM could be said to be found in
the latter subject. However, the order of presentation is not important as
the processes are iterative and never entirely self-contained.

The underlying purpose of each of the operative functions is to achieve
performance and what is said is based on the view that if individuals within
an organisation are allowed to progress in their professional roles (and this
includes support staff of all kinds), this will enhance the quality of performance of students' learning, of the organisation and of themselves. There
are tensions between meeting organisational demands for performance and
individual needs, but a culture of collaboration is vital to progress along all
fronts (Law and Glover, 1996). This requires accepting people where they
are (as well as for what they might become), an emphasis on the present
(and future) rather than the past and trust in others. However 'responsible
professionals take accountability seriously' (Hoyle and Jones, 1995, p. 74),
and the pull of the sometimes countervailing forces of responsibility and
autonomy has to be addressed.

Staff selection

Within any area of HRM the core activities of management apply. Selection
has to be planned for; the need for staff has to be justified as part of that
planning, recruitment to obtain the best field of candidates requires careful

forward planning and the process itself cannot be allowed to just happen. Similarly, organising, commanding, leading, co-ordinating and evaluating are all called for within the selection function. Another vital aspect of selection is to remember that one is invariably selecting on the basis of *predicting* performance (particularly in the case of teachers/lecturers seeking management posts) through various selection measures.

The underlying principles of any selection process should be based on equity (fairness), effectiveness (it does what it purports to do) and efficiency (the selection process can be overextended and create unreasonable costs). Like all policies relating to the management of people, selection should be within the bounds of ethical principles, taking into account equal opportunities relating to gender, age, race and disabilities. Trained people are needed to select, preferably as an ongoing team. The final decision and the process used has to be made within the specific and general contexts in which recruitment and selection are managed, with the question, 'Which candidate has the best potential to perform here?' Chapter 10, by David Middlewood, gives extended consideration to these issues.

Leadership

Leadership is capable of numerous, and often misleading, definitions and interpretations. It is basically about having the ability to influence others – individuals, groups and teams – to take them in a desired direction. Leadership can happen at a number of different levels throughout an organisation and is a process in which people to varying degrees make 'especially salient contributions in leading' (Hosking, 1988, p. 151). There is considerable debate about how leadership differs from management and whether effective leadership for performance involves management and *vice versa*. However, it is useful to look upon effective performance in leadership as relating to inspiration, mission, transformation, direction, pathfinding and 'doing the right things' (e.g. Gronn, 1996), and effective performance in management as the designing and carrying out of plans, transactions, means, systems, getting things done, working effectively with people at the tactical level and 'doing things right'.

There are many leadership theories including 'trait theory', the 'great man theory', the 'situationist critique', leadership styles, functional leadership and finally leaderless leadership, to say nothing of bureaucratic leadership, charismatic leadership, democratic-autocratic-*laissez-faire* leadership, group-centred leadership, reality-centred leadership, leadership by objective and so on (Bennis, 1959). These theories are too often translated from descriptions to prescriptions without much justification. A current emphasis is on gender-related leadership, which points out that women have a significant and unique contribution to bring to the process of leadership (Hall, 1996), but even this can be overstated, as feminine characteristics of leadership are present in male leadership behaviour and *vice versa*. No matter how leadership is defined, theorised and developed it is vital to performance in an organisation.

How does leadership assist the performance of individuals and the organisation as a whole? Whether one is planning, organising, co-ordinating or evaluating, in establishing mission, goals, strategies, policies, plans or programmes in a school or college, at any level, leading should be the core activity. It enables human beings to grow in effectiveness and, in Drucker's phrase, to enable ordinary people do extraordinary things.

Motivation

'Motivation' has been defined as a person's will to do something; motivations are the 'whys' of behaviour (Hersey and Blanchard, 1993). Not all the members of an organisation are motivated by the same mix of goals, and motivation may change over time. Motivation is certainly a key operative function in HRM and effective quality leadership is of pivotal importance within it. A basic model of motivation has the following building blocks:

1) needs or expectations,
2) behaviour,
3) goals and
4) some form of feedback.

The variables affecting motivation are numerous, confusing and sometimes conflicting, covering the demands of the job, the capacity of the individual, the environment of the organisation, and internal and external human pressures, which seem to be over-ridden by mental and physical capacity and the 'intermediate situations of unfairness, injustice, upset with colleagues and changes in duties' (Betts, 1993, p. 145). In some ways motivation is akin to *eustress* or good stress, the opposite of which is *distress*, commonly known as 'stress' (see Chapter 8).

Theories of motivation abound but can be loosely classified into content and process theories (Riches, 1994a). To summarise, the former theories are concerned with identifying specific things which motivate the individual to work and the relative strengths of those needs. For Maslow (1943), there is a hierarchy of needs ranging from the physiological to self-actualisation. For McGregor's (1970) 'X' person motivations are mainly physiological and lethargic, but for the 'Y' person motivation happens at the self-actualisation level and the proposition is that most work because it is natural to do so. Herzberg (1959) claimed that a distinction could be drawn between hygiene factors concerned with job dissatisfaction and 'motivators', generally relating to job content, with job satisfaction. Critics have concluded that empirical evidence does not support this two-factor theory of motivation.

Process theories look at the dynamic relationships between motivational variables which keep the action going. Expectancy theories (e.g. Neider, 1980) stress the way people are influenced motivationally by what they expect to be the impact of their actions. In equity theories (Adams, 1965) the roots of motivation are to be found in whether individuals feel they are being treated fairly or not, while goal theories stress the importance of goal setting in motivation. Within a high performance cycle (Locke and Latham, 1990), it is claimed that motivation to work and satisfaction are relatively independent outcomes. Job satisfaction comes from rewards as measured against one's own self-appraisal of the job and the consequences of satisfaction and dissatisfaction spring from the individual choices which people make. These are very simplified summaries of theories of motivation, but sufficient evidence can be drawn from their fuller versions to draw some conclusions about what general actions arise from them (based on Steers and Porter, 1991):

1) To improve performance and work attitudes those responsible must manage motivational processes and accept responsibility for improving attitudes. Appreciation of work performance has to be recognised in a tangible way – if rarely financially then by expressions of thanks!
2) 'Physician heal thyself': to improve motivational performance leaders need to go through a process of self-examination; their own strengths and limitations, desires and expectations and self-perceptions.
3) There is a need to recognise that people are motivated in different ways. Each has his or her own abilities, traits and preferences (valences) in motivation. This is positive action because it makes allowance for the utilisation of a diversity of talents, e.g. in a team.
4) People respond to challenge; tasks should not always be easy and should have diversity to meet personal satisfactions.
5) Proper attention should be given to the overall work environment in relation to the climate and dynamics of the group. Effective teamwork is an important factor in motivation.
6) To increase motivational levels – and consequently performance – it is important to involve staff as fully as they wish and co-operatively in the processes aimed at organisational effectiveness.

How these principles of action will be translated into one's own motivational schemes will depend on a variety of contingent factors. It is important to the spirit of performance in individual institutions to tease out what motivates individuals within it and how this can be applied to team and total organisational performance.

Staff appraisal and development

This is a major operative function in HRM which is dealt with more fully in Chapters 12 and 13. Appraisal provides one means of needs identification for staff development in an organisation. The ultimate purpose of needs identification is to improve performance by recognising either skills or non-skills discrepancies and growth points. If these are not recognised this benefits neither the individual, the team(s) or the work organisation's performance. The *spirit* with which one deals with them is vital: 'the provision of development opportunities rather than sanctions in response to "weaknesses"' (Oldroyd and Hall, 1996, p. 26). There seems no reason why mutually negotiated performance criteria cannot be established from the outset of the development procedure. The starting point for relating professional and organisational development to performance has to be needs identification measured against performance criteria. There are different needs foci for middle managers and for senior posts. In all cases the needs of individuals have to be matched against the needs of the groups to which they belong and to total institutional needs. Identifying needs on a serial basis is highly important for effective continuing professional development (CPD).

Poster and Poster (1991) have identified four approaches to appraisal: developmental which can easily merge in to the *laissez-faire* approach, the managerial (a hierarchical system chiefly concerned with shorter-term assessment), which merges into the judgemental view. There are weaknesses in all these positions on appraisal, and there seems a need for a balance between the need in appraisal to be accountable for one's action and performance, to address individual weaknesses when they exist and to relate the developmental model for the individual to development of the organisation as a whole.

Interpersonal relationships

Interpersonal relationships can be both rewarding and frustrating; they are certainly complex. People bring to their professional lives a set of experiences from childhood; we have developed attitudes, beliefs and values, our personality consists of a unique pattern of motivations and our striving to satisfy them, and 'in the end our behaviour will depend on the ways in which our intentions', shaped by the influences listed above, 'are empowered into action' (Whitaker, 1993, p. 8–9). This is what the latter calls 'the interpersonal landscape' and 'building and developing relationships is a process matching the elements of our own unique world with that of others' (*ibid.*). Uncomfortable relationships can present themselves and anxiety, tensions and dissonances build up which hinder effective H RM either at the giving or receiving of an exchange. Theoretical and empirical evidence on this topic is derived from various sources and is a distillation from a number of disciplines.

At the centre of all successful interpersonal relationships is the ability to communicate effectively (Riches, 1994b). Communication consists of 'sorting, selecting, forming, and transmitting symbols between people to create meaning' (Rasberry and Lemoine, 1986, p. 23). There are many models of communication concerned with the process of 'Who says what, to Whom, in Which channel, with What effect' (Laswell, 1948, p. 2). For the human resource manager in a school or college it is important to be aware of the barriers which hinder communication, such as problems of language, of attitude, of different perceptions, undue emphasis on status, the withholding of information, premature evaluation of what is being communicated and so on. Communication flow both upwards and downwards is vital as is the building up of communication networks, an analysis of which tells us much about interpersonal relationships within an institution. Communication skills include active listening, appropriate non-verbal communication and effective negotiation through open communication channels.

The above summary does no more than alert the reader to issues within the field of communication. Certain general conclusions arise from the evidence. The first is for each institution to examine closely the stages, content and processes of communication which it uses. Secondly, consideration should be given to how more empathy could be achieved in the communication process, i.e. understanding the communication receiver's needs and attitudes more. Thirdly, the better transmission of messages and feedback to ensure that the message has been accurately conveyed. This is one of the most neglected areas of HRM in practice, and much could be done to smooth the way to better interpersonal relationships, with limited effort for extremely beneficial outcomes. However like all the aspects of HRM we have considered there seems to be no single 'Holy Grail' for effective performance.

CONCLUSION

It is tempting to look for some single overall answer to the problems and possibilities of HRM such as the application of TQM. The term 'quality' in education has been defined as:

(1) providing teaching and challenging educational situations fit for students' needs, interests and expectations;
(2) working for continuous improvement in all processes to make students satisfied;
(3) working to maintain and/or add value to life.

(Tofte, 1995, p. 470)

TQM has been characterised as arrangements to ensure that the customer, both internal and external, is always heeded; her or his requirements are the only definition of quality. Other features include meeting those requirements, covering every aspect of the organisation, responsibility residing with everyone, a standard which gets things right first time, prevention of mistakes rather than the detection of them and a culture of continuous improvement. West-Burnham (1992) raises a number of possible objections to this philosophy and practice and attempts to deal with them *en passant*:

1. Managerialism denies professionalism,
2. Hierarchical accountability diminishes collegiality and autonomy,
3. The emphasis on leadership denies democracy,
4. Managerialism denies educational values,
5. Management is inevitably manipulative,
6. Educational outcomes cannot be managed.

As with TQM, HRM celebrates professionalism (in the best sense of the word), argues that accountability provides room for participative arrangements in management, stresses that leadership is a collegial activity, makes educational values central to the enterprise, contests the view that management is inevitably or generally manipulative, and believes firmly that for effective outcomes and performance it is essential that quality management takes place.

There is little doubt that the philosophy of TQM has much to commend it. Vision is valuable and its aims give a shared commitment to improvement in educational institutions which have embraced it. However, as we have discussed, total commitment to an organisation's aims and activities is unlikely; remedial and positive action alike are called for. The various operative functions discussed in this chapter with their theoretical underpinnings and guidance into general and detailed actions seem to be a sounder way forward than a single good idea, although 'the vision thing' should never be undervalued in HRM.

REFERENCES

Adams, J.S. (1965) Inequality is social exchange, in Berkowitz, L. (ed.) *Advances in Experimental Psychology, Vol. 2*, New York, Academic Press.

Bennis, W.G. (1959) Leadership theory and administrative behaviour: the problem of authority, *Administrative Science Quarterly*, Vol. 4, pp. 255–71.

Betts, P.W. (1993) *Supervisory Management* (6th edn), London, Pitman.

Boyatzis, R.E. (1982) *The Competent Manager: A Model for Effective Performance*, New York, Wiley.

Cascio, W.F. (1991) *Applied Psychology in Personnel Management* (4th edn), Englewood Cliffs, NJ, Prentice-Hall.

Dennison, B. (1993) Performance indicators and consumer choice, in Preedy, M. (ed.) *Managing the Effective School*, London, Paul Chapman.

Drucker, P. (1974) *Management: Tasks, Responsibilities, Practices*, London, Heinemann.

Drucker, P. (1988) *Management*, Oxford, Heinemann.

Drucker, P.F. (1989) The spirit of performance, in Riches, C. and Morgan, C. (eds.) *Human Resource Management in Education*, Milton Keynes: Open University Press.

Elliott, G. and Hall, V. (1994) FE Inc. – business orientation in further education and the introduction of human resource management, *School Organisation*, Vol. 14(1), pp. 3–10.

Fitz-Gibbon, C.T. (1996a) Judgements must be credible and fair, *The Times Educational Supplement*, 29 March, p. 21.

Fitz-Gibbon, C.T. (1996b) *Monitoring Education: Indicators, Quality and Effectiveness*, London, Cassell.

Graystone, J. (1996) Governors' performance goes under the spotlight, *The Times Educational Supplement*, 12 April.

Gronn, P. (1996) From transaction to transformations, *Educational Administration and Management*, Vol. 24, No. 1, June pp. 7–30.

Hall, V. (1996) *Dancing on the Ceiling: A Study of Women Managers in Education*, London, Paul Chapman.

Hersey, P. and Blanchard, K. (1993) *Management and Organisational Behaviour*, London, Prentice-Hall.

Herzberg, F. (1966) *Motivation to Work*, New York, Wiley.

Hosking, D.M. (1988) Organising, leadership and skilful process, *Journal of Management Studies*, Vol. 25, no. 2, pp. 148–65.

Hoyle, E. and Jones, K. (1995) *Professional Knowledge and Professional Practice*, London, Cassell.

Kydd, L. (1996) Towards a restructuring of teachers' professional development, in Kydd, L., Crawford, M. and Riches, C. (eds) *Professional Development for Educational Managers*, Milton Keynes, Open University Press.

Laswell, H.D. (1948) The structure and function of communication in society, in Bryson, L. (ed.) *The Communication of Ideas*, New York, Harper & Bros.

Law, S. and Glover, D. (1996) Towards coherence in the management of professional development planning, paper delivered at the BEMAS Research Conference, March (unpublished).

Locke, E.A. (1968) Towards a theory of task motivation and incentives, *Organisational Behaviour and Human Performance*, vol. 3, pp. 157–89.

Locke, E.A. and Latham, G.P. (1990) Work motivation: the high performance cycle, in Kleinbeck, U., Quast, H.-H. and Hacker, H. (eds.) *Work Motivation*, Lawrence Erlbaum Associates.

Management Charter Initiative (1991) *Managing Standards Implementation Pack*, London, MCI.

Maslow, A. (1943) A theory of work motivation, *Psychological Review*, Vol. 50(4), pp. 370–96.

McGregor, D. (1970) *The Human Side of Enterprise*, Maidenhead, McGraw-Hill.

Neider, L. (1980) An experimental field investigation utilising an expectancy theory view of participation, *Organisational Behaviour and Human Performance*, Vol. 26(3), pp. 425–42.

Ofsted (1993) *Handbook for the Inspection of Schools*, London, HMSO.

Oldroyd, D., Elsner, D. and Poster, C. (1996) *Educational Management Today: A Concise Dictionary and Guide*, London, Paul Chapman.

Oldroyd, D. and Hall, V. (1996) *Managing Staff Development*, London, Paul Chapman.

O'Neill, J., Middlewood, D. and Glover, D. (1994) *Human Resource Management in Schools and Colleges*, Harlow, Longman.

Pollard, A. and Tann, S. (1994) *Reflective Teaching in the Primary School*, London, Cassell.

Poster, C. and Poster, D. (1991) *Teacher Appraisal, A Guide to Training*, London, Routledge.

Preston, D. (1989) *Personnel Management*, Harmondsworth, Penguin Books.

Rasberry, R.W. and Lemoine, L.F. (1986) *Effective Managerial Communication*, Boston, Mass., Kent Publishing.

Riches, C. (1994a) Motivation, in Bush, T. and West-Burnham, J. (eds) *The Principles of Educational Management*, Harlow, Longman.

Riches, C. (1994b) Communication, in Bush, T. and West-Burnham, J. (eds.) *The Principles of Educational Management*, Harlow, Longman.

Riches, C. and Morgan, C. (eds) (1989) *Human Resource Management*, Milton Keynes, Open University Press.

Rogers, L. and Badham, L. (1994) Evaluation in the management cycle, in Bennett, N., Glatter, R. and Levacic, R. (eds) *Improving Educational Management through Research and Consultancy*, London, Paul Chapman.

Ronan, W.W. and Prien, E.P. (1971) *Perspectives on the Measurement of Human Performance*, New York, Appleton-Century-Crofts.

Steers, R.M. and Porter, L.W. (1991) *Motivation and Work Behavior* (5th edn), New York, McGraw-Hill.

Tofte, B. (1996) A theoretical model for implementation of total quality leadership in education, *Total Quality Management*, Vol. 6, pp. 469–86.

West-Burnham, J. (1992) *Managing Quality in Schools*, Harlow, Longman.

Whitaker, P. (1993) *Practical Communication in Schools*, Harlow, Longman.

3

THE LEARNING ORGANISATION

Jacky Lumby

The term 'learning organisation' has attracted interest from many in education, as seeming to hold out the hope of providing new ideas which will aid those charged with managing educational institutions in times of unprecedented change. This chapter will discuss whether the concept of the learning organisation merits serious attention from educational managers, by exploring the origins of the term, how it has been differently understood by practitioners and theorists, and the variety of ways it has been implemented. Its value to education as a concept and as a practical tool to increase school and college effectiveness will be assessed. Finally the implications for managing people will be explored.

THE ORIGINS OF THE LEARNING ORGANISATION

The accelerating speed of change and the proliferation of sources of pressure on people in organisations has led to renewed emphasis on the centrality of learning. Since Revans (1982) formulated the equation that the rate of learning in an organisation must equal or be greater than the rate of change, the focus of managing people has moved further towards securing the means to help all staff learn. In schools and colleges, the role of creating a learning organisation is doubly important, not only in terms of making the institution itself as effective as possible, but also in providing a role model for all other organisations. For, as Clark (1996, p. 115) points out: 'If it fails here, what hope is there for all those institutions whose focal task is not an educational one?'

Jones and Hendry (1994) give a useful summary of the history of the term 'learning organisation', pointing out that although the actual phrase may be of relatively recent origin, research on the nature and relevance of learning within organisations has been taking place over a much longer period of time. They outline the contribution of researchers such as Argyris and Schon (1981), Revans (1982) and Pedler (1987) into company learning in business and industry. At the same time a parallel if smaller body of literature has been growing, exploring similar interests in the nature of learning in educational organisations.

The impetus to link the idea of the learning organisation to education has derived from three sources. First, the recognition of the speed and magnitude of change has led to the belief that the many education reforms present: 'the most fundamental challenge to prevailing orthodoxies of the management of educational institutions. The changes are so profound that any attempt to respond to them using established principles and processes is likely to be dysfunctional' (West-Burnham, 1992, p. 46). The implication is that new concepts and tools are needed to meet the difficulties of managing schools and colleges in the third millennium.

Secondly, there has arisen a rethinking of the capacity of educational organisations to develop their staff, and the ability of staff to learn. Writing of higher education, Boud (1995, p. 213) comments:

> It is a wonderful irony that, until now, institutions which are so professionally committed to education at the highest level and to the importance of learning, have in the past been so lacking in their ability to organize themselves to prompt learning for their own employees for the benefit of their organization.

Allied to the distinct lack of complacency in terms of education's ability to achieve effective development of staff, is a growing questioning of the nature of the way teachers learn, and a move from an emphasis on individually based learning to a more holistic and communal approach as the basis of effective teacher development. Recent writing on developing teachers (Yinger and Hendricks-Lee, 1993; Clark, 1996) explores the implications of a shift in perceptions, from an individually focused process of development to one where the whole teacher in the context of the whole organisation is the centre of planning development.

The third pressure to give serious consideration to the relevance of the learning organisation arises from research into school effectiveness. Sammons *et al.* (1995, p. 23) use a wide-ranging review of the research into school effectiveness to arrive at a list of eleven factors for effective schools, the last of which is 'A learning organisation':

> Effective schools are learning organisations, with teachers and senior managers continuing to be learners, keeping up to date with their subjects and with advances in understanding about effective practice. We use the term 'learning organisation' in a second sense which is that this learning has most effect when it takes place at the school itself or is school-wide, rather than specific

to individual teachers. The need for schools to become 'learning organisations' is increasingly important given the pace of societal and educational change.

Everard and Morris (1990) had earlier referred to schools which become learning organisations, as a way 'to stave off ossification'. Southworth (1994, p. 52) writes of the idea of a 'learning school':

> Peter Holly and I adopted this term because our work with teachers told us that just as there can be no curriculum development without teacher development, . . . so schools will not develop unless their staff groups develop, and staff development meant, for us, teachers learning. In short, a learning school is a developing school.

To summarise, the concept of the learning organisation is relevant to educational institutions because

- new means are needed to manage change on an unprecedented scale;
- educational institutions may not be sufficiently effective in developing staff;
- the understanding of the paradigm underlying teacher development is changing; and
- research on school and college effectiveness points to a relationship between effectiveness and achieving a learning organisation.

The developing concept of a learning organisation directs those who manage people in educational organisations to a reconsideration of the purpose and processes of their role.

DEFINITIONS OF THE LEARNING ORGANISATION

The connection made between educational effectiveness and the learning organisation should lead towards a possible agenda for action to achieve development of the individual and the organisation. The problem is that the term 'learning organisation' has collected a multiplicity of definitions and there is no common understanding of just what the term means. At one level it is a question of semantics, with discussion about whether organisational learning and the learning organisation are the same thing (Jones and Hendry, 1994).

A paradox is at the heart of the difficulty of definition. Individuals learn, but the sum of that learning does not necessarily equal organisational learning. For the latter to occur, other conditions may have to be satisfied, so that some synthesis occurs and the abstraction, the organisation, in some sense learns. The paradox is that an abstract concept cannot learn, and yet, for some writers (Handy, 1989; Senge, 1993; Jones and Hendry, 1994) this is exactly what they believe to happen in a learning organisation. There are implications here not only for those with a responsibility for the development of staff, but also for the structures of organisations, and the way an educational organisation is led, to ensure a communal focus for learning.

Further definitions range from concepts of improved HRM to more visionary descriptions of a process or state which implies more fundamental change. The concept of transformation is central to the understanding of many writers. Jones and Hendry (1994) criticise those who, in their attempts to get to grips with the nebulous concept of a learning organisation, rely on superficial changes in human resource processes or structures. For them, the core of the issue is the nature of learning itself, and any definition which glibly proposes improving learning without an in-depth understanding of how people learn is of little value: 'The concept of the learning organisation is therefore a challenge to explore more fully what learning is and how we can create organizational structures which are meaningful to people so that they can assist, participate and more effectively control their own destiny in an unhampered way' (*Ibid.*, p. 160).

The definitions above relate to generic management. Definitions specific to educational management have not proliferated to the same degree. Southworth (1994, p. 53) offers one example of applying similar ideas within the context of a school:

A learning school has five interrelated characteristics. In the learning school:
- the focus is on the pupils and their learning;
- individual teachers are encouraged to be continuing learners themselves;
- teachers (and sometimes others) who constitute 'staff' are encouraged to collaborate by learning with and from each other;
- the school (all those people who constitute the school) learns its way forward, i.e. the school as an organization is a learning 'system' (Schon 1971);
- the headteacher is the leading learner.

This definition encompasses many of the ideas of the generic definitions. There is an emphasis on all staff learning individually and together, focusing on the central objective of the institution (students' learning) and with a strong role for the leader in creating the right culture and climate. It also makes clear that, unlike business in general, educational institutions are learning organisations in a double sense. They have as their central purpose the promotion of learning, and they must create a learning organisation where all those involved, not just students, must learn individually and collectively to provide a model of lifelong learning which, in itself, is focused on the learning of students.

Southworth (*ibid.*) states that creating a learning school is 'neither simple nor straightforward'. The implications in practical terms will be explored in the following section.

CREATING THE LEARNING ORGANISATION: CREATING LEARNING

One of the common features of learning organisations, identified in the preceding section, is a challenging of assumptions about learning, and the requirement to harness learning which is different in nature and scale from that which has previously been the norm. Senge (1993, p. 13) defines how 'learning' has come to be understood:

> The problem with talking about 'learning organizations' is that the 'learning' has lost its central meaning in contemporary usage. Most people's eyes glaze over if you talk to them about 'learning organizations'. Little wonder — for, in everyday use, learning has come to be synonymous with 'taking in information'. 'Yes, I learned all about that at the course yesterday.' Yet, taking in information is only distantly related to real learning.

A number of writers (Argyris, 1991; Schein, 1993; West, 1994) challenge the notion that managing people's learning is straightforward. They point to the fact that although learning occurs almost constantly, it is trammelled by the culture and mythology of the organisation, by the micropolitical interests of the individual, and by the personal defence mechanisms that may have been established to circumvent painful lessons for many years.

The phrase to summarise the theories explored in relation to the learning organisation is perhaps that people need to learn how to learn. The assumption that staff trained to help others to learn will be automatically good at learning themselves may not be justified. Perhaps schools and colleges must take as a premise that their highly skilled staff are unlikely to be able to overcome the many barriers to positive organisational learning without a great deal of help. Managing people therefore involves providing structures, resources and support which will help staff learn.

Although there are general descriptions of the need to create an experimental and non-blame environment, specific practical means of offering the help needed are rather rare. Empirical evidence of educational organisations' attempts to foster a learning organisation is sparse.

An exception is the work of Southworth (1994), who builds up a case study of a primary school striving to become a 'learning school'. Southworth draws out the implications for other schools as being the need for information to flow freely in all directions, so that there is a base of commonly held knowledge. He also stresses (*ibid.*, p. 70) the need for a diversity of approach to joint learning:

> One conclusion of the Whole School Curriculum Development project is that the project team generally believe schools need more rather than fewer ways of fostering learning. A reliance on only one or two ways in which teachers learn is not sufficient; a rich mix is needed. Although we have not attempted any quantitative assessment of our data, our view is that senior staff in schools need to foster and sustain a high number of strategies by which teachers learn together and which are regularly and repeatedly used so as to develop a critical mass of them.

Southworth also emphasises the need for the school leader to lead by becoming a living example of a commitment to continuous collaborative learning. This case study focuses on the needs of teachers, and consequently misses one of the central features of a learning organisation, which is that *all* staff must be involved in the collaborative learning.

Although not explicitly linked to the creation of a learning organisation, Henry's (1994) description of the steps he took to change the culture of his further education college outlines a process to draw everyone into a central excitement of learning how best to meet the needs of students. The minimum of structure and frequent change are used to undermine any sense of stasis. He asks (*ibid.*, p. 218):

> Do your cleaners have pigeon holes? Is there a weekly bulletin or newsletter which updates staff on what is happening in the college? Did you stop sending memos six years ago? . . . do all members of your staff have an opportunity to work with a computer from their homes? Is every member of staff in a team? Are all staff given regular weekly time off to attend team meetings? . . . Do you have totally free unmetered access to photocopying? Do you encourage the borrowing of college equipment by staff and students? Has your college changed its structure at least a dozen times in the last three years? Has your college refused to introduce any appraisal system in recognition of the fact that appraisal is Deming's third deadly disease? Is upward appraisal encouraged at all levels within the college?

The first point emerging is an emphasis on the holistic management of all staff, not just teaching staff. Trust is demonstrated in a number of ways. Central bureaucracy is dismantled. The whole focus is a reversal of the traditional mode of managing people which centres on communication and development directed down the organisation. The emphasis in Henry's strategy is on an upward flow of communication. Development of the staff, and thereby the college, is no longer centred on training and downward appraisal. The new approach demands the willingness of every member of the organisation to respond to endemic change, and to listen to those for whom they provide a service. The need to learn is embedded in the system.

Ralph (1995) outlines in detail the process of developing her further and higher education college as a learning organisation, involving a sustained piece of research to identify the conditions needed to support the effectiveness of the 'change agents' within the college. She examined staff's needs in relation to communication, motivation, creativity, stress and support. In effect she listened to staff in detail, over time, and responded with a range of changes designed to contribute to the effectiveness of staff in understanding and implementing their role. She found that the organisation was sabotaging the very changes it wished to achieve by 'Flawed communication processes involving ineffective decision-making, inappropriate gatekeeping, inefficient information dissemination and inadequate participation' (*ibid.*, p. 665). She draws on the literature of the learning organisation to suggest eight programmes to address the needs of staff to be effective change agents (*ibid.*, pp. 672–6):

• Communication process development

- Corporate values dissemination
- Management development programme
- Peer support programme
- Fostering reflection
- Team empowerment programme
- Staff welfare programme
- Environment enhancement programme.

These programmes are not vague wish lists, but developed in detail with concrete plans and timescales. The reality of an organisation with competing agendas, stressed staff and failed communication is accepted as a starting point for an in-depth review and response to the real needs of staff. The learning involved is not comfortable but necessary to discover possible ways to motivate staff and to release their creativity.

The examples of the primary school and the further and higher education colleges are not presented as ideal types of achieving a learning organisation. Rather they are examples of approaches which have tried to achieve learning of a different nature to that which existed previously. In the primary school example, it is the diversity and quantity of learning activity which it is hoped will lead to 'a critical mass'. In the example of the further education college, the emphasis is on establishing a way of acting which invests absolute trust in the staff, alongside a willingness of managers to listen constantly to what the staff are saying. The further and higher education college demonstrates an approach which establishes the full set of circumstances needed to sustain individual endeavour to improve the college. In none of the three is the issue of staff learning seen as a discrete matter which can be tidily encompassed under the heading 'staff development'. Rather establishing the capacity to learn is a central strategic task of those with the responsibility of managing people and involves looking at the whole range of circumstances which will support or impede their effectiveness.

CREATING THE LEARNING ORGANISATION: CREATING STRUCTURES

If to focus on the development of the individual is not enough, what whole organisation implications are there for change? The attitudes and vision of the person initiating change must be the first consideration. Argyris believes this must be the person at the top of the organisation, and that without this commitment, the process of creating a learning organisation may be counterproductive. Honey (1991, p. 33) argues that development can be more piecemeal:

> If top management are out of sympathy with the notion of a Learning Organisation that is unfortunate but not the end of the matter. Simply use the steps to create a mini learning organisation in the parts you *can*

influence. Small incremental changes, *if sustained,* have a habit of gaining momentum to the point where they become transformational.

The ideal process would therefore involve the commitment of the person who leads the educational institution, but Honey's suggestion implies that the head of department, section, faculty, or those with a specific responsibility for the development of staff, could initiate change.

The actual structures required cannot be prescribed, but there does seem to be a degree of agreement, that what Morgan (1986) refers to as the ability to 'self-organize', is important. Henry's (1994) description of the college reorganizing a dozen times in three years presupposes a fluidity and looseness which is the opposite of rigidly defined hierarchies and networks. Southworth (1994, p. 70) echoes this belief:

> A measure of looseness may be needed. In other words, learning schools are not always tight or organizationally 'tidy' places and the staff who work in them need to be tolerant of ambiguity. Indeed, alongside the plans which create a clear picture of the goals at which we are aiming, needs to go a measure of flexibility. Learning schools are not soft and unfocused but neither are they hard and tight institutions. Informality abounds . . .

This links to the research on school effectiveness (Mortimore *et al.,* 1988; Sammons *et al.,* 1995), which indicates that a participative approach to management, rather than hierarchical decision-making structures, is the more effective.

The 'loose-tightness' needed will not arrive without careful planning and implementation. All the evidence reviewed points to the necessity for staff to be freed and empowered as far as possible, but if this were the sum of the process, the end point might well be a renewed emphasis on individual, and not collective, learning. A tension exists between the flatter structures which distribute the power of decision-making more widely in schools and colleges, and the need for communication and collaboration between constituent parts. More autonomy increases motivation and the capacity to respond, but may lessen the incentives to communicate widely.

Turner (1991) describes colleges' experiments with different forms of grouping to ensure cross-sectoral learning. Of particular interest is the distinction between formal working groups and informal network groups, which come together from widely dispersed parts of the organisation to ensure communication and collaboration. Southworth (1994, p. 55) discusses the same difficulty in relation to primary schools:

> Undoubtedly, where staff have the capacity to collaborate professionally they increase their opportunities to learn from one another both informally and formally (e.g. staffroom conversation, staff meetings, working parties, committees). In fact, whenever staff work together they learn from one another. However, the challenge is for staff to organize themselves so that their professional growth is a central and explicit concern rather than a serendipitous process.

Southworth suggests that professional development days provide time for this process, but does not offer any further suggestions as to how the process can be embedded through the rest of the school year. Each educational organisation perhaps needs to adopt a multistranded approach:

- Review the effectiveness of formal means in existence to ensure collaborative learning, such as departmental/year/section teams, professional support days, specific development activities in-house or elsewhere.
- Support informal networking needs.
- Improve the physical environment for staff relaxation and contact.
- Manage staff pressures, ensuring time management helps reduce stress and overload.
- Create occasions for informal discussion, such as common non-contact hours across institutional boundaries.

All these may be areas that require a long-term strategy to support collective learning.

CONCLUSIONS: IMPLICATIONS FOR EDUCATIONAL ORGANISATIONS

There are many pressures in existence which militate against the creation of learning organisations in schools and colleges. The stringencies of development or strategic planning and the requirements of the inspectorate for documented systems all push against maintaining the looseness needed. For further education particularly, the large numbers of part-time staff, almost half of all those employed (FEDA, 1995), do not make it easy to create collaborative learning. Given these forces working towards organisations which are more tightly controlled and less centred on a permanent community of staff, what can the concept of a learning organisation offer to schools and colleges? Is the concept likely to remain a rather nebulous vision or can it contribute to increasing school/college effectiveness?

It is clear that the idea of a learning organisation does not offer a single practical agenda. Rather it provides an overarching concept which redirects the attention of those who manage people in education, which as Fidler and Cooper (1992, p. 57) point out: integrates 'the classroom and the staffroom', teachers are engaged in the same systematic and continuous learning process as their pupils/students. The first implication for those who manage people then is how they can place learning at the centre of all activities. This may result in part from a number of small contributions, such as Tann's (1995, p. 46) suggestion that each potential new member of staff is asked at interview: 'What did you learn last year?' and 'What are you hoping to learn this year?', indicating the organisation's demand for lifelong learning. There may also be a more sustained emphasis on continuous learning, as implied in Southworth's (1994, p. 68) description of the role of the headteachers:

> The heads monitored the extent to which school policies were implemented; they took an active interest in the teachers' work and lives; they promoted curriculum initiatives by encouraging experimentation; they attended to teachers' individual and collective needs and interests; they established ways in which staff could share and talk about their work in their classrooms (e.g. showing assemblies, staff meetings, informal visits by the head to teachers in their classrooms after school). In much of this heads were seeking to establish and sustain an organisational culture that facilitated openness and sharing.

Secondly, if defence mechanisms which militate against learning are to be overcome, fear must be banished. Again there is not a single means to achieve this, but educational leaders could adopt people management systems which communicate trust. Henry's (1994) technique was to use only upward appraisal. Argyris (1991) suggested challenging the hidden communication at meetings by discussing people's real thoughts and feelings and fears of expressing them prior to the actual meeting. Such techniques contain risk, but a very strong message may be required to liberate people from what is often the constrained communication of 'professional' discussion.

Finally, the strategic performance of educational organisations may be seen in the light of ongoing learning for the whole staff. Tann (1995) surveyed a number of further and higher education institutions and identified that a 'learning approach to strategy' and 'participative policy-making' in a number of them contributed to moving them towards becoming a learning organisation. As she noted (*ibid.*, p. 55): '. . . these characteristics imply a more flexible, facilitative and long-term approach than is usually deemed possible in a rapidly changing environment with a downward driving of the resource unit.'

The concept of a learning organisation does not offer an obvious and simple series of practical steps in managing people, but it is none the less, a powerful tool. Ideas in themselves have power to shift people's thinking and, ultimately, their actions. The vision of a learning organisation, despite or perhaps because of the variety of ways in which it is understood, can be a useful catalyst in refocusing people's efforts. It directs people to reassess in two ways. It challenges schools and colleges to rethink how far the means they have adopted to manage staff are effective, and suggests that many of the textbook techniques may be too superficial. As Henry (1994, p. 218), taking this approach to an extreme, states: 'Any colleague with a function described as human resource management obviously would be ruled out', implying that a discrete approach to managing people, with one person seen as having the major responsibility, is no longer appropriate.

The notion also points people to reconsider the appropriate structures to create a dynamic responsive environment, and in this it has much in common with the philosophy of total quality management, with its emphasis on structures which empower and liberate.

The concept therefore has worth as pointing towards a journey of reassessment and engagement with the reality of organisational cultures, but it increasingly offers a number of practical agendas for steps which may be taken to achieve an organisation which is able to cope with the enormous demands of the third millennium, as educational institutions consider and enact their understanding of the implications of the concept. It is not a route for the faint hearted. The concept challenges existing systems and wisdom:

> . . . there is a danger of overlooking important conflicts between the requirements of learning and self-organization on the one hand, and the realities of power and control on the other. Any move away from bureaucracy toward self-organization has major implications for the distribution of power and control within an organization, since the increase in autonomy granted to self-organizing units undermines the ability of those with ultimate power and control within an organization to keep a firm hand on day-to-day activities and developments. Moreover, the process of learning requires a degree of openness and self-criticism that is foreign to traditional modes of management.
> (Morgan, 1986, p. 108)

Moreover, it is clear that not all organisations will be ready to embark on this path. As well as leaders prepared to operate in a way which sees their central role in managing people as nurturing organisational learning, the values of the school or college need to be well established: 'You cannot have a learning organization without shared vision. Without a pull toward some goal which people truly want to achieve, the forces in support of the status quo can be overwhelming. Vision establishes the overarching goal' (Senge, 1993, p. 209).

As long ago as 1977, the HMI report *Ten Good Schools* (DES, 1977) recognised that to promote the learning of students successfully, schools had to do more than adopt the technical means of delivering teaching; they had to in some sense embody the very commitment to learning as of central importance to human existence: '"Success" does not stem merely from the existence of certain structures of organisation, teaching patterns or curriculum planning, but is dependent on the spirit and understanding that pervades the life and work of a school, faithfully reflecting its basic objectives' (quoted in Sammons *et al.*, 1995, p. 7). In this sense, the concept of the learning organisation offers to educational institutions a powerful idea and an emerging set of tools to underpin their effectiveness at the most fundamental level. Those managing people in education can see the development of all staff, not as a peripheral support activity, but as an intrinsic and strategic process to be embedded in every aspect of the institution's activity.

REFERENCES

Argyris, C. (1991) Teaching Smart People How to Learn, *Harvard Business Review*, May–June, pp. 99–109.

Argyris, C. and Schon, D.A. (1981) *Organizational Learning*, Reading, Mass., Addison-Wesley.

Boud, D. (1995) Meeting the challenges, in Brew, A. (ed.) *Directions in Staff Development*, Buckingham, Society for Research into Higher Education and Open University Press.

Clark, D. (1996) *Schools as Learning Communities*, London, Cassell.

Department for Education and Science; HM Inspectorate of Schools (1977) *Ten Good Schools: A Secondary School Enquiry*, London, HMSO.

Everard, B. and Morris, G. (1990) *Effective School Management*, London, Paul Chapman.

FEDA (1995) *Mapping the FE Sector*, London, FEDA.

Fidler, B. and Cooper, R. (1992) *Staff Appraisal in Schools and Colleges*, Harlow, Longman.

Handy, C. (1989) *The Age of Unreason*, London, Random House.

Henry, T. (1994) Changing college culture, in Gorringe, R. and Toogood, P. (eds) *Changing the Culture of a College*, Bristol, The Staff College (*Coombe Lodge Report*, Vol. 24, no. 23).

Honey, P. (1991) The learning organisation simplified, *Training and Development*, July, pp. 30–3.

Jones, A.M. and Hendry, C. (1994) The Learning Organization: Adult Learning and Organizational Transformation, *British Journal of Management*, Vol. 5, pp. 153–162.

Morgan, G. (1986) *Images of Organization*, London, Sage.

Mortimore, P., Sammons, P., Stoll, L., Lewis, D. and Ecob, R. (1988) *School Matters: The Junior Years*, Wells, Open Books.

Pedler, M. (1987) *Applying Self-Development in Organizations*, Sheffield, Manpower Services Commission.

Ralph, M. (1995) *Developing the College as a Learning Organisation*, *Coombe Lodge Report*, Vol. 24, Nos. 7 and 8, Bristol, The Staff College.

Revans, R.W. (1982) *The Origins and Growth of Action Learning*, Bromley, Chartwell-Bratt.

Sammons, P., Hillman, J. and Mortimore, P. (1995) *Key Characteristics of Effective Schools: A Review of School Effectiveness*, London, Ofsted.

Schein, E.H. (1993) How can organizations learn faster?, *Sloan Management Review*, Winter, pp. 85–92.

Schon, D. (1971) *Beyond the Stable State*, London, Temple Smith.

Senge, P. (1993) *The Fifth Discipline*, London, Century Business.

Southworth, G. (1994) The learning school, in Ribbins, R. and Burridge, E. (eds) *Improving Education: Promoting Quality in Schools*, London, Cassell.

Tann, J. (1995) The learning organisation, in Warner, D. and Crosthwaite, E. (eds) *Human Resource Management in Higher and Further Education*, Buckingham, Society for Research into Higher Education and Open University Press.

Turner, C. (1991) *Structures – Fact and Fiction*, *Mendip Paper* 015, Bristol, The Staff College.

West, P. (1994) The Concept of the Learning Organization, *Journal of European Industrial Training*, Vol. 18, no. 1, pp. 15–21.

West-Burnham, J. (1992) Total quality management in education, in Bennett, N., Crawford, M. and Riches, C. (eds) *Managing Change in Education*, London, Paul Chapman.

Yinger, R. and Hendricks-Lee, M. (1993) Working knowledge in teaching, in Day, C., Calderhead, J. and Denicolo, P. (eds) *Research on Teacher Thinking*, London, Falmer Press.

Section B: organisational issues

Managers in schools or colleges can only achieve effective performance from people who work in them, or develop the appropriate culture for this to occur, if the appropriate devices are in place. Three of these are discussed in this section. Tony Bush examines the purpose and relevance of structures in Chapter 4. He describes how conventional bureaucratic structures have been challenged in the 1990s and the subsequent development of structures which are 'flatter'. He argues that structures illustrate the potential for tension between individual needs and organisations' requirements. In Chapter 5, Valerie Hall discusses the concept of role and its application in education. She analyses how many of the current assumptions about roles bring conflict and ambiguity but argues that the emphasis on self-development means that there is considerable potential for individuals to shape their own roles. John O'Neill in Chapter 6 re-examines some of the conventional approaches to working through teams, arguing that these assumptions ignore some of the realities of collaborative working. Disagreements are inevitable and should be accepted as being a positive and healthy part of effective teamwork. A nominal but ineffective team approach may be counterproductive in a profession where the key work is essentially individual.

4

MANAGEMENT STRUCTURES

Tony Bush

INTRODUCTION: WHAT DO WE MEAN BY STRUCTURE?

Structure refers to the formal pattern of relationships between people in organisations. It expresses the ways in which individuals relate to each other in order to achieve organisational objectives. O'Neill's (1994, p. 109) definition captures the main features of structure: 'Structure embodies both a formal description of roles, authority, relationships, and positions within the organisation . . . and also the pragmatic notion that structural design should promote and facilitate organisational effectiveness. Structure . . . is created to distribute and co-ordinate the work of people in the pursuit of organisational goals and objectives.' The notion of 'creation' is significant because it serves to stress the potential for managers to restructure the organisation to meet changing requirements. While, as we shall see later, pre-existing structures may inhibit change, leaders do have the power to shift the organisation to reflect new circumstances.

Structures are often represented by organisation charts which show the authorised pattern of relationships between members of the institution (Bush, 1995, p. 29). However, there is a tension between the focus on structure and the individual characteristics which people bring to organisations. Janes *et al.* (1989, p. 429) emphasise that 'management structures have to be both interpreted and implemented by human beings'. Effectiveness depends on both the nature of the structure and on the individual qualities that people bring to the organisation. Janes *et al.* (*ibid.*, p. 431) summarise the connection in further education:

> The behaviour of staff and the attitudes that underpin their behaviour can be thought of as being influenced by the college's structure . . . One of the

things that organisation structure does is to articulate who does what and in association with whom. This identifies those who are to be brought together and influences decisions about who should be kept apart.

Gray (1982, p. 34) is sceptical about the perceived centrality of structure in management and prefers to focus on relationships: 'Structure is simply a description of what people do and how they relate; organisation structure is a grossly simplified description of jobs and relationships.' This view is a useful counter to those who assert that perfecting structure is the most significant element in organisational effectiveness. There is an iterative and dependent relationship between people and structure: 'An emphasis on structure leads to the notion of individuals being defined by their roles while a focus on people leads to the predominance of personality in determining behaviour' (Bush, 1995, p. 25).

It can be argued that there is likely to be greater variability in people than in structures, and outcomes are likely to depend more on the human dimension than on the formal organisation. When there are staff changes, it can often be seen that the new occupant fills the role in a different way but it is rare for the position to be unrecognisable following the change. Structure provides stability and predictability while people introduce human variables arising from their personality and unique experience.

OBJECTIVES OF STRUCTURES

Mullins (1989, p. 113) emphasises that structure is not an end in itself but provides a means of improving organisational performance. He identifies six objectives of structure:

- The economic and efficient performance of the organisation and the level of resource utilisation;
- Monitoring the activities of the organisation;
- Accountability for areas of work undertaken by groups and individual members of the organisation;
- Co-ordination of different parts of the organisation and different areas of work;
- Flexibility in order to respond to future demands and developments, and to adapt to changing environmental influences;
- The social satisfaction of members working in the organisation.

While it can be argued that the objectives of structure may be common to all types of organisation, the precise nature of that structure varies according to the size and type of institution. O'Neill (1994, p. 111) claims that the actual structure depends on three variables:

1) the organisation's activities;
2) the existing roles of people in management positions;

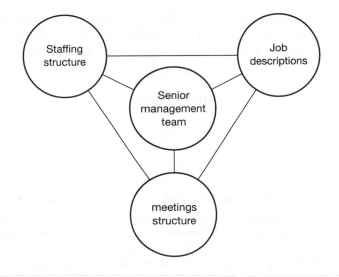

Figure 4.1   The parts of the management structure
Source: Roberts and Ritchie, 1990

  3) the degree of motivation of people within the organisation.

The structure is also likely to be influenced by the capability of individuals within the organisation and on the preferences of the principal. All these factors mean that each school or college requires a unique structure to meet its individual needs.

  Roberts and Ritchie (1990) claim that structures in secondary schools comprise four elements:

- Senior management team.
- Staffing structure.
- Meetings structure.
- Job descriptions.

The centrality of the SMT is stressed by the authors' diagrammatic representation of the relationship between these four elements (see Figure 4.1). The components of structure identified by Roberts and Ritchie (*ibid.*) do not include governors. While the governing body and its committees constitute the government structure of the institution, the management structure usually comprises senior managers and staff but not lay governors.

STRUCTURES AND ORGANISATIONAL THEORY

Structure is an important element in the theory of educational management (Evetts, 1992; Bush, 1995). The treatment of structure depends on certain underlying assumptions about the nature of management in education. Changes in structure in schools and colleges are often underpinned by a conceptual dimension reflected in one or more of these theories.

Bureaucracy

Most management structures in education, particularly those in secondary schools and colleges, tend to be consistent with bureaucratic assumptions and some could be regarded as pictorial representations of bureaucracy. Packwood (1989, p. 9) argues that a bureaucratic structure is the most effective device for organising work and dealing with imposed change:

> Organisation is an artefact for achieving work, so it is worth getting it as right as possible for the benefit of those who perform, or depend upon, that work . . . If schools are to make the best of the new demands that have, to a great extent, been imposed upon them, they have no choice but to make the best of bureaucracy.

Packwood's emphasis on improving bureaucratic structures is characteristic of this approach; maximising efficiency through modification rather than radical change. His view that bureaucracy is 'inevitable' is reflected elsewhere in the literature, for example in Smith's (1986) discussion of structures in higher education. The main features of bureacratic structures are indicated by Bush (1995, p. 36):

> [Bureaucracy] stresses the importance of the *hierarchical authority structure* with formal chains of command between the different positions in the hierarchy. This pyramidal structure is based on the legal authority vested in the officers who hold places in the chain of command. Office holders are responsible to superordinates for the satisfactory conduct of their duties.

Evetts (1992, p. 84) emphasises the hierarchical nature of school structures and reinforces the authority of the head: 'A high degree of authority is vested in the headteacher and transmitted through heads of departments/years. . . [it implies] agreement about the headteacher's ability to direct the management of the school without disagreement or opposition.' The bureaucratic model subordinates individuals to the needs of the organisation. In the dialectic between structure and personality, the former wins 'hands down': 'A central assumption of this [bureaucratic] approach is that personnel may change but the structure is an enduring feature of the organisation' (Bush, 1989, p. 3)

Collegiality

The traditional emphasis on bureaucracy has been challenged by a normative preference for collegiality in the 1990s. Wallace (1989, p. 182) describes it as 'the official model of good practice'. Structures are lateral or horizontal rather than vertical and hierarchical, reflecting the view that all teachers should be involved in decision-making and 'own' the outcome of discussions. Authority in collegial structures is based on professional expertise rather than position.

Johnston and Pickersgill (1992, p. 239) argue that, in primary schools, it is 'imperative that managerial behaviour is centred on leadership for collegiality . . . the "collegial" school offers the most attractive and persuasive basis for the provision of educational experience of the highest quality'. Collegiality provides the conceptual underpinning for the view that management structures should be 'flat', with few levels and short communication chains.

Culture

The concept of structure may be contrasted with that of culture which refers to the informal aspects of organisations. Harling (1989, p. 20) claims that 'networks of informal relationships and unofficial norms . . . arise from the interaction of individuals and groups working within the formal structure'. While this chapter focuses on structure, the cultural aspects of the organisation may be equally significant, as O'Neill (1994, p. 103) suggests:

> A distinction between culture and structure is helpful because it highlights the potential tensions between structures and policies, which constitute the official goals and formal relationships in the organization, and the values and informal networks of relationships which represent the practice and aspirations of the people who make up the organization.

The nature of structure may influence the culture of the organization. Complex structures, such as those in secondary schools and colleges, may lead to multiple cultures whereas the typical simple primary school structure is more likely to lead to a single dominant culture.

Micropolitics

The departmental structure of many secondary schools and colleges may allow micropolitics to thrive with subunits competing for influence and resources (Evetts, 1992; Bush, 1995). The formal structure becomes the setting for conflict between interest groups: 'In the conventional departmental structure . . . the primary interest of the HoDs is their self-interest in the success and growth of their section rather than what might be the over-riding interest of the college as a whole' (Janes *et al.*, 1989, p. 433).

DETERMINANTS OF STRUCTURE

O'Neill (1994) argues that management structures have to serve two distinct, and potentially conflicting, purposes. First, they should determine the nature of *differentiation*, that is the allocation of tasks and duties and the definition of specific roles and responsibilities. Secondly, they should encourage *integration*, the linking together of roles to promote interdependence.

Evetts (1992, p. 89) points to the need for organisational change in response to the demands facing self-managing schools in the 1990s, including, in England and Wales, the National Curriculum, local management of schools and increasing parental choice of schools: 'The impact of such educational changes has influenced headteachers' construction and development of management structures and has increased the amount of micro-political negotiations in schools over tasks and responsibilities.'

Most heads and principals inherit the previous management structure when they take over their institutions and this is certain to be a strong influence on their planning, at least in the short term. Inherited structures may constrain change, partly because of the expectations of the existing staff, which are likely to be focused on the previous status quo. More significant, though, is the inhibiting effect of the existing pattern of responsibility allowances: 'Schools inherit organisational structures, and proposed changes to those structures can be problematic. Current postholders need to be persuaded of the benefits of change, allocation of incentive allowances may need revision and new teams may have to be formed' (Fincham, 1991, p. 246).

As Fincham suggests, new principals may experience difficulties when they seek to adapt structures. Johnston and Pickersgill (1992, p. 242) refer to the problems arising when staff resist change: 'People, and therefore the organisations they create, often resist change and their resistance may be greatest when they feel that they have some investment in the original design.'

Change may be particularly painful if it occurs during, and perhaps prompted by, declining student numbers and income. The existing organisation may be overelaborate and very expensive if the school or college is significantly smaller than it was when the structure was established. This situation prevailed at the Pensnett Comprehensive School in the West Midlands in the late 1980s. The new head inherited a management structure, designed when the school had 900 pupils, which was palpably 'top heavy' with a roll of fewer than 600. Bush (1989, pp. 4–5) identifies two problems arising from falling rolls: 'First, it seems likely to limit promotion opportunities and may lead to the build-up of resentment among junior staff . . . Secondly, the specific responsibilities held by senior staff may be a constraint on organisational change especially where they combine to defend the status quo.'

Despite these limitations, leaders do have the opportunity to create their own structures, even if progress is slow, uneven and incremental rather than immediate and seismic. As long as they can secure the support of governors, they have control over the allocation of responsibility allowances (or 'points') and can gradually develop their own preferred pattern: 'The allocation of promotion allowances to particular responsibilities is an important indication of a headteacher's priorities and values. School structures of management are one of the ways in which headteachers can create their own schools' (Evetts, 1992, p. 96).

THE ACADEMIC/PASTORAL 'DIVIDE' IN SECONDARY SCHOOLS

We noted earlier O'Neill's (1994) view that a central purpose of structure is differentiation, that is the allocation of tasks and duties to individuals and groups. In secondary schools and colleges, in particular, it is necessary to share responsibilities so that individuals have discrete, and manageable, loads. The corollary of such arrangements is the need for effective co-ordination of disparate activities.

Evetts' (1992, p. 92) research shows that many secondary schools achieve differentiation through separate academic and pastoral structures. However, her respondents were concerned about the dysfunctional effects of these arrangements: 'For the majority of . . . headteachers these were two separate and distinct systems of management. However, some . . . headteachers saw such a separation as a defect in terms of effective management of schools and also in terms of the career development of individual teachers.' One concern expressed by Evetts' respondents was the lower status of pastoral care. A related factor was the tendency for women to take pastoral roles, a bias that might limit their subsequent promotion opportunities. Marianne Coleman gives extended consideration to this issue in Chapter 9.

Fincham (1991, pp. 246–7) argues that the 'typical' secondary school structure (see Figure 4.2) tends to promote division and conflict:

> In this pattern, pastoral and curricular interests of the school are managed through deputy head-teachers with specific responsibilities. Their job definitions reflect a bias either towards pastoral or academic functions and they might chair meetings of pastoral middle-managers or heads of department respectively . . . it may give rise to a spurious division between pastoral and academic concerns.

Research at the Pensnett School (Bush, 1989) illustrates the problems that can be created by separate pastoral and academic structures. A strong team of faculty heads was perceived as 'insular' by some staff. The pastoral heads subsequently developed as a separate team with both groups operating as 'secret societies': 'There is a definite split; The academic/pastoral divide is unfortunate; There are two separate empires; Two compartments with

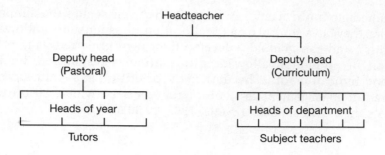

Figure 4.2 A typical model of school organisation and management
Source: Fincham, 1991

a partition; Backbiting existed between faculty heads and pastoral staff'
(teacher, quoted by Bush, *ibid.*, p. 5).

The separation between the academic and pastoral aspects of the school
was sustained by three structural elements:

1. Specialist curriculum and pastoral roles at the deputy level;
2. Designation of senior and middle management posts as either academic
   or pastoral;
3. Separate meetings for academic and pastoral senior staff.

(Ibid.)

At Pensnett, and in many of the schools discussed by Fincham (1991) and
Evetts (1992), heads inherited these separate structures. As we suggested
earlier, existing organisations provide rigidities which may be difficult and
slow to overcome. Fincham (1991, p. 248) argues that resistance to change
should not be allowed to inhibit reform:

> A school may, for example, inherit a system of pastoral heads and heads of
> department with corresponding salary allowances and responsibilities which
> preclude radical and immediate changes in the management structure . . .
> However, schools must also find ways of meeting the charge that pastoral
> and academic concerns are artificially segregated and that the management
> structure and organisation is contributing to unintended conflicts and
> divisions . . . What is being advocated is an attempt at the integration
> of pastoral and academic interests which enables staff to realise their dual
> role of teaching and caring.'

The reference to 'integration' reinforces O'Neill's (1994) view that this is one
of the central purposes of structure. Some heads have responded to concerns
about divisive structures by making changes designed to promote cohesion.
For one of the heads interviewed by Evetts (1992, p. 93), the motivation was
provided by the National Curriculum and local management of schools:
'We decided that we wanted lower, middle and upper school with a much
more integrated pastoral/academic responsibility, to look at the curriculum

in a horizontal way, possibly to become cost centres under LMS . . . We have made the heads of school, lower, middle and upper, pastoral *and* academic.'

A similar approach to this problem is suggested by Whalley and Watkins (1991). They advocate the use of the year team as the 'building block' of secondary school structures. This should avoid the pastoral/academic split and lead to whole-school management: 'Inappropriate structures can undermine . . . the deployment of people in achieving particular goals. Without appropriate structures talk of "whole school" remains empty rhetoric' (*ibid.*, p. 20).

Another advantage of horizontal structures is that they may serve to facilitate cross-curricular work. It is often regarded as a low-status activity (Todd, 1994) and this is unlikely to change within traditional structures because of the power of departmental heads.

The academic/pastoral issue is a powerful illustration of the risks attached to any division of responsibilities, particularly when they are institutionalised in the formal structure. In large organisations, a measure of differentiation is inevitable but issues of integration should be given equal attention to avoid the development of separate empires, the breeding ground for potentially damaging micropolitics.

STRUCTURES IN FURTHER EDUCATION

Further education colleges in the UK share many of the structural features of secondary schools but they are larger, their activities are more diverse and their structures are often more complex. The traditional departmental model is hierarchical (Turner, 1991) with many levels and often weak lateral co-ordination. Janes *et al.* (1989, p. 433) point to the limitations of this model: 'In the conventional departmental structure HoDs are appointed to manage one section of the college . . . a number of relatively self-contained "mini colleges" are created, each with a "mini principal" exercising control over all the roles within the domain . . . The SMT has a built-in conflict of interests.'

Following incorporation in 1993, there has been a review of structure in many colleges. More flexible frameworks are being developed to respond to the many changes in funding and accountability (FEDA, 1995). Lumby (1996) refers to dissatisfaction with traditional departmental structures and to attempts to achieve a more student-centred approach. One purpose of the new structures may be to counter the curriculum power and micropolitical interests of departmental heads. In one college, senior management were given functional roles to neutralise the power of academic middle managers:

We felt that functional heads were less likely to be wedded to the interests of any vocational or teaching area. Therefore our middle managers who do relate to particular areas of teaching are managed by functional managers who don't have that sort of narrower perspective. We believe this has decreased the micropolitical imperatives which might previously have been driving the curriculum.

(College manager, quoted by Lumby, *ibid.*, p. 345)

Lewis (1994) points to the need to abolish a 'rigid departmental structure' in order to achieve organisational change at Broxtowe College, Nottingham, where he is the principal. He argues that radical restructuring was needed in order to overcome resistance to major policy changes, including staff redundancies and increased class size:

These changes . . . produced forms of dissent and blocking behaviour in some individuals who were able to use college structures to undermine the attempt to implement a corporate re-alignment of the college. To ensure the success of the survival strategy . . . it became necessary to destroy certain rigid organisational structures which were restraining cultural change.

(*Ibid.*, p. 256)

Field (1993, p. 94) also stresses the need to relate structure to function and to 'deal effectively with any existing power structures' which may inhibit change.

The radical changes discussed by Field (1993) and Lewis (1994) are redolent of the approach often taken in the private sector. Elliott and Hall (1994) refer to the infusion of business values since incorporation and express concern about the impact of these approaches on the core educational purpose of colleges. It remains to be seen whether the power accumulated by senior managers, at the expense of academic units, produces more effective colleges and better quality for students.

PRIMARY SCHOOL STRUCTURES

Most primary schools, in sharp contrast to secondary schools and colleges, are small and operate a relatively straightforward system for managing teaching and learning, and pupil welfare. The class system means that children spend much of their time with the same teacher who takes responsibility for their learning and care.

In most schools only the head has significant 'non-contact' time and those in small schools often have a substantial teaching role. This means that heads are typically the only people with time for management during the teaching day and even this may be limited by their own classroom responsibilities.

Bennett (1995) questions whether primary schools can have middle managers and points to two structural factors which cast doubt on the notion:

1) The small size of most primary schools restricts the extent to which a formal hierarchy of posts can be created.
2) Classroom teachers are not accountable to someone intermediate between them and the head. Only the head has time available to overcome the insularity of the classroom teacher.

Helps (1994) claims that the primary deputy is the head's 'partner in management' and cites Bolam *et al.*'s (1993) view that the role of deputy head has been enhanced since the *Education Reform Act* 1988. However, Helps' research confirms Bennett's comment about deputies having little time for management. Almost 50 per cent of his respondents had no non-contact time while another 20 per cent had less than one hour each week. Only one respondent was not a class teacher:

> This survey has highlighted the fundamental problem that there is so little non-contact time allocated to deputies during the normal school day that it is almost impossible for them to function effectively as senior managers, even though this is becoming an increasingly important aspect of the deputy's role.
>
> (Helps, 1994, p. 245)

Purvis and Dennison's (1993) research confirms Helps' findings. Of their respondents, 42 per cent are full-time class teachers and only 10 per cent have non-contact time for as much as half the week: 'Obligations directly associated with their own classrooms can prevent deputies from sustaining a school-wide responsibility for significant parts of the working day . . . the opportunity (and the energy) to practise the managerial duties which might be associated with deputy headship continue to be curtailed' (*ibid.*, p. 16). The implication of these two research projects is that management remains pre-eminently the function of the head, who has had to bear most of the extra responsibilities arising from the introduction of the National Curriculum and the shift to self-management. Despite all the changes of the 1980s and the 1990s, primary school structure has scarcely changed. What the author (Bush, 1981, p. 77) described as a 'typical' primary school structure at the beginning of the 1980s (see Figure 4.3) would still be valid in many schools in the second half of the 1990s.

The main feature of this structure is that it is relatively flat and unstratified. Most staff are classroom teachers and only the head has a managerial relationship with other staff. The deputy's ambiguous position, identified by Purvis and Dennison (1993) and Helps (1994), is shown by including it in two places. The classroom role is dominant and the weakness of the managerial relationship between the deputy and other teachers is reflected by a dotted line. Little appears to have changed since 1976 when Coulson (1976, p. 43) was able to assert that 'the day-to-day work of most deputy heads appears to be similar to that of other primary school teachers'.

The relatively small size of most primary schools, and their 'flat' structures, serve to facilitate collegiality, regarded (see p. 48) as the most

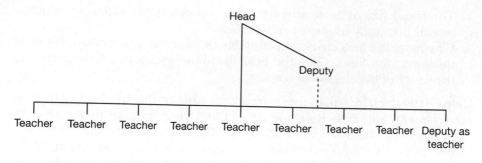

Figure 4.3 'Typical' primary school management structure
Source: Bush, 1981

appropriate model of management for 'successful' schools: 'Successful primary school heads . . . have succeeded through and with other staff in moving their schools in the direction of collegial structures and processes and to practice that is grounded in co-operative teamwork' (Johnston and Pickersgill, 1992, p. 239).

Flat structures may be preferred in primary schools but they are also inevitable as long as only the head has the opportunity to manage other staff during the teaching day. Bennett's (1995, p. 97) research shows that 'there was a hierarchical relationship between heads and assistants, but the hierarchical elements of that authority could not, apparently, be delegated to anyone else'.

THE IMPACT OF SALARY STRUCTURES ON SCHOOL ORGANISATION

Management structures, especially in secondary schools, have inevitably been shaped by the national salary arrangements. National bodies, in prescribing, allowing or limiting appointments at particular levels, have had a powerful influence on school structures and contributed strongly to a large measure of conformity in the organisation of schools.

Wallace (1986) traces the impact of salary structures on the development of management hierarchies in schools in England and Wales. From the 1950s, graded and, later, scale posts allowed the development of management structures. In practice, however, the responsibility attached to scale posts 'was often nominal, the reason for promotion often being to reward past performance or to attract or retain teachers with particular expertise rather than for accepting new responsibilities' (*ibid.*, p. 205).

As the management demands on schools became more evident, scale posts were increasingly allocated for specific responsibilities:

The organisational structures of management in schools are greatly influenced and constrained by the system of salary and promotion posts ... In the organisation of secondary schools, virtually every allowance involves some management/administrative responsibility. In organising and allocating a division of tasks and responsibilities, and in rewarding those undertaking such responsibilities, headteachers are both enabled and constrained by the career structure.

(Evetts, 1992, p. 87)

The 1995 pay and conditions document for England and Wales (DFEE, 1995) allows 'points' on the salary spine to be allocated for six reasons. As well as qualifications and experience, these are responsibilities, 'excellence', recruitment and retention, and special educational needs. The document emphasises that schools may determine their own pattern of allowances. The DFEE (*ibid.*) also stresses the management role of deputy heads and allows discretion for schools to determine the number of deputies to be appointed.

TOWARDS 'FLATTER' STRUCTURES

Flat structures are typical in primary schools but, as we have seen, hierarchical structures are the norm in secondary schools and colleges. There is a growing recognition of the potentially dysfunctional consequences of complex structures, as we noted earlier. Communication is regarded as more difficult in elaborate structures, particularly where it cuts across functional units such as departments. Staff may also be more likely to give their prime loyalty to the subunit rather than the school or college, leading to competition for power and resources, a prime indicator of micropolitics.

The preference for 'flat' structures is increasingly evident in the general management literature. Mullins (1989, p. 113) argues that structures should contain the least possible number of management levels: 'The chain of command should be as short as possible. Every additional level makes for difficulties in direction and mutual understanding, distorts objectives, sets up additional stresses, creates inertia and slack, and increases the difficulties of the development of future managers moving up through the chain.'

Management 'guru' Charles Handy (1994, p. 117) claims that the 'horizontal organisation' is in fashion. The central features of these structures are

- work is organised around processes not functions;
- hierarchy is 'flattened'; and
- teams not individuals are the principal building blocks of organisations.

According to Holbeche (1995), 90 per cent of UK-based organisations have undertaken 'delayering' exercises.

A recognition of the value of flat structures is also evident in some writing on management in education. Smith (1986, p. 227) says that 'hierarchies ... [are] generally not regarded as the most desirable or appropriate for higher education' while further education colleges in Scotland are being exhorted to adopt flatter structures with more emphasis on teamwork (Gartside, 1991).

There is also some evidence of limited shifts towards flatter structures in schools. Doe (1995, p. 2) refers to 'the imminent disappearance of more than one in ten deputy heads in secondary schools' and adds that primary schools may also lose deputies, albeit at a slower rate. One example is the primary school where the head decided not to replace the departing deputy head but to restructure by creating three team-leader posts for infants, lower juniors and upper juniors (Bush *et al.*, 1996, p. 130).

The 1995 pay and conditions document for England and Wales (DFEE, 1995) makes it clear that structures may be determined or modified to meet the perceived needs of individual schools and explicitly acknowledges the tendency for schools to reduce the number of senior posts:

> Schools should be free to determine the right management structure having regard to their own particular circumstances, including in particular the educational and management needs of the school. They should review their management structures from time to time, and should not feel obliged to retain a pattern of senior posts which is no longer prescribed by statute.
>
> (*Ibid.*, p. 9)

It should not be assumed that adoption of flatter structures is a panacea for organisational tension. Holbeche (1995) argues that attention should be given to motivating and rewarding people who no longer have a clear career path through promotion: 'While flatter structures offer clear advantages to the organisation, benefits to the employee are less obvious . . . Flatter structures work on the basis that employees are willing to adjust expectations about career development.' The pay and conditions arrangements for schools in England and Wales allow managers to reward excellent classroom performance and a shift in this direction may help to maintain motivation while supporting effective teaching and learning by keeping good practitioners in the classroom. However, this possibility assumes that money saved by implementing flatter structures will be spent in rewarding classroom excellence. In practice, such savings may be used for other purposes, particularly in the tight budgetary climate of the 1990s. A survey for the Secondary Heads Association showed that 66 per cent of schools identified financial reasons for non-replacement of deputy heads (Arkin, 1995).

Financial pressures underpinned plans to simplify the structure at Notley Secondary School in Essex. The incoming head inherited a 'top heavy' structure which had not been adjusted despite falling rolls. The school had 25 of its 39 staff in senior or middle-manager posts and the financial implications of this 'inheritance' had several dysfunctional consequences:

1) Increases in the size of teaching groups.
2) Higher teaching loads for all staff.
3) *Ad hoc* gaps in the organisational structure arising from non-replacement of departing staff.

The head and governing body introduced a new staffing structure in 1995, with fewer senior and middle-manager posts. These changes enabled the school to recruit two new staff and to reduce 'contact time' for all teachers. A reduction in management costs enabled funds to be diverted to support teaching and learning.

CONCLUSION

Structures are an important expression of the values of leaders and serve to represent the formal pattern of relationships between members of organisations. The traditional bureaucratic model has been criticised for its emphasis on potentially dysfunctional hierarchies and for underestimating the significance of lateral relationships. The normative preference for collegial structures arises from the recognition that expertise is widespread in schools and colleges and that structures should facilitate the involvement of all staff in the decisions that affect their working lives.

The tentative shift to flatter structures is consistent with the principles of collegiality but may lead to demotivation for teachers whose career development is likely to be constrained by a reduction in the number of promoted posts. The benefits for the institution should be matched by advantages for staff, as at Notley, if structural change is to succeed. In modifying structure, leaders must consider the impact on staff as well as notions of organisational effectiveness.

REFERENCES

Arkin, A. (1995) It's time to debunk delayering, *The Times Educational Supplement: School Management Update*, 10 November.

Bennett, N. (1995) *Managing Professional Teachers*, London, Paul Chapman.

Bolam, R., McMahon, A. Pocklington, K. and Weindling, D. *Effective Management in Schools*, London, HMSO.

Bush, T. (1981) Key roles in school management, in *E323: Management and the School*, Milton Keynes, Open University.

Bush, T. (1989) School management structures – theory and practice, *Educational Management and Administration*, Vol. 17, No. 1, pp. 3–8.

Bush, T. (1995) *Theories of Educational Management* (2nd edn), London, Paul Chapman.

Bush, T., Coleman, M., Wall, D. and West-Burnham, J. (1996) Mentoring and continuing professional development, in McIntyre, D. and Hagger, H. (eds) *Mentoring in Schools: Developing the Profession of Teaching*, London, David Fulton.

Coulson, A. (1976) Leadership functions in primary schools, *Educational Administration*, Vol. 5, No. 1, pp. 37–48.

Department for Education and Employment (1995) *School Teachers' Pay and Conditions of Employment 1995* (Circular 5/95), London, DFEE.

Doe, B. (1995) A dearth of deputies, *The Times Educational Supplement: School Management Update*, 10 November.

Elliott, G. and Hall, V. (1994) FE Inc. – business orientation in further education and the introduction of human resource management, *School Organisation*, Vol. 14, No. 1, pp. 3–9.

Evetts, J. (1992) The organisation of staff in secondary schools: headteachers' management structures, *School Organisation*, Vol. 12, No. 1, pp. 83–98.

Field, M. (1993), *APL: Developing More Flexible Colleges*, London, Routledge.

Fincham, D. (1991) Horizontal or vertical? Integrating pastoral and academic concerns, *School Organisation*, Vol. 11, No. 2, pp. 241–51.

Further Education Development Agency (1995) *Mapping the FE Sector*, London, DFEE.

Gartside, P. (1991) *Managing Flexible College Structures: part III*, *Coombe Lodge Report*, Vol. 22, No. 3., Further Education Staff College, Blagdon.

Gray, H. (1982) A perspective on organisation theory, in Gray, H. (ed.) *The Management of Educational Institutions*, Lewes, Falmer Press.

Handy, C. (1994) *The Empty Raincoat: Making Sense of the Future*, London, Hutchinson.

Harling, P. (1989) The organizational framework for educational leadership, in Bush, T. (ed.) *Managing Education: Theory and Practice*, Milton Keynes, Open University Press.

Helps, R. (1994) The allocation of non-contact time to deputy headteachers in primary schools, *School Organisation*, Vol. 14, No. 3, pp. 243–6.

Holbeche, L. (1995) *Flattening Organisational Structures*, Roffey Park Management Institute, Horsham, Sussex.

Janes, F., Gartside, P., Havard, B. and Kershaw, N. (1989) *Managing Flexible College Structures: Practice and Principles*, *Coombe Lodge Report*, Vol. 21, No. 6., Further Education Staff College, Blagdon.

Johnston, J. and Pickersgill, S. (1992) Personal and interpersonal aspects of team-oriented headship in the primary school, *Educational Management and Administration*, Vol. 20, No. 4, pp. 239–48.

Lewis, N. (1994) Re-engineering the culture of a college, *Coombe Lodge Reports*, Vol. 24, No. 3, pp. 253–64.

Lumby, J. (1996) Curriculum change in further education, *Journal of Vocational Education and Training*, Vol. 48, No. 4, pp. 333–48.

Mullins, L. (1989) *Management and Organisational Behaviour* (2nd edn), London, Pitman.

O'Neill, J. (1994) Organisational structure and culture, in Bush, T. and West-Burnham, J. (eds) *The Principles of Educational Management*, Harlow, Longman.

Packwood, T. (1989) Return to the hierarchy!, *Educational Management and Administration*, Vol. 17, No. 1, pp. 9–15.

Purvis, J. and Dennison, W. (1993) Primary school deputy headship – has ERA and LMS changed the job?, *Education 3–13*, Vol. 21, No. 2, pp. 15–21.

Roberts, B. and Ritchie, H. (1990) Management structures in secondary schools, *Educational Management and Administration*, Vol. 18, No. 3, pp. 17–21.

Smith, T. (1986) Faculty governance – professionals and bureaucrats, *Educational Management and Administration*, Vol. 14, No. 3, pp. 227–30.

Todd, M. (1994) Squeeze tightens across curriculum, *The Times Educational Supplement*, 26 August.

Turner, C. (1991) *Structures – Fact or Fiction?*, *Mendip Papers*, Blagdon, The Staff College.

Wallace, M. (1986) The rise of scale posts as a management hierarchy in schools, *Educational Management and Administration*, Vol. 14, No. 3, pp. 203–12.

Wallace, M. (1989) Towards a collegiate approach to curriculum management in primary and middle schools, in Preedy, M. (ed.) *Approaches to Curriculum Management*, Milton Keynes, Open University Press.

Whalley, C. and Watkins, C. (1991) Managing the whole curriculum in the secondary school – a structure, *Management in Education*, Vol. 5, No. 3, pp. 19–22.

5

MANAGEMENT ROLES IN EDUCATION

Valerie Hall

MAKING THE FAMILIAR ACCEPTABLE

Within the language of education management, 'management roles' is a concept whose taken-for-grantedness belies its complexity. Earlier functionalist views of role theory suggested that, as long as a school's or college's purposes and structures could be identified, roles could be ascribed and subsequent behaviour predicted. More recent interactionist perspectives on social life, in which individual subjective realities are as important as 'social facts', have shown how an understanding of roles helps us make sense of the everyday world. In the early 1970s, Silverman (1971, p. 134) described roles as merely clusters of related meanings perceived to be appropriate to certain social settings. As such, and together with structures, they provide a framework for action but do not determine it. They constitute a 'social stock of knowledge' in the form of a series of assumptions about appropriate behaviour in different contexts. In this way they render social life both more intelligible and more problematic, since, as Berger and Luckman (1966, p. 75) point out, meanings are not only given, they are socially sustained: 'The realization of the drama depends upon the reiterated performance of its prescribed roles by living actors. The actors embody the roles and actualize the drama by presenting it on the given stage. Neither drama nor institution exist empirically apart from this current realization.'

In this chapter I want to explore the complexities of the roles education managers are currently undertaking in schools and colleges. The discussion is grounded, wherever possible, in research findings which portray the reality of life in schools and colleges. A number of research projects completed in Britain since the Education Reform Act 1988 (ERA) testify to the multitude of meanings that the players bring to their parts, however prescribed the scripts appear to be. They show how, even if the concepts of management and roles are now acceptable in education, there are considerable difficulties in identifying the precise nature of management roles. These difficulties arise from a number of sources, including the diversity of goals in education, teachers' perceptions of themselves as 'professionals' and the interaction of central government's prescriptions and individual teachers' interpretations. Additionally, there are the global changes that influence teachers' work and culture in the postmodern age. Writing on this theme, Hargreaves (1995, p. 66) uses Toffler's metaphor of the 'moving mosaic' to describe the patterns characterizing new organizational structures in a new society. Toffler asks his readers to picture

> a moving mosaic composed not on a flat, solid wall, but on many, shifting see-through panels, one behind the other, overlapping, interconnected, the colors and shapes continually blending, contrasting, changing. Paralleling the new ways that knowledge is organized in data bases, this begins to suggest the future form of the enterprise and of the economy itself. Instead of a power-concentrating hierarchy, dominated by a few central organizations, we move toward a multidimensional mosaic form of power.

These changing patterns reflect changing roles in organisations in which not just the structures but also the membership are in constant flux. In spite of the problematic aspects of the moving mosaic, Hargreaves welcomes the greater flexibility and responsiveness that such schools would demonstrate.

The research studies, on which this chapter draws, as well as trends in other countries, generally show schools and colleges to be in a transitional state between bureaucratic certainties (including tightly defined structures, roles and responsibilities) and the postmodern uncertainties (in which boundaries are permeable, roles blurred and tasks constantly changing). The evidence for the relevance of Toffler's 'moving mosaic' to education is there, but only dimly glimpsed. It does, however, provide a beacon for where the future might lie; a future in which power is decentralised and shared.

In this chapter, I aim to integrate what we know about role theory with what recent research tells us about management roles in education. Researchers have, in the main, absorbed the interactionist version of roles and moved away from the formal descriptions of tasks and responsibilities that characterised earlier writings on education management (e.g. Lyons, 1976). As a result they often raise more questions than answers about management roles in education, including such questions as follows:

- Who holds management roles in education?
- What is distinctive about management roles, particularly in education?
- Who defines management roles in education and are they defined

differently in each of the sectors (primary school, secondary school, further and higher education)?
- How do concepts associated with role theory (e.g. role conflict, role ambiguity) contribute to understanding management roles in education?
- What do management roles consist of?
- How can managers be supported in the skilful performance of their roles?

In discussing issues raised by these questions, I will draw particularly on recent research in Britain in primary and secondary school management. Although the examples are all taken from the British context, the implications of the concepts, questions and issues they address have applicability across education systems. All relate to people at work in education, and schools and colleges as social organisations.

ROLE-TAKING AND ROLE-MAKING

At their simplest, roles constitute the parts people expect and are expected to play in the daily drama of educational life. Turner (1969) distinguishes between 'role-taking' (i.e. accepting the role as it is presented) and 'role-making' (i.e. actively reconstructing it). From one perspective, management roles provide the formal mechanism through which people are matched with tasks and responsibilities, to ensure the smooth running of the organisation. To this extent, the players are provided with scripts in the form of job descriptions and other written agreements (e.g. performance targets agreed in appraisal interviews). They thus become 'role-takers'. Yet the theatrical analogy falls down when we consider the complexity of the scripts facing managers in education in the 1990s and their right to interpret and play them out according to their own understanding of the purposes of management in education. An individual's performance in a job is as much about 'role-making' as 'role-taking'. Job descriptions vary in the degree to which they reflect what a person is expected to do once in post. The source of the variation between formal and actual role is external to the role holder, but the individual is still 'role-taking'. Alternatively, the reasons why an individual behaves differently from his or her formal job description may derive from the individual's attempts to make the role his or her own, by fitting it to his or her own interpretation.

Accepting the validity of different interpretations of roles makes it all the harder to pin down management role definitions in education. When Hoyle (1974) first introduced his ideas about teachers as professionals in the early 1970s, teacher autonomy was the norm and the freedom for some managers to 'make' roles was considerable. Even in the 1980s, the POST project studying the selection of secondary headteachers in England and Wales found only one of a hundred or more local education authorities having a formal job description for headteachers (Morgan *et al.*, 1983). Headteachers therefore had considerable latitude in interpreting their roles, as the follow-up study to POST confirmed (Hall *et al.*, 1986). Now, in all education systems which have shifted responsibilities to self-managing schools, those managing in education are confronted by a variety of role prescriptions, many of which include clashing or inconsistent expectations. These emanate from government (e.g. the job descriptions for headteachers and other managers in official documents outlining teachers' pay and conditions), or from writings about management roles that also address what constitutes skilful role performance (e.g. Earley and Fletcher-Campbell, 1989, on heads of department; Jirasinghe and Lyons, 1996, on competent heads). Equally influential on definitions of role are the expectations held by tax payers (including parents) of those who work in schools and colleges and their responsibilities in educating students.

Teachers, lecturers and principals, within the framework of their under-standing of others' expectations of their roles, attempt to interpret them in ways which are comfortable, rewarding and manageable. The problem is in the failure of these myriad interpretations to match each other. Government expectations of how teachers should work with young people (e.g. continu-ously measuring their performance) may not fit with teachers' preferred ways of behaving. Government requirements for heads and governors to use formal inspections to rid schools of underperforming teachers clash with professional expectations of collegiality. Within a school or college, an individual head of faculty's preferred management style (i.e. the way they act out their role) may be at odds with senior managers' expectations of what is appropriate. In all these cases, conflict may occur while staff interpret their own and others' roles in ways which may or may not resemble others' interpretations. This dynamic of expectation and interpretation around roles extends beyond the school or college to include governors, parents, students and the wider community, all of whom are stakeholders and have a part to play in managing the institution.

WHOSE MANAGEMENT ROLE IS IT ANYWAY?

It is unlikely that this question would need to be asked as a prelude to the discussion of management roles in other sectors such as industry and commerce. There management roles are more clearly delineated. People are more likely to know who the managers are and what they are expected to do. In education, the picture is murky. If management roles in education are defined as those which carry any responsibilities for the work of other adults in the organisation, then the list of management roles in each sector of education is potentially very long. At its most extreme, we might argue that in education, 'we are all managers now'. When the School Management Task Force (DES, 1990) launched its training initiative, one of their recommendations was that management training for teachers should begin while they were still undergoing initial teacher training. This proposal derived from the transformation of teachers' roles as a result of government initiatives, which require all teachers to take on some 'management' responsibilities. As a result, management roles in all sectors in education are filled, in the main, by academic staff, with support from administrators. In schools, most headteachers continue to teach; in universities, heads of department continue to publish. Generally, senior and middle managers are forced to squeeze their management tasks in to already-crowded timetables leading to a situation in education in which there is no time to manage. Nowhere is this more clearly demonstrated than in primary schools, where responsibilities have increased yet postholders, deputies and many heads still have full teaching timetables.

It is in primary schools, too, that ambiguities surrounding what constitutes a 'management' role are most clearly demonstrated. As I suggested earlier, defining someone's role as 'management' depends on a combination of the role-holder's own perceptions, others' expectations and their formal job description. For example, in primary schools in Britain, as research by Webb and Vulliamy (1996) shows, heads retain a clear leadership role; and the management role of the deputy has expanded, though it is still controlled largely by the headteacher. They conclude that 'deputies' job satisfaction, effectiveness and personal well-being is largely determined by her or his perceptions of, and relationship with, their headteacher' (*ibid.*, p. 109). More ambiguity surrounds the roles of promoted postholders. Bennett's (1995) research on middle managers in primary and secondary schools leads him to ask whether postholders are, in fact, managers. He offers (*ibid.*, p. 74) this interesting distinction between managers and co-ordinators:

> The distinction between 'managers' and 'co-ordinators' or 'consultants' is important, and lies in the underlying concept of the individual's work. Co-ordinators relate to teachers as professionals or artists (Wise et al. 1984). They work with teachers who have high levels of autonomy and discretion in their classroom work, and must therefore work by consensus and the negotiated individual consent of each teacher. Managers may *choose* to operate in this way but are assumed to retain some measure of control over what teachers do.

After 1987, the conditions of service laid down by government for mainscale teachers in England and Wales included 'coordinating or managing the work of other teachers' (DES, 1987). As Bennett (1995) points out, this endorsed the view that all teachers have management responsibilities and that postholders are paid for additional duties. His survey over four years, of the job descriptions and postholders' accounts of their roles, reveals a confused picture in which the role of middle managers in primary schools remains blurred, varying between 'basic administration and a wide-ranging involvement in generating new classroom practice' (*ibid.*, p. 84).

Some of the same ambiguities surrounding the definition of management roles continue in the context of secondary schools. There, the debate is less whether a role is managerial or not (although Bennett still asks the question 'can secondary schools have middle managers?'). It focuses more on the nature of the role, how it is performed and its contribution to school effectiveness. The main impact of changing definitions of senior management roles comes from the shift in many secondary schools towards teamwork as the most effective way of responding to the growing multiplicity of management tasks. Some fear the loss of individual status and identity (as well as power) that might come with teamwork. Yet Wallace and Hall's (1994) study of teamwork in secondary school management shows how the value placed on equal contribution by team members has confirmed, not undermined, the status of the individual management roles represented. Bolam *et al.*'s (1993) study of effective management in schools in England and Wales concludes that teamwork has, for example, considerably enhanced the role of the deputy headteacher. It now embraces new areas of responsibility, greater overall responsibility and more autonomy (*ibid.*, p. 45).

This expansion has also contributed to solving the dilemma which so often characterises the deputy head's role, poised between staff and the headteacher with no authentic identity of his or her own (Spence, 1985, p. 9). As a result, some primary deputies continue to occupy a named position but fulfil no commonly defined role.

Defining the headteacher's or principal's role as managerial appears less problematic, in spite of the unprecedented scale of changes to the role in recent years. Many studies of headship (e.g. Bolam *et al.*, 1993; Ribbins and Marland, 1994; Grace, 1995; Southworth, 1995; Hall, 1996) demonstrate its continuing centrality to the increasingly complex management task of running schools and colleges. Earlier research showed the head's role to be poorly defined, with inadequate preparation, and performed in an *ad hoc* rather than a strategic manner (e.g. Hall *et al.*, 1986). In the 1990s, headteachers are more likely to have job descriptions and expanded opportunities for training and development. Where competition is encouraged, it would be a naive head who did not think and act strategically. Unlike other management roles (e.g. deputy headteachers and middle managers), the head's role has been subject to intense scrutiny. This intensity is reflected, for example, in Jirasinghe and Lyons' (1996) study of 'the competent head' in which they report the results of a rigorous job analysis of 280 headteachers in England and Wales. As well as providing a profile of the skills and behaviours needed by school leaders to deal effectively with current reforms, they identify heads' preferred personality dimensions, indicating their favoured ways of working, leadership styles and team roles. The resulting competency model of headteachers includes five competence areas: the planning and administrative process; dealing with people; managing the political environment; professional and technical knowledge; and personal skills (*ibid.*, p. 96).

ERA of 1988 and the Further and Higher Education Act 1992 have created deep anxieties among teachers in further and higher education (FHE), particularly in response to the new management regimes. Warner and Crosthwaite's (1995, p. 10) research shows how the manager's role in FHE has changed, as staff interpret the external demands, position their departments or institutions against these requirements, and interpret for their colleagues what can or should be accommodated or resisted. New 'professional' contracts in FE have reframed the role of the lecturer who, as in schools, must give other activities the same priority as teaching.

In higher education, the middle-management role of the head of department has expanded, making heavy demands on the individual academics who are appointed or elected to the post. In her case study of one new university's approach to developing a human resource strategy, Launchberry (1995) describes the appointment of a senior human resource professional at assistant-director level. The post in itself was a novelty. The decision to recruit a former personnel manager who was not an academic caused an outcry (*ibid.*, p. 21).

Her example highlights another feature of changing management roles in education; the reappraisal of the necessity for them to be filled by academic staff. Since 1986, governors in schools in Britain have played an increasingly large and potentially powerful part in their management. Thody (1992) entitles her book on school governors in the 1990s *Moving into Management*, thereby capturing the transformation in the role open to them. In grant-maintained schools, as Bush *et al.* (1993, p. 178) show, the governors have additional responsibilities without the 'fall-back' of the local education authority. The experiences of their case-study schools highlight the importance of clarifying the governors' proper role, if trust and a productive partnership between the professional and lay managers are to emerge. From her viewpoint as an advocate for governing bodies, Joan Sallis summed up the difficult and extensive task of governors as follows: 'to build productive relationships with staff; to cope with the workload and the jargon; to organize their time; to develop as an effective team with no powerful groups taking over; to keep upright on the shifting sands of law and regulations' (reported in *The Times Educational Supplement*, 18 March 1994, p. 5).

In her view, building a partnership with the head is the biggest challenge, since it depends on the head's willingness to share. Hargreaves (1994) sees this unquestioning acceptance of the desirability of collaboration as the possible downside of the moving mosaic referred to earlier. Collaborating teams are potentially exclusive since in identifying some staff as members they simultaneously create an outgroup. This limits rather than expands the roles open to people. While collaboration provides a means for easing role overload, it also requires recognition of changing roles reflecting shared authority and staff involvement in major decisions.

BLURRING THE BOUNDARIES

Another significant shift in management roles from academic to non-academic is manifest in changes in the nature of the work of those whom Mortimore and Mortimore (with Thomas, 1994) term 'associate staff'. In particular, in response to the demands of school-managed budgets, many school secretaries have become bursars. With their increased responsibilities comes a place in some secondary schools on the senior management team (SMT) with the potential of becoming a main policy-maker. In their discussion of individual contributions to teamwork on SMTs, Wallace and Hall (1994) note the ambiguities that can surround these non-teaching management roles. Those who hold them are both part of the team, and separate from it. One secretary was described as 'almost like a minister without portfolio'; another was keenly aware of how her own and other members' interpretation of her position constrained her participation.

This recent blurring of the academic–non-academic interface between management roles in education is one way in which they differ from management roles outside education. For some educators, delegating to or sharing management responsibilities with others leaves them more freedom to act out their preferred interpretation of the 'professional' dimensions of their role, particularly those relating to teaching and learning. The formal power and influence that accompany most promoted posts in education empower some but leave others feeling uncomfortable. The latters' concern is that the requirement to be both a teacher and a manager may constrain their critical perspectives on education. There are also different views on where accountability lies. For example, a major task facing many education managers in a time of education cuts is in making staff redundant. When the heads in Hall's (1996) study were confronted with this issue, conflict occurred as a result of their and the teacher unions' different perspectives. The heads saw themselves managing the issue as professionals concerned primarily with the needs of children. The teacher unions were primarily committed to protecting individual and collective staff interests (sometimes, in the heads' view, at the expense of the children). In one particular instance, when a primary head clashed with the union representatives over the redundancy issue, she was angered by their suggestions that, as management, she did not have the teachers' interests at heart (*ibid.*). The impact of what many educators see as a mismatch between pedagogic and managerialist cultures is reflected in other studies too. Elliott (1996) explores its implications for lecturers' and managers' roles in FE, suggesting that it is only by significantly modifying managerialist approaches that college managers can turn staff resistance to their strategies into co-operation and collaboration.

Education managers' credibility in their role depends on keeping in touch with the central tasks of learning and teaching. In his survey of headteachers working in English schools, Grace (1995) identifies different types of responses to the moral, ethical and professional dilemmas generated by the changed culture of school leadership. Some whom he describes as 'headteacher-managers' are excited by the possibilities of new roles in the education marketplace. Others, whom he calls 'headteacher-professionals', feel their allegiance to professionality is undermined by the ways in which they are required to be managerial. These conflicts and tensions experienced in different sectors all reflect the outcomes of the varied perceptions and powers of different role definers, whether the government, professional associations, the role holder, the institution or others associated with it.

ROLE THEORY REVISITED

So far I have concentrated on the difficulties of identifying the precise nature of management roles in education. The trend has been for many in education to find an increasing number of management responsibilities as part of their formal role description. The democratisation implied by this apparent sharing of management is offset by educators' concerns about the nature of management, particularly management goals, and the part they are expected to play in achieving them.

If the reality is that those working in education have management roles, whether they like it or not, then what can role theory contribute to our understanding of their experience within these roles? Earlier in the chapter I pointed to the tensions between ascribed roles and individual's choices of how to behave. Turner (1969) suggests that the ascribed role acts as a device to set the 'real' role in motion, as individuals reinterpret their roles through interaction with others. To understand and predict the behaviour and performance of individuals in management roles in education, we need to be able to dissect the dynamic of the interaction arising from the tensions between ascribed and 'real' role.

Given the nature and scale of change in education, and its diverse goals, role strain would seem inevitable. Role strain occurs when individual expectations are either contradicted or not shared with others. Predictably, role strain can contribute to stress. In the context of further education, Brain (1994, p. 97) describes the amoeba-like growth of the FE lecturer's role:

> Over the past 20 years we have ad hoc added to the role of lecturer that of learning facilitator/supporter, learning resource producer, information technology specialist, pastoral worker, marketeer, course/programme manager, deliverer of integrated core skills, raiser of European awareness, team worker, tester, assessor, examiner, deliverer of open/flexible/distance learning, administrator and increasingly manager. By anyone's standards this is surely exhausting rather than enriching.

In her view the consequences are an undervaluing of staff, low morale, prolonged and intermittent union disputes, all leading to the low public regard for teaching as a profession.

In schools, the stressful outcomes of role strain are manifest in the numbers of headteachers taking early retirement, often through ill-health; the low numbers of applicants for headship posts in different parts of the country; and difficulties in recruiting to governing bodies. Premature retirement through ill-health is just one response to the many ambiguities, conflicts and stresses of increasingly complex management roles. Expansion of headship training opportunities has helped some become better equipped for management challenges, but many remain reluctant to engage in the battle. As Southworth (1995) shows, in his study of one primary school headteacher, headship is no longer just a job, but a way of life. Although role strain is not inevitable for everyone with management responsibilities in education, it represents a strong undercurrent that can tug even the strongest swimmer temporarily or permanently under.

Most people are likely to be exposed to one or more of a range of sources of strain at different points in their career (and personal lives). These sources of strain can be summarised in terms of role conflict, role ambiguity and role incompatibility. Role conflict arises from the contradictory expectations held for the incumbent of a single position. The conflict can occur between roles, within a role and within a role set. Handy (1985, p. 59) defines a role set as including all those with whom an individual, as the focal person, has more than trivial interactions. One important contribution to understanding management roles, particularly as they are affected by role conflict, has come from perspectives that take gender into account and link the personal and the professional. Androcentric views of management (which take men's behaviour as the norm) compartmentalise work and non-work roles, associating the former mainly with men, the latter with women. While it has usually been assumed that women prefer not to seek promotion because the additional demands would clash with their family responsibilities, no such assumption is made about men in management roles. Yet recent research on both men (e.g. Harris, 1995) and women (e.g. Marshall, 1995) shows role conflict as a reality for both men and women. The increasing popularity of self-development as a route to management development demonstrates managers' and aspiring managers' concerns to know their whole self, if they are to be more effective in working with others (Hall *et al.*, 1996). Identifying personal priorities as part of one's professional persona is no longer seen as the prerogative of women.

Wallace and Hall (1994), for example, describe the situation of a senior teacher expected, as a member of the SMT, to attend an evening function at school, yet required by his teacher wife to look after the children, while she fulfilled what was expected of her professionally. His decision to support his wife on this occasion made life uncomfortable for him for some time after in the team. This conflict arose from the need for decisions by both partners about how to allocate personal and professional time. Within the SMT, the same teacher and a colleague were faced at times with conflicts of loyalty within the school. Both had been co-opted on to the team, although they were not 'senior managers'. As a result they were conscious of their 'poacher turned gamekeeper' identities arising from their SMT membership and, at times, were uncertain about the form their contribution should take (*ibid.*, p. 101).

Changes in the roles of others within any one individual's role set can also lead to conflict for an individual within a role. Take, for example, a headteacher's role set in the 1990s. In many contexts, legislation now specifies the parameters of the head's role, including any new responsibilities resulting from education reforms. At the same time, it may also specify transformations in the roles of those with whom heads work, e.g. school governors, including their relative powers. In Britain, both Thody's (1994) research on governing bodies, and Hall's (1996) research on headteachers found that governors prioritised the 'consent' and 'protection' dimensions of their role, thereby constituting little threat to heads' construction of their leadership role. Thody (1994, p. 165) concludes: 'Legitimation by governors' consent lends support to principals and can help protect them from some of the stresses of school management. Heads can gain protection from governors, providing a forum to which heads can refer decisions.'

Changes in expectations within role sets can create role ambiguity as well as role conflict. This occurs when an individual is uncertain about the precise nature of his or her role at any given time. A major problem facing teachers as they assume management responsibilities is in knowing what is expected in a role for which they have often had little relevant preparation. The studies by Bennett (1995) and Webb and Vulliamy (1996) both show the confusion surrounding the boundaries, powers and expectations of middle managers' roles in primary and secondary schools. Bennett (1995, p. 143) proposes a strategy for addressing this ambiguity through personal management development. He suggests to middle managers:

> First, consider yourself. What view do you hold of yourself as a teacher, are you a labourer, a practitioner of craft skills, a professional, or an artist? What kind of advice, guidance, support or direction do you seek from others, and whom do you seek it from and why? Which teachers do you admire and respect most, and why? Do those you respect most hold the most senior positions in the school? If not, where do they fit in to the formal hierarchy of seniority? When, if at all, do you think it is acceptable to ignore instructions or directions? What degree of discretion do you think you should be allowed by others in carrying out your teaching responsibilities?

Another source of role strain is uncertainty about whether one is performing well in the job. Roles carry expectations of quality performance and the need for individuals to have the basic qualities required to achieve this. The current drive in education towards measuring the performance of both staff and pupils (through, for example, testing, appraisal, external inspections) arguably reduces role uncertainty, since these approaches theoretically leave individuals in little doubt about how they are doing. In practice the picture is less clear, not least because of appraisers' reluctance at times to give 'frank' feedback to colleagues. Both the methods of evaluation and the criteria for judging performance are made explicit. The problems arise in how managers respond to difficulties or inadequacies in an individual's ability or motivation to perform a role effectively, particularly where they feel they must impose sanctions rather than provide support for development.

Role incompatibility can arise from other people's incompatible expectations within a role set; that is, different individuals or different groups have conflicting expectations of the role holder. Sometimes, others' role expectations are incompatible with an individual's self-concept. The headteachers in Wallace and Hall's study of senior management teams were often faced with incompatible expectations of them as team leader and team member. In common with other team members, they wanted to be both leaders and followers, but felt at times the need to assert their authority. This undermined the team's usual commitment to the belief that all contributions were equal.

Individuals may experience role incompatibility when the behaviour expected of them does not match their view of themselves. This tendency has been commented on regarding women's career ambitions. Both Al-Khalifa (1989) and Evetts (1990) have suggested that the image of management as masculine, with its associations of being tough, calculating and competitive, discourages many women teachers from seeking promotion. A view of management roles in education as masculine suggests the need for women (and some men) to perform in ways which are unfamiliar and uncomfortable. The incompatibility that some women discern between their own qualities and those required in management roles is reflected too in the uncertainties of those who are responsible for selecting for management posts. Both men and women selectors often hold deep-seated views about the role of women in society which influence their beliefs about whether a woman would be as effective as a man, if appointed to a senior management post.

IT ISN'T ALL BAD NEWS

So far, this review of the usefulness of role theory for understanding roles in education appears to offer only bad news; of strain, conflict, ambiguity and uncertainty, all leading to stress. What then is the good news? First, there is a positive side to role ambiguity. It is located in the space it allows for an individual to shape his or her own role. Recent headship studies (Grace, 1995; Woods, 1995; Hall, 1996) testify to the positive responses of many heads to education reforms which decentralise management responsibilities. These heads relish the possibilities provided by the reforms to develop their schools and the opportunities they create for professional renewal. Not only do they have considerably more room for role-making than their senior and middle manager colleagues but they also play a key part as school or college leaders in setting the parameters for others' roles. Role theory suggests that all role holders have space but some have more space than others.

The other good news is in the recognition in education management of the desirability of managers being good role models. Pedler and Boydell (1985, p. 8) describe the 'New Age Manager' as one who attempts to combine thinking and doing to take action in full awareness of what he or she is doing and why, and its consequences for other people and the organisation. Reviewing his earlier work on team roles at work, Belbin (1993, p. 82) questions the value of role models and the notion that managers can learn from outstanding managers and leaders 'by osmosis'. He exhorts managers to avoid becoming pale shadows of others and seek their 'real' selves through self-assessment and assessment from others. While welcoming his emphasis on self-development for management development, my own research on women headteachers demonstrates the value of their concern to be good role models for other teachers and managers. By prioritising self-knowledge as a basis for action, they tried to model through their own behaviours how they wanted others to work and relate with each other in the school. Underpinning their search for credibility in the role models they provided for others were their values about being 'authentic' and being 'consistent' at work (Hall, 1996, p. 186). As Oldroyd (1996, p. 19) has noted:

> Leading by example is a powerful process of modelling positive attitudes and a commitment to and belief in success. As the saying goes – 'attitudes and values are caught not taught'. To become a model of positive, success-oriented thinking is then a key role of the leader of an organization striving for success and high performance from the rest of its members, from the least talented student to the caretaker.

How can this positive note about management roles in education be sustained? Are they to be part of Toffler's 'moving mosaic', challenging and creative; or smashed to pieces under the heavy weight of imposed change? The ambiguities and conflicts that arise from changing roles are offset by greater clarity about what those in management roles have to be able to do, and more feedback about whether they are doing it effectively. Using defined competencies as a basis for selecting, developing and assessing managers in education is potentially both limiting and liberating. Most managers in education are human resource managers. Their roles include ensuring that their institution competes successfully in the marketplace. This means not only performing their own role effectively but also supporting others in carrying out what is required in their roles. They must be able to select, develop, motivate and provide support. The centrality of their human resource management function has implications for how they themselves are selected, developed, motivated and supported.

The emphasis of many management development programmes is now on self-management as a basis for managing others. Their focus reflects the possibilities for 'role-making' to combat the negative consequences of just 'role-taking'. This self-appraisal needs to be accompanied by a thorough reappraisal of the role of teachers and lecturers, as they become defined as managers as well as teachers. Brain (1994, p. 98) concludes her own reappraisal of changing roles in FE with the hope that

> this process would produce a clear definition of the professional lec-turer/teacher as a highly skilled manager of the learning process, whose training and experience enables them to understand and control the com-plexity of the learning situation and to manage a team of para-educationalists who assist in ensuring the right environment, resources and general instruc-tion and assessment are available for students.

Recognising the Utopian quality of her vision, it still provides an apt conclusion to this survey of management roles in education.

REFERENCES

Al-Khalifa, E. (1989) Management by halves: women teachers and school manage-ment, in De Lyon, H. Migniuolo, F. (eds) *Women Teachers*, Milton Keynes, Open University Press.

Belbin, M. (1993) *Team Roles at Work*, Oxford, Butterworth-Heinemann.

Bennett, N. (1995) *Managing Professional Teachers: Middle Management in Primary and Secondary Schools*, London, Paul Chapman.

Berger, P. and Luckman, T. (1966) *The Social Construction of Reality: A Treatise in the Sociology of Knowledge*, New York, Doubleday.

Bolam, R., McMahon, A., Pocklington, K. and Weindling, D. (1993) *Effective Management of Schools: A Report for the Department for Education via the School Management Task Force Professional Working Party*, London, HMSO.

Brain, G. (ed.) (1994) *Managing and Developing People*, Blagdon, The Staff College/Association for Colleges.

Bush, T., Coleman, M. and Glover, D. (1993) *Managing Autonomous Schools: The Grant-Maintained Experience*, London, Paul Chapman.

Department of Education and Science (1987) *The Education (School Teachers' Pay and Conditions) Order*, London, HMSO.

Department of Education and Science (1990) *Developing School Management: The Way Forward, a Report by the School Management Task Force*, London, HMSO.

Earley, P. and Fletcher-Campbell, F. (1989) *The Time to Manage: Department and Faculty Heads at Work*, Slough, NFER/Nelson.

Elliott, G. (1996) *Crisis and Change in Vocational Education and Training*, London, Jessica Kingsley.

Evetts, J. (1990) *Women in Primary Teaching: Career Contexts and Strategies*, London, Unwin Hyman.

Grace, G. (1995) *School Leadership: Beyond Education Management: An Essay in Policy Scholarship*, Lewes, Falmer Press.

Hall, V. (1996) *Dancing on the Ceiling: A Study of Women Managers in Education*, London, Paul Chapman.

Hall, V., Cromey-Hawke, N. and Oldroyd, D. (1996) *Management Self-Development in Secondary Schools*, Bristol, University of Bristol, National Development Centre for Educational Management and Policy.

Hall, V., Mackay, H. and Morgan, C. (1986) *Headteachers at Work*, Milton Keynes, Open University Press.

Handy, C. (1985) *Understanding Organizations*, Harmondsworth: Penguin Books.

Hargreaves, A. (1994) *Changing Teachers, Changing Times: Teachers' Work and Culture in the Post-modern Age*, London, Cassell.

Harris, I.M. (1995) *Messages Men Hear: Constructing Masculinities*, London, Taylor & Francis.

Hoyle, E. (1974) Professionality, professionalism and control in teaching, *London Educational Review*, Vol. 3, no. 2, Summer, pp. 13–19.

Jirasinghe, D. and Lyons, G. (1996) *The Competent Head: A Job Analysis of Heads' Tasks and Personality Factors*, Lewes, Falmer Press.

Launchberry, E. (1995) Developing a human resource strategy, in Warner, D. and Crosthwaite, E. (eds) *Human Resource Management in Higher and Further Education, Buckingham*, SRHE and Open University Press.

Lyons, G. (1976) *Heads' Tasks: A Handbook of Secondary Schools Administration*, Slough, NFER.

Marshall, J. (1995) *Women Managers Moving On: Exploring Career and Life Choices*, London, Routledge.

Morgan, C., Hall, V. and Mackay, H. (1983) *The Selection of Secondary Heads*, Milton Keynes, Open University Press.

Mortimore, P. and Mortimore, J. (with Thomas, H.) (1994) *Managing Associate Staff: Innovation in Primary and Secondary Schools*, London, Paul Chapman.

Oldroyd, D. (1996) Developing self and school by positive affirmation, in Hall, V., Cromey-Hawke, N. and Oldroyd, D. (eds) *Management Self-Development in Secondary Schools*, Bristol, University of Bristol, National Development Centre for Educational Management and Policy.

Pedler, M. and Boydell, T. (1985) *Managing Yourself*, London, Fontana.

Ribbins, P. and Marland, M. (1994) *Headship Matters: Conversations with Seven Secondary School Headteachers*, Harlow, Longman.

Silverman,. D (1971) *The Theory of Organisations: A Sociological Framework*, London, Heinmann.

Southworth, G. (1995) *Looking into Primary Headship: A Research Based Interpretation*, Lewes, Falmer Press.

Spence, B.V. (1985) Secondary school deputy headship: the search for a new role, in Spence, B.V. (ed.) *Secondary School Management in the 1980s: Changing Roles*, Hull, University of Hull.

Thody, A. (1992) *Moving into Management: School Governors in the 1990s*, London, David Fulton.

Thody, A. (ed.) (1994) *School Governors: Leaders or Followers?*, Harlow, Longman.

Toffler, A. (1990) *Power Shift*, New York, Bantam Books.

Turner, R. (1969) Role-taking: process versus conformity, in Lindesmith, A. and Strauss, A. (eds) *Readings in Social Psychology*, New York, Rinehart & Winston.

Wallace, M. and Hall, V. (1994) *Inside the SMT: Teamwork in Secondary School Management*, London, Paul Chapman.

Warner, D. and Crosthwaite, E. (eds) (1995) *Human Resource Management in Higher and Further Education*, Buckingham, SRHE and Open University Press.

Webb, R. and Vulliamy, G. (1996) *Roles and Responsibilities in the Primary School: Changing Demands, Changing Practices*, Buckingham, Open University Press.

Woods, P. (1995) *Creative Teachers in Primary Schools*, Buckingham, Open University Press.

6

MANAGING THROUGH TEAMS

John O'Neill

INTRODUCTION

The concept of 'the team' is now firmly embedded in the educational management literature and appears at first glance to have suffered none of the tissue rejection difficulties which have afflicted many other attempts to transplant approaches from mainstream management into the working processes of schools and colleges. Part of the reason may be that 'team' status is awarded unconditionally by practitioners to any number of different functioning groups within the institution (the course team, the senior management team, the learning support team, the office team). Yet, the little research which has been conducted in this area within education suggests that, if the group dynamics and achievements of these self-styled 'teams' were evaluated according to normative descriptions of 'teamwork', many would not qualify as such (e.g. Tansley, 1989; Walker and Stott, 1993).

In contrast, theoretical definitions of teams tend to be succinct yet extremely challenging (for a review of the literature, see Coleman and Bush, 1994) in terms of the demands they make on team members. The issue is that these definitions, many of them expressed as taxonomies of behaviours or norms, are merely frameworks which need to be given organisational contexts and specific management issues if we are to gain meaningful insights into the extent to which the working patterns of professional teacher-managers are being enhanced through teamwork.

Since the mid-1980s in England and Wales, a succession of education and broader employment Acts have served to redefine the official relationships between laity and professionals with regard to governance (Grace, 1995), and between senior staff and other professionals in terms of management (Ball, 1993). Seen through a political lens, the moves represent a realignment of power and authority in education. Moreover, financial autonomy in the staffing of schools and colleges, combined with a growing government insistence that public sector pay increases shall be funded predominantly by 'productivity gains', has led to the widespread use of part-time and temporary contract staff within educational institutions together with a blurring of the historical occupational divide between teaching and support staff (Mortimore *et al.*, 1992).

At site level, these trends combine to generate a problematic management context in which issues of status, remuneration, commitment, time, access, responsibility and accountability all inform individual staff members' perspectives and actions in any number of 'team' settings. Is it equitable, for instance, to encourage classroom support staff or hourly paid course tutors to attend staff meetings for which they may receive no pay and at which their voice is largely without influence? Similarly, from a large-scale survey of teachers' work, Campbell and St J. Neill (1994) identify a consistent pattern of secondary school organisation in which

1) senior staff tend to teach smaller, more academically oriented classes; and
2) there is a clear separation of the work of 'managers' and 'teachers'.

The intention, through teamwork, to increase staff commitment via greater involvement in decision-making processes is laudable but remains a double-edged sword in practice. On the one hand, Sinclair (1992), for example, cuttingly refers to the unfettered and unethical application of this management approach as the 'tyranny of a team ideology'. Her pessimistic assessment is given some justification by reports of research conducted in England and Wales (Mortimore *et al.*, 1992) and Aotearoa/New Zealand (NZEI/Te Riu Roa, 1995) which confirm that many primary and secondary schools make unrealistic demands on the goodwill of their support staff. On the other hand, Hopkins and Ainscow (1992, p. 299), commenting on their work with a number of institutions in a school improvement project, observe that 'organisational structures such as senior management teams and the use of school-wide task groups seem at times to have a dramatic impact on development activities'.

Four specific issues are addressed in this chapter. First, there is an analysis of the role of conflict in team development. Secondly, I provide a brief critique of the canons of team literature, namely the models developed by Tuckman, Adair and Belbin. Thirdly, we explore a number of the potential benefits and pitfalls of teamwork in schools and colleges by drawing on some of the evidence provided from empirical studies in education. In the concluding part of the chapter a tentative 'model' for teamwork in educational settings is discussed.

CONFLICT IN TEAMS

Let us begin with a working definition: 'A team is a small group of people who recognise the need for constructive conflict when working together in order for them to make, implement and support workable decisions.' This description of a team is unconventional inasmuch as it highlights the notion of conflict as an integral feature of effective teamwork. Stephenson (1985, p. 105) argues that conflict is present in all organisations and is 'the inevitable outcome of interdependence linked with the scarcity of resources.'

As a result of the curriculum reforms of the last decade, schools and colleges are clearly made up of a number of increasingly 'interdependent' subject areas and staff teams. Moreover, these groups are frequently required to compete actively against each other for their slice of a shrinking resource cake, be it in terms of personnel, materials, room allocation or timetable space. Arguably, then, educational managers are now more likely to encounter conflict within the institution than they did ten years ago.

However, Stephenson also makes an essential distinction between 'constructive' and 'destructive' conflict. In the former, managers attempt to use inevitable differences of opinion and values to seek better solutions to problems. In the latter, such differences are by-passed or ignored. The positive potential of conflict is elegantly summarised by the Scandinavian academic Per Dalin who was, for a number of years, involved in a structured school improvement programme (IDP) throughout northern Europe:

> Instead of avoiding conflicts, the IDP 'uses' conflicts as opportunities for understanding the reality of the school, for raising key issues related to participants' perceptions of reality, and for exploring ways in which energy 'stored' in conflicts can be released for the benefit of the school. Conflicts offer opportunities for learning because they often provide a chance for clarifying issues, for putting unresolved issues on the table and for helping to understand another point of view.

> (Dalin and Rolff, 1993, p. 28)

Dalin's observations consider conflict in general terms and at the whole-school level yet similar conclusions have been drawn from focused studies of smaller groups and teams in educational settings. Knight (1993, p. 293, emphasis added), for example, analyses the process of curriculum policy development by a school council in Melbourne, Australia:

> This mix of parents and staff empowered to make curriculum decisions immediately ran into traditional forms of antagonism. . . . From the outset, the formation of school curriculum policy at Duke Park High was not going to be a consensus model of decision-making. '*It started and still remains, four years later, a conflict model, though this does contain some advantages*'.

In one sense, this antagonism between community and staff members on the school council is not surprising. Traditionally, professionals are reluctant to cede control over their activities to 'outsiders'. None the less, Knight's conclusion implies that the quality of curriculum decision-making was enhanced because of, not in spite of, the way in which conflict was used to confront entrenched professional positions: 'Parents and community representatives on the school council brought a pluralist perspective to issues and provided links to diverse and minority community opinion. Well-managed conflict can provide a healthy mechanism for problem-solving' (*ibid.*, p. 298).

Conversely, a recent study of teams by Harrison and colleagues (1995) demonstrates the negative consequences of conflict that remains unacknowledged or is avoided altogether. They document (*ibid.*, p. 55) the experience of one respondent who, when reflecting on his regular meetings with the school's senior management team, '. . . identified the sometimes bland response that he encountered, when offering constructive criticisms or proposals to the team, as the "we all work very hard" reaction. Senior managers had established and encouraged this culture as a means of fending off uncomfortable ideas'.

Similarly, another head of department recalled the occasion when she led a 'task team' to develop a whole-school information technology policy. She commented on the resentment exhibited towards the team by a vocal group of long-serving staff. The policy was eventually put in place despite this opposition, but the team leader was left with negative memories of her experience.

Thus, in my definition articulated above, conflict is accepted as endemic but, to elaborate on Stephenson's distinction, is viewed as a means of constructively challenging the status quo rather than destructively stifling open discussion. I recognise that, in choosing to describe teams in this way, I have omitted four of the most frequently invoked criteria in this field. Typically, effective teams are described as having

- defined tasks
- inclusive processes
- deep commitment
- collective expertise.

Often, these are overlaid with an emotional gloss which maintains that teams are as much about socialising and developing individual members as they are to do with meeting task objectives (e.g. Schein, 1988; Bell, 1992). In such definitions, the presence of conflict is rarely acknowledged in any meaningful way, yet the manner in which inevitable differences are handled is essentially what distinguishes a team from the looser notion of a 'group': 'The new senior management team is working well as a team. There is a good balance of personalities and experience. *We are now comfortable enough to disagree with each other* and it is very productive' (Bolam *et al.*, 1993, p. 96, emphasis added).

In short, according to my understanding, a team is, or becomes, confident in its ability to exploit conflict as a vehicle for making better decisions. Effective teams assume that members will hold different and, occasionally, irreconcilable views on certain issues. In the two senior management teams they studied over the course of a year, for example, Wallace and Hall (1994, p. 190) 'were aware of some difficult moments when consensus could not be reached, soaking up time; or when grappling with new ideas, which, for most members, posed a threat to the existing culture of teamwork'. A group, however, is more likely to be concerned with merely avoiding such conflict altogether or, alternatively, with either socialising or excluding from the group those who are perceived to have different values and norms.

THEORIES ABOUT TEAMS

Some thirty years ago, whilst working for the US navy, Tuckman (1965) constructed a model of team development which has proved remarkably enduring in many other occupational sectors. Based on an analysis of the extant literature, Tuckman suggested that teams go through several basic stages of growth. These have since been labelled, in mnemonic fashion,

- forming
- storming
- norming
- performing.

The key point is that a period of 'storming' or turbulence is essential if the team is to establish shared norms which will enable it to function effectively. A further developmental option has since been added to the model suggesting that performing teams go on either to 'underperforming' if they become too complacent or outlive their usefulness, or to 'grieving' if a team member leaves and the group thus reforms.

With regard to team development, new policy areas, time constraints and competing priorities are all examples of the sorts of routine pressures which impact on professed team norms and thereby produce the potential for conflict. Indeed, it appears naive to imply, as many models do, that the process of developing team norms in schools and colleges can be readily isolated from external accountability constraints and the internal pressures induced by

- limited resources;
- the cultural and historical context within which the team works; and
- its relationships with other teams within the institution.

To acknowledge the presence of conflict, latent or active, within teamwork is implicitly to make a case for astute, creative orchestration of the relationships, work and membership of the team. Adair's model of leadership (1988) is frequently cited to illustrate the three areas of concern for team leaders; namely, the need to balance their wish to get things done with the development of individuals and that of the team as a whole. As with many other traditional leadership models, Adair embodies these activities in terms of an individual – the leader.

This singular form of leadership is now regarded as dated in many occupational sectors. Nevertheless, in permanent work groups in schools and colleges such as departmental, key stage or senior management teams it is relatively easy to envisage similar 'leadership' and associated 'deference' expectations being tied to the formal authority of a postholder as designated team leader. This person clearly has a vested interest in balancing the three domains identified by Adair. One difficulty, though, is that permanent teams are likely to have settled work and social patterns, norms which are highly resistant to change even on the part of an active leader. Hence, the leader's freedom to act is subtly constrained by the habitual actions of other members of the team.

Groups formed to address *ad hoc* tasks, crosscurricular issues or whole-school projects, however, begin life as embryonic teams, in the early stages of evolution, and are unlikely to possess these idiosyncratic shared norms from the outset. Consequently, such groups are possibly more vulnerable, or amenable, to radical leadership action. In a similar vein, *de facto* 'leadership' activity, exercised by one or more individuals, may emerge informally from within the group in such situations as members 'form', 'storm' and 'norm'. Conversely, as Paechter (1995) reveals in her report on interdisciplinary coursework initiatives in 29 schools and colleges, without sufficient time set aside at the outset for the clarification and acknowledgement of participants' different purposes and viewpoints, these crosscurricular groupings may never achieve a worthwhile, workable consensus: 'Carrying on as if everyone had the same motives, however, is likely to lead to dissatisfaction on the part of those whose agendas are not being addressed, with a consequent failure of commitment' (*ibid.*, p. 101).

In education, individuals frequently belong to more than one established team; staff members may teach in several subject areas, and often have pastoral duties as well. Senior management staff routinely have some classroom delivery responsibilities, and heads of department are usually members of a middle management group which has whole-curriculum considerations as part of its brief. As a result, those working in schools and colleges can expect to have to adopt a number of different roles each of which imposes discrete expectations. In a reference to primary school headteachers, Yeomans (1987) describes this dualism as 'leading the team and belonging to the group'. Equally, with many teams consisting of a fluid mixture of full-time, part-time and temporary staff, experienced and inexperienced teachers, and professional, para-professional and lay members, it is reasonable to assume that team development is a fragmented, non-linear process and considerably more complex than many normative models imply.

The importance of having team members who are capable of making different but complementary contributions was identified and developed by Belbin (1981; 1993). Belbin discovered that teams made up solely of high-achievers were unlikely to work productively together. He suggested that a more considered mix of team roles was necessary. For example, he identified the need for someone who could 'shape' or 'chair' the work of the team. Equally important was the presence of a 'completer-finisher' to keep the team focused and on-task. His model was originally derived from observations made in artificial situations, yet in terms of its potential for analysis and development of teams the taxonomy continues to enjoy great currency in many occupational sectors. Recently, as Wallace and Hall (1994, p. 67) observed, it has gained credibility in education:

> Four heads had been influenced by the work of Belbin on complementary team roles, and sought to achieve heterogeneity in teamworking styles within the SMT. The head at Underhill was unique in being able to create a team from scratch. He used a typology of complementary team roles to assess candidates during the selection process for both deputies, having become aware of his preferred team role as a result of his recent training.

In short, Belbin's work is helpful because it

1) allows individuals to identify their own preferred or natural team role; and
2) enables teams to identify gaps in the range of natural roles amongst team members.

More challenging, however, is the notion that members need to take on unaccustomed roles according to the demands of the task in hand in order to keep the team functioning effectively. This dictum applies especially to small functioning groups and institutions where the nine possible Belbin roles may significantly outnumber the actual membership of the team!

TEAMS, TEACHING AND MANAGEMENT

In this part of the chapter, I wish to explore some potential limitations on the use of teams in school and college settings and, in particular, the assertion that teams are an ineffectual medium for developing classroom teacher expertise. We also examine the impact of feminine management perspectives on our analysis of teams in education. Finally, some likely difficulties within crosscurricular teams are identified.

The limitations of teams

In attempting to develop team structures, educational managers need to take into account two characteristic features of teaching:

- Teachers spend most of their working day physically isolated from colleagues.
- Teachers value authority and the ability to exert control.

My view is that these two factors militate strongly against the successful adoption of team approaches by classroom teachers.

According to their champions (e.g. Everard and Morris, 1990; Jenkins,

1991; Bell, 1992; West-Burnham, 1992; Caldwell, 1994) the considered application of team approaches in education would appear to have immense
potential to break down the traditional 'egg crate' (Lortie, 1975) or cellular
pattern of teachers' work. I want to proceed with considerably more caution,
however, and argue that there is one historical 'no-go' area in schools and
colleges where team models have yet to make any real inroads; namely, the
classroom. Teaching is almost invariably a solitary activity.

Despite an apparent move towards more collegial and collaborative forms
of management in schools and colleges, the underlying, deeply entrenched
occupational culture of teaching continues to value strongly the notion of
'control'. This reification of authority appears pervasive in schools and
colleges. It is manifested most clearly both in respect for formal status –
most notably that of the headteacher or principal – and in the expectation
that individual teachers must develop the ability to 'control' their students
(see Nias, 1992; Brown and McIntyre, 1993; Court, 1994). Indeed, until the
introduction of compulsory teacher appraisal and a national inspection
regime in England and Wales, achievement of control traditionally conferred
the right to enjoy autonomy in one's classroom and, in doing so, reinforced
the idea of teaching as an activity practised in isolation by 'self-managing'
professionals.

Nevertheless, burgeoning external accountability demands and the requirement to provide a seamless learning experience for students have created
pressures for collaborative planning, resourcing, delivery, assessment and
evaluation of the official curriculum. Teams are thus easily seen as a ready
solution to the intensification of teachers' and managers' work in schools and
colleges. Dimmock (1995), for example, anticipates the possible renaissance
of 'team teaching' as a means of reorganising the delivery of a curriculum for
the secondary school of the twenty-first century. At the level of institutional
practice, however, staffing structures, demarcations of responsibility and
salary scales all remain predominantly hierarchical and, as such, constitute
a powerful organising framework within which those working in education
continue to conceptualise 'the natural order'.

According to Clement and Staessens (1993, p. 147), an additional, persistent difficulty is that the practice of teaching and the process of teamwork
may simply be incompatible bedfellows:

> . . . there is a fundamental difference between a team of football players and
> a team of teachers. The core events in the two professions differ entirely in
> nature. For a football team, the core event is a collective event: a football
> game. Of course, the individual players have to be well trained for this
> collective event. The core event for a team of teachers is what happens in
> the classroom between teacher and pupils. This is not a collective event,
> although teachers can benefit from good collegial relations and support. By
> denying this state of affairs, one denies the fundamental nature of teaching
> and being a teacher.

On the basis of their study of teacher development in a number of Flemish primary schools, the authors argue that both collegiality and autonomy are necessary. However, the way in which schools choose to manage this tension between the various forms of collegiality and autonomy is crucial in terms of stimulating or stunting the growth of opportunities for professional development. We can usefully apply this argument to our present discussion and suggest that team approaches, used selectively, provide an appropriate and important context in which curriculum and teacher development might be nurtured.

However, asking teacher-managers to adopt routinely 'authentic' team approaches may undermine the basic tenets of their workplace culture and, consequently, these approaches may not be readily attainable through the management structures currently in place in the vast majority of schools and colleges. At an individual level, Convery (1992) captures the paradox perfectly when he distinguishes between his willingness to dissect curriculum prescriptions with colleagues in the staffroom and his reluctance to talk openly through personal anxieties about his own teaching with the very same people; the former is largely about agreeing how to accommodate external, official requirements within existing departmental patterns of work, whilst the latter would involve giving control and autonomy over 'his' teaching space to the group. The one can be dealt with anonymously within the already 'performing' team, the other is much more closely tied to the teacher as a person. But, if Convery's ambivalence is typical of that amongst teachers generally, then the potential benefits of teamwork in schools and colleges may be limited to management activities *per se* and not extend to the collective analysis of individual teaching practice.

Teams and teacher development

The literature suggests that formal team approaches have succeeded in education where the focus is removed from the domain of individual teacher development priorities and is concerned with arguably less sensitive administrative or management issues. This would make sense inasmuch as many management activities are, sooner or later, capable of reduction to rational processes and procedures in a way which is problematic for those intuitive, spontaneous and highly individualised facets of the art or craft of classroom teaching.

I want to suggest that mandated team approaches are too threatening and demanding a vehicle for the development of individual teaching expertise in many schools and colleges. For example, in Lloyd's account of his early years as a teacher in Canada (Butt *et al.*, 1992, p. 65), he recounts how his negative experience of grade-level (year-group) teacher meetings adversely affected his attitude to these group sessions:

I became a 'closet teacher', in that I would listen to suggestions, not offering any suggestions, and then 'do my own thing'. I found great success with this mode of operating and up to a few years ago, I hesitated to share any of my strategies/worksheets/lessons I developed on my own. Becoming an administrator forced me into sharing, for I wanted to provide teachers with access to as many resources as possible – the better the programmes they had, the better it was for the school.

The idea that 'wanting to' is a necessary precondition for collaboration or teamwork amongst teachers is given further credence in empirical studies conducted by Nias *et al.* (1989) and Wallace and Hall (1994). In their study of successful primary schools, Nias and colleagues observed that effective teamwork, including the open and good-humoured discussion of classroom successes or failures, became possible only when colleagues already liked each other on a personal level. Similarly, Wallace and Hall (1994, p. 198) concluded, from their analysis of SMTs in secondary schools, that 'the culture of teamwork is no stronger than individuals' commitment'.

By implication, collaborative management models such as quality circles (FEU, 1987; Stewart and Prebble, 1993), which are intended to encourage team approaches to enhancing classroom practice, may only experience the essential early success where individuals can elect to work on the basis of existing friendship groups or where they feel that they personally will gain more by collaborating than by acting in isolation. Indeed, Brown and McIntyre (1993, p. 115) are absolutely forthright on this point: 'The benefits of such attempted sharing of expertise are likely to be realized only if an exclusively positive perspective is taken on the observed teaching and if time is set aside and used for post-observation discussion of the observed teacher's thinking.'

This soft approach, of course, appears more frequently in the literature related to the induction, mentoring and appraisal of individual teachers (see Chapters 11 and 12 in this volume); it is antithetical to the usual managerial understanding of a team which places greater emphasis on altruism and comparatively impersonal processes, roles and tasks.

Teams and feminine management styles

In their analysis of primary school staff teams, Nias *et al.* (1989) raised the issue of whether the 'culture of collaboration' they identified could be attributed directly to gender factors. Was this less structured version of teamwork, based on closely interwoven personal relationships, an example of feminine management (see Chapter 9) and thus a unique manifestation of the preferred work styles of women? At the time, Nias *et al.* were content simply to ask the question. However, there is now an emerging body of theory and research in the field of educational management which has as its central argument the idea that feminine management approaches are distinguished by their concern with empathy and negotiation and their lack of emphasis on role and status. More significantly, they are claimed to offer a more educationally appropriate, holistic alternative to traditional, masculine educational management approaches. The latter are perceived to depend on compartmentalised understandings of rationality and authority.

In her study of a middle-school syndicate (year group) of women teachers, Court (1994) recounts the effects – on the three participants, on the principal and on other syndicates within the school – of an atypical leadership model in which the responsibilities and additional remuneration of the former senior teacher postholder were shared equally amongst all three teachers. Court draws two particularly insightful conclusions from her study of this team at work:

1) Unlike their male counterparts, women tend not to distinguish between team teaching and team management but, consistent with other research on women administrators, see the two as 'similar and part of the same field of endeavour' (*ibid.*, p. 41).
2) While the three women found this 'official' team arrangement a natural extension of the way they liked and needed to collaborate as teachers, the shared leadership model had little impact on existing hierarchies elsewhere in the school. Indeed, the principal made a unilateral decision to discontinue the 'trial' after less than a year. Court observes that a principal's official 'sovereign' status continues to limit the development of non-hierarchical management approaches throughout an institution.

Tensions in cross-curricular teams

Court's second finding is consistent with those derived from other studies (Earley and Fletcher-Campbell, 1989; Bolam *et al.*, 1993; Wallace and Hall, 1994; Paechter, 1995) of larger schools and colleges which have examined the relationships between, and within, groups in the same institution. In essence, establishing an inclusive, collaborative management approach in the subject department 'team' is generally unproblematic, given appropriately sensitive and tactful leadership. In contrast, it is much more difficult to develop true teamwork characteristics in middle management or crosscurricular groups where sectional interests may take precedence. The difficulties appear to be twofold:

1) These groups are reluctant to accept ownership of decisions concerning initiatives which are perceived to have originated elsewhere.
2) With regard to the group's authority to act, designated areas of responsibility and accountability are often vague.

Not surprisingly, the participants within such groups may remain fiercely partisan and consequently are unable to develop either the whole-school or college perspectives necessary for informed decision-making, or the sense of altruism needed to turn an essentially amorphous group into a fully functioning team.

To summarise my argument thus far, there is an important caveat to be applied to the introduction of off-the-shelf team approaches in schools and colleges. Resistance to the analysis of individual teaching practice in a formally constituted team forum may be attributable more to the inappropriateness, and lack of intimacy, of the approach itself than to the recalcitrance of teachers. If team approaches are to begin to influence the analysis and development of individual teacher practice, perhaps they will do so more readily with greater acknowledgement and proliferation of feminine styles of collaborative management.[1] Finally, whilst the process of developing a team ethos within discrete subject, pastoral or management teams may prove comparatively straightforward, attempts to create whole-school or college teams tend to be less successful.

CONCLUSION: TOWARDS EFFECTIVE TEAMS

Despite these various caveats, however, it is clear from studies which have been carried out in educational contexts that a team model does offer a feasible, challenging and supportive means of enhancing *management* practice – and here we must include the teaching-*related* activities of curriculum design, assessment and evaluation. It does so by encouraging norms of openness, interdependence and a clarity of focus together with a clear task-driven purpose and an explicitly collaborative process. Gillborn (1989, p. 78), for example, writes of 'an increasing interdependence between headteachers and their senior staff' in the secondary schools he researched. Similarly, the authors of the one major study which deals specifically with teams in education (Wallace and Hall, 1994) are cautiously optimistic in their assessment of the potential teams have for enhancing management effectiveness. Furthermore, Bolam *et al.* (1993) also identified effective team norms operating within their self-selecting sample of schools. The more significant point is that team approaches can help challenge existing, conventional management structures through their focus on collective rather than unitary sources of authority and responsibility. Bolam *et al.* (*ibid.*, pp. 95–6) describe the steps taken by a newly appointed special school headteacher to dismantle the previous management structure:

> The restructuring consisted of an enlarged senior management team [seven] with new people and new roles; all staff working in three curriculum groups [primary/secondary/FE]; six administration teams and cross-curricular co-ordinators. The headteacher pointed out that the new structure gave a flattened hierarchy so that in addition to the school teacher management team, eleven of the twenty four staff had leadership roles. Each of the groups and teams had a devolved budget and took on decision-making roles.

In this extract we have some indication of the major preconditions for effective management teams in education. First, and most importantly, the revised management structure serves the actual working priorities and organisational arrangements of the school; it is not a historical anachronism. Secondly, and related to this, is the principle that these reconstituted groups, with newly defined roles and briefs, have power and authority to act autonomously; they also possess the financial resources necessary to help implement any decisions they make without, one assumes, having to refer decisions back for approval. Thirdly, there is a clear attempt to provide functional curriculum groupings of staff with administrative support, and to link their work by using crosscurricular co-ordinators. Finally, the notion of distributed or collective leadership is evident in the assertion that a large number of staff are expected to take on leadership roles. Interestingly, the positive staff feedback on the effectiveness of this revised management structure, as reported by Bolam *et al.*, fully supports the headteacher's claims of involvement, commitment and autonomy.

However, not all schools and colleges are in a position to undertake major restructuring along these lines; and therein lies the difficulty for teacher-managers who wish to operate on the basis of teamwork. To a certain extent, historical staffing, responsibility and remuneration structures can be modified on paper, and nominal teams can be created, but habits and attitudes are relatively immune from such simple panaceas. Thus, a more pragmatic assessment of when and where to encourage teams is needed. This assessment may lead to the realisation that team approaches need to be cultivated in piecemeal fashion when the conditions are favourable. The analysis undertaken in this chapter suggests that management through teams is likely to succeed only where all members are committed to the process. This commitment requires team members to acknowledge and value differences of opinion and to recognise that consensus may not always be possible. Similarly, there is a real possibility that different teams within the one institution may have incompatible priorities and, particularly in larger schools and colleges, that team members may have conflicting loyalties. These too need to be taken into account.

Equally, I have argued that a team approach is an inappropriate vehicle for the collective analysis of classroom teaching practice. Thus, a team structure needs to be leavened with other management approaches, such as induction, mentoring and appraisal, for individual teachers. Finally, if the ultimate purpose of all this management activity is to enhance the quality of learning for both staff and students, then senior staff in schools and colleges need to recognise and have faith in the benefits which derive from continued teacher autonomy together with informal collaborative initiatives which are based on friendship groups; in effect, a valuing of the enduring occupational culture of teaching itself.

NOTE

1.   Currently, in Aotearoa/New Zealand, an understanding of Maori 'management' approaches is also contributing to a questioning of the universal applicability of conventional management structures in education. Parallel with the growth of Kohanga Reo and Kura Kaupapa Maori, which provide education in Maori, by Maori, for Maori, there has emerged an awareness of the need to organise these institutions in the same way as the extended

family groupings they serve. This cultural awareness has been articulated recently by one secondary school head of department:

I do not see myself as the 'head' of my department. Being a Maori institution implies that the way the Maori Department functions should reflect the cultural values found on the marae. In our situation, there is what I call the 'Tatou tatou' concept. This means that we operate as a whanau or family unit. The managerial and leadership roles are shared. Who takes the lead depends on who is best qualified to do the job. Furthermore, another key concept which underlies what we do and how we do things in our Department is the notion of 'Tautoko'. Tautoko means that we collectively help one another to perform our tasks. This also implies that we share the accountability of our department (Tibble, n.d.).

REFERENCES

Adair, J. (1988) *Effective Leadership*, London, Pan Books.

Ball, S. (1993) Education policy, power relations and teachers' work, *British Journal of Educational Studies*, Vol. 41(2), pp. 106–21.

Belbin, M. (1981) *Management Teams, Why they Succeed or Fail*, London, Heinemann.

Belbin, M. (1993) *Team Roles at Work*, London, Butterworth-Heinemann.

Bell, L. (1992) *Managing Teams in Secondary Schools*, London, Routledge.

Bolam, R., McMahon, A., Pocklington, D. and Weindling, D. (1993) *Effective Management in Schools*, London, HMSO.

Brown, S. and McIntyre, D. (1993) *Making Sense of Teaching*, Buckingham, Open University Press.

Butt, R., Raymond, D., McCue, G. and Yamagishi, L. (1992) Collaborative autobiography and the teacher's voice, in Goodson, I. (ed.) *Studying Teachers' Lives*, London, Routledge.

Caldwell, B. (1994) Structural reform in a global context: an international perspective on self-managing and self-governing schools and their potential for improving the quality of schooling, paper given at Loughborough University, March.

Campbell, J. and St. J. Neill, S. (1994) *Secondary Teachers at Work*, London, Routledge.

Clement, M. and Staessens, K. (1993) The professional development of teachers and the tension between autonomy and collegiality, in Kieviet, F. and Vandenberghe, R. (eds) *School Culture, School Improvement and Teacher Development*, Leiden, DSWO Press.

Coleman, M. and Bush, T. (1994) Managing with teams, in Bush, T. and West-Burnham, J. (eds) *The Principles of Educational Management*, Harlow, Longman.

Convery, A. (1992) Insight, direction and support: a case study of collaborative enquiry in classroom research, in Biott, C. and Nias, J. (eds), *Working and Learning together for Change*, Buckingham, Open University Press.

Court, M. (1994) *Women Transforming Leadership*, Palmerston North, NZ, ERDC Press.

Dalin, P. and Rolff, H.-G. (1993) *Changing the School Culture*, London, Cassell.

Dimmock, C. (1995) Restructuring for school effectiveness: leading, organising and teaching for effective learning, *Educational Management and Administration*, Vol. 23, pp. 5–18.

Earley, P. and Fletcher-Campbell, F. (1989) *The Time to Manage? Department and Faculty Heads at Work*, Windsor, NFER/Nelson.

Everard, B. and Morris, G. (1990) *Effective School Management* (2nd edn), London, Paul Chapman.

Further Education Unit (FEU) (1987) *An Evaluation of Quality Circles in Colleges of FE, Planning Staff Development*, No. 7, March, London, FEU.

90 *Managing people in education*

Gillborn, D. (1989) Talking heads. Reflections on secondary headship at a time of rapid educational change, *School Organisation*, Vol. 9 (1), pp. 65–83.
Grace, G. (1995) *School Leadership, Beyond Education Management*, Lewes, Falmer Press.
Harrison, B., Dobell, T. and Higgins, C. (1995) Managing to make things happen: critical issues in team management, in Bell, J. and Harrison, B. (eds) *Vision and Values in Managing Education. Successful Leadership Principles and Practice*, London, David Fulton.
Hopkins, D. and Ainscow, M. (1992) Making sense of school improvement: an interim account of the 'Improving the Quality of Education for All' project, *Cambridge Journal of Education*, Vol. 23 (3), pp. 287–304.
Jenkins, H. (1991) *Getting it Right, a Handbook for Successful School Leadership*, Oxford, Blackwell.
Knight, T. (1993) Setting a democratic base for effective schooling, in Crump, S. (ed.) *School Centred Leadership, Putting Policy into Practice*, Melbourne, Nelson.
Lortie, D. (1975) *Schoolteacher, a Sociological Study*, Chicago, Ill., University of Chicago Press.
Mortimore, P., Mortimore, J. with Thomas, H., Cairns, R. and Taggart, B. (1992) *The Innovative Uses of Non-teaching Staff in Primary and Secondary Schools Project, Final Report*, London, Institute of Education.
Nias, J. (1992) Introduction, in Biott, C. and Nias, J. (eds) *Working and Learning Together for Change*, Buckingham, Open University Press.
Nias, J., Southworth, G. and Yeomans, R. (1989) *Staff Relationships in the Primary School*, London, Cassell.
NZEI/Te Riu Roa (New Zealand Educational Institute) (1995) *Breaking New Ground, Support Staff in Today's Schools*, Wellington, NZ, NZEI/Te Riu Roa.
Paechter, C. (1995) *Crossing Subject Boundaries, the Micropolitics of Curriculum Innovation*, London, HMSO.
Schein, E. (19880 *Organizational Psychology* (3rd edn), Englewood Cliffs, NJ, Prentice-Hall.
Sinclair, A. (1992) The tyranny of a team ideology, *Organisation Studies*, Vol. 13 (4), pp. 611–26.
Stephenson, T. (1985) *Management, a Political Activity*, London, Macmillan.
Stewart, D. and Prebble, T. (1993) *The Reflective Principal*, Palmerston North, NZ, ERDC Press.
Tansley, P. (1989) *Course Teams, the Way Forward in FE?*, Windsor, NFER/Nelson.
Tibble, K. (n.d.) Unpublished MEDAdmin assignment, Massey University.
Tuckman, B. (1965) Developmental sequences in small groups, *Psychological Bulletin*, Vol. 63, pp. 384–99.
Walker, A. and Stott, K. (1993) The work of senior management teams, some pointers to improvement, *Studies in Educational Administration*, Vol. 58, pp. 33–40.
Wallace, M. and Hall, V. (1994) *Inside the SMT, Teamwork in Secondary School Management*, London, Paul Chapman.
West-Burnham, J. (1992) *Managing Quality in Schools, a TQM Approach*, Harlow, Longman.
Yeomans, R. (1987) Leading the team, belonging to the group, in Southworth, G. (ed.) *Readings in Primary School Management*, Lewes, Falmer Press.

Section C: individual issues

One clear manifestation of the changed context within which managers of people in education work is the rising concern about pressures on time and the related stress caused to individuals. The research carried out by Jim Campbell and Sean Neill is described in Chapter 7 and the implications for managers drawn out. These include strategies which enable individuals to reflect upon and manage the use of their own time, but also to consider what actions are needed by managers since many pressures upon time come from external bodies. In Chapter 8, Megan Crawford argues that, whilst stress affects individuals, managers need to develop support strategies in organisations to offset the damage to people and to performance which may result from negative stress. Marianne Coleman addresses one of the equal opportunities issues, that of gender, in Chapter 9, and argues that managers should be aware of inequality and take action to improve the situation. Stereotyping is proving difficult to break down and managers may need to re-examine their structures and processes to enable the growth of cultures which will encourage development for all staff.

7

MANAGING TEACHERS' TIME UNDER SYSTEMIC REFORM

Jim Campbell and Sean R. St J. Neill

BACKGROUND

The purpose of this chapter is to report research conducted into the use of teachers' time in primary and secondary schools, and to analyse its implications for school management. In doing so, we draw upon some of the relevant international evidence and upon analyses of the occupational culture of teaching.

As the Education Reform Act 1988 began to be implemented in England, Wales and Northern Ireland from 1989, we were commissioned to carry out a series of empirical studies over four years into the impact of the 'reforms' upon the work of teachers. The full details of these studies have been reported elsewhere (Campbell and Neill 1994a; 1994b; 1994c; Evans *et al.*, 1994). Teachers completed a diary log (for the period from 0700 hours to 2400 hours) over seven consecutive days and a questionnaire. In all we had a database of over 7,000 working days from over 700 teachers over the period from 1989 to 1993. It included a small ($n = 97$) longitudinal sample of Key Stage 1 (infant) teachers across the whole period of the curriculum reform process for that Key Stage. Twenty-four teachers in the longitudinal sample were interviewed.

ANALYSIS: CLASSIFICATION OF TEACHERS' USE OF TIME

We analysed the diary data using a five-fold classification of work activity common to both primary and secondary samples. These were

1) teaching
2) preparation/marking
3) professional development
4) administration
5) other activities.

Within this overall classification each main category was broken down, on the coding system used by the teachers to record their time use, into smaller subcategories which allowed for finer analysis and took into account differences between primary and secondary teaching. For example, under the main category of Teaching, primary teachers' time was allocated to five subcategories, viz., Teaching Mathematics, Teaching English, Teaching Science, Teaching Other Subjects and Assessment/Recording for the National Curriculum. Secondary teachers' time, on the other hand, under the Teaching category was subdivided into components, viz., Teaching your Main Subject, Teaching Other Subjects, Assessment/Recording for the National Curriculum, Assessment and Testing Excluding National Curriculum Assessment.

The adoption of a common framework of main categories had two advantages; it enabled a comparison between primary and secondary teachers' use of time, and the framework was broadly similar to that used in the only previous studies (Hilsum and Cane, 1971; Hilsum and Strong, 1978) thereby permitting comparison with the nature of teachers' work some fifteen to twenty years before this study (and before the 1988 reforms).

CONCEPTUALISING TEACHERS' WORK

We adopted two relatively simple ways of conceptualising teachers' work. As can be seen from the above, the first was the most basic; we assumed that there were two principal dimensions to teachers' work, viz.:

1) The amount of time spent.
2) The activities upon which time was spent.

It can be seen from this that *time* was central to the analysis of their work because, as Hargreaves (1989) argues, time is the fundamental measure by which work is structured and controlled.

A second way of conceptualising work is from the perspective of individual teachers, as indicated in Figure 7.1, with the time on each descending level being a subset of the one above. It is, to use a different analogy, like a sequence of the pictures of the earth's surface relayed by satellite, where each picture is of a smaller area, in sharper focus, than the preceding one.

Figure 7.1 is simple and rather self-evident, but it has two virtues. Time is usually thought of from the *institutional* point of view, with regard to the needs of the school and its management (see Bell, 1988; Knight, 1989,

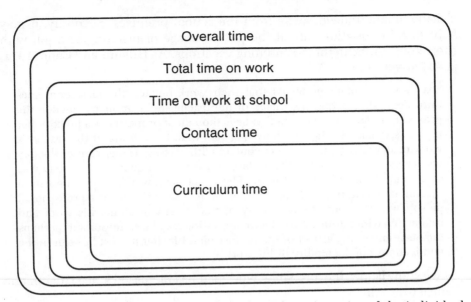

Figure 7.1 Framework for time analysis from the perspective of the individual teacher

Level 1 Overall time: i.e. 24 hours per day, whether spent on work or not

Level 2 Total time on work: i.e. all time spent on work, whenever it is spent, including school days, evenings, weekends

Level 3 Time on work at school: i.e. all time spent on work during the school day, including teaching, registration, supervision, assembly, meetings, administration and non-contact time

Level 4 Contact time: i.e. all time spent with pupils, including teaching, registration, supervision and assembly

Level 5 Curriculum time: i.e. all time spent teaching and assessing pupils

for examples). The framework in Figure 7.1, however, directs us to think about time from the *individual* point of view and how work fits into the individual's life overall (see Campbell, 1992, for an elaboration of this point). This was important when we examined the impact of work on teachers' personal lives (see Evans *et al.*, 1994), and identified conflict arising from the differing time demands at Levels 1 and 2. Secondly, the framework does not restrict itself to work in the school day, reflecting, by the inclusion of Level 2, time taken up with work outside it. We were able, therefore, to take two dimensions of teachers' work into account: 'visible' work, that is, work that can in principle be seen by parents and other members of the public; and 'invisible' work, which is mainly carried out in private (or in professional seclusion on training courses, etc.) and which is not in the public domain.

The importance of taking this comprehensive view of teachers' work is twofold. First, much of teachers' work is now conducted outside the classroom and, indeed, away from the school premises. Secondly, it may help to raise questions about the public image of teaching as a job with short hours ('nine to three') and long vacations. As Hilsum and Cane (1971, p. 91) noted:

> Teachers have often protested that their work outside the classroom goes unrecognised, and that the image of the teacher held by many outside the profession is far too narrow, in that he is thought of primarily as a practitioner in a classroom. Our figures show that less than three-fifths of the teacher's working day was spent in direct contact with classes; 15 per cent of the day was spent in school but without class contact, and a quarter of the day was spent entirely outside school hours. These facts lend weight to the suggestion that an understanding and appreciation of the teacher's role as a professional person will not come from a study of the classroom alone; his work and interaction with pupils in the classroom setting may be an important, perhaps the most important, aspect of his professional life, but it must be seen in the wider context of the totality of his work.

As we show below, the 'invisible' workload has increased since Hilsum and Cane's research.

FINDINGS: MAIN CATEGORIES OF WORK

Our findings for primary and secondary teachers are presented separately in respect of the five main categories of activity outlined earlier, together with the total time spent on work, in Table 7.1. From the perspective of time management six points emerge from Table 7.1. First, as is indicated by the note, the sum of hours spent on each main category exceeds the total

Table 7.1 Time spent on five main categories, expressed in hours and as percentages of total time on work

Main category	Primary (*n* = 374)		Secondary (*n* = 348)	
	Hours	%	Hours	%
Teaching	18.70	35	16.9	31
Preparation/Marking	15.90	30	12.9	24
Administration	14.10	27	18.1	33
Professional Development	5.90	11	5.3	10
Other Activities	5.40	10	4.1	8
Total	52.60		54.4	
Note: Sum of main categories	60.18 hrs		57.3 hrs.	

NB: The sum of categories exceeds the total since activities within two or more different categories could be carried on simultaneously. The program written to analyse the data was designed to avoid such double counting when arriving at the total hours.

time spent on work. This is because the teachers sometimes carried out two or more activities simultaneously (e.g. teaching pupils (Teaching) and mounting a display (Administration)). More of primary teachers' time was spent on this 'simultaneous working', probably reflecting a more pressurised working school day. Secondly, only about one third of the teachers' working time was spent Teaching, reinforcing the point made in the Hilsum and Cane research. Thirdly, the ratio of Teaching to Preparation/Marking (1:0.85 primary; 1:0.76 secondary) implies that, for every hour teachers are directed to teach, another 51 minutes (primary) and 45 minutes (secondary) will, on average, be required in the teachers' 'own', or non-directed, time. Fourthly, there was substantial time spent on Administration. This category included two elements: administration or management (e.g. helping to run the school or a department, examinations, pastoral care) and time spent on the routines of school life (e.g. supervising pupils, registration and transition, participating in assemblies, mounting displays, etc.). Thus it covers much more than administrative activities as commonly understood. The latter element illustrates that for both groups a substantial amount of time was spent on activities which, whatever their importance for the smooth running of a school, are low-level routines not requiring a graduate qualification. Fifthly, the time spent on Professional Development, even allowing for the fact (somewhat optimistically) that staff meetings were included within this category, was between five and seven hours a week, the longer time at primary level reflecting the more substantial professional development programmes directly related to the implementation of the National Curriculum and assessment, especially at Key Stage 1. Using a stricter definition of professional development (i.e. only in-service training) primary teachers spent 2.3 hours and secondary teachers 2.0 hours a week, roughly equivalent to 4 per cent of their working week, at a time when what were acknowledged to be major reforms were being implemented. None the less, by comparison with the evidence from Hilsum and his colleagues (Hilsum and Cane, 1971; Hilsum and Strong, 1978) these figures represent substantial increases in time and therefore substantial educational resources devoted to teachers' professional development. Sixthly, Other Activities, including time spent on extracurricular activities, clubs, orchestra, etc., attendance at governing bodies and activities that were uncodable in our classification, amounted to just under 10 per cent of the teachers' working week, with the largest specific time commitment being to extracurricular activities with just over one hour (primary) and one-and-a-half hours (secondary) per week.

Finally, the total time spent on work at over 50 hours per week in term time fits closely, as has been said, with the other studies in the field (Coopers and Lybrand Deloitte, 1991; Lowe, 1991; NAS/UWT, 1991; School Teachers' Review Body, 1995). The average, of course, disguises significant variation, typically from 35 hours to over 65. Consistent correlations with long hours on work were not found in respect of *positional* factors (e.g. range of responsibilities, salary status, size of class, age or experience). Highly significant

correlations were found (linear trend $p < .001$) between long hours and a
personal response – the subjective perception of the number of hours it
was reasonable for the teacher to be expected to work in his or her own
time ('non-directed time' in England and Wales). (The only exception to this
finding was for deputy heads, where longer hours were worked than other
teachers. The numbers involved were fairly small, but the finding is worth
further research.) Because this response was broadly and systematically
correlated with working time over which teachers had discretion, we called
it the 'conscientiousness' factor. In doing so we intended to signify two
dimensions to 'conscientiousness' - first, that teaching remains a vocationally oriented occupation (cf. Acker, 1987) with teacher motivation driven
largely by a personal and professional sense of obligation and, secondly, that
the management of teachers' time overall is ultimately a matter of personal,
rather than institutional, control, even though institutional arrangements
can help or hinder the extent of personal control.

STRUCTURAL CHANGE OVER THE PAST TWENTY YEARS

It is worth drawing attention to one main finding common to both groups of
teachers. We were able to analyse the overall time spent on work by teachers
according to whether it was spent with pupils or away from them (e.g. in
meetings, professional development, at home, etc.) and to compare it with
the findings of Hilsum and his colleagues reported in 1971 (primary) and
1978 (secondary). The findings are illustrated in Figures 7.2 and 7.3.

Figure 7.2 shows our primary teachers spending approximately 45 per
cent of their time in contact with, and 55 per cent out of contact with,
pupils. Although precise comparison is difficult, Hilsum and Cane's (1971)
junior teachers spent 58 per cent of time in contact and 42 per cent out
of contact – almost inverse proportions. Figure 7.3 shows our secondary
teachers spending approximately 39 per cent of time in contact and 61
per cent out of contact with pupils. Hilsum and Strong's (1978) secondary
teachers spent 45 per cent of time in contact and 55 per cent out of contact with pupils. The pie charts illustrate an important structural change
occurring in teachers' work, especially clear at the primary-school level.
The explanation for the different patterns of time is not that teachers in
the early 1970s were spending less time absolutely on teaching pupils but
that *proportionately* (within an overall increase of working time of about ten
hours a week) less time was spent teaching in the early 1990s. Moreover, in
absolute terms, much more time was spent on work not involving pupils,
especially upon activities in the 'extended professional' (Hoyle, 1974) or the
'teacher-as-educationist' (Keddie, 1971) role. The structure of teaching as an
occupation seems to have shifted to require teachers to spend more time in
activities, such as staff meetings, training days, professional development
and managerial/administrative tasks, which require them to work with other

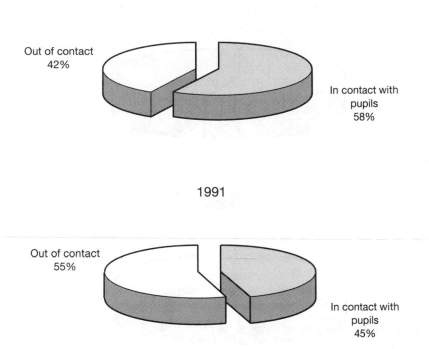

Figure 7.2   Primary school contact time

adults rather than with pupils, and to engage in educational discourse. Whatever the long-term advantages of such excursions into adult collaboration and professional discourse, for primary teachers certainly (Nias, 1989) and for many secondary teachers also (Poppleton and Riseborough, 1990) the main sources of job satisfaction, as Lortie (1969) has shown, have traditionally been within the classroom arising from relationships with pupils. From the point of view of managing systemic reform, this structural shift is problematic, since teachers will need external motivation and incentive to engage in extended professional activities which have relatively little intrinsic reward for them.

DIFFERENCES IN TIME USE: PRIMARY AND SECONDARY

The general pattern of working time illustrated above has been painted in broad brush. At the level of the finer detail of subcategories there were, as might be expected, some considerable differences between primary and secondary teachers which might affect time management.

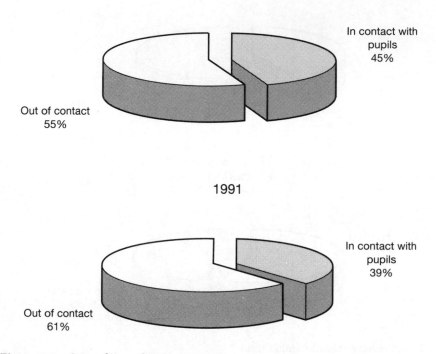

Figure 7.3   Secondary school contact time

The use of primary teachers' time

The overall pattern of working time for primary teachers is given in Table
7.2. Three features of time use in Table 7.2 are relevant to the management
of the curriculum. First, our primary teachers, in line with all research on
curriculum time allocations in primary schools (e.g. Bassey, 1977; Bennett
et al., 1980; Galton and Simon, 1980; DES, 1987; Tizard *et al.*, 1988; Meyer
et al., 1992; Alexander 1992), allocated roughly 50 per cent of curriculum
time to the two 'basic' subjects of English and Mathematics. (It will be
seen that the sum of the hours given over to different components of the
curriculum is 32.7 hours, exceeding the 18.7 hours total teaching time by
more than 70 per cent, reflecting the classroom practice of teaching more
than one subject at a time and giving a '170 per cent curriculum'.) Whatever
the merits of this concentration of time on the basics, it left primary teachers
with inadequate amounts of time available for delivering the rest of the
statutory curriculum (NCC, 1993; Ofsted, 1993; Campbell and Neill, 1994c).
Secondly, registration and transition (crocodiling pupils round the school
from one location to another, such as the classroom to the hall) took up some

Table 7.2 A profile of primary teachers' work in 25 subcategories (time in hours per week)

Category	Hours per week
Teaching (total)	*18.7*
English	9.8
Mathematics	6.3
Science	3.4
Other subjects	9.6
Assessing while teaching	2.7
Preparation (total)	*15.9*
Planning lessons	10.5
Marking/recording	7.1
Organisation	2.7
Administration (total)	*14.1*
Parents	1.2
Displays	2.2
Liaison	0.7
Real break	3.0
Working break	2.2
Non-contact time	0.2
Registration/transition	2.7
Supervision	1.5
Worship/assembly	1.3
Professional Development (total)	*5.9*
In-service courses	1.0
Travel to in-service courses	0.4
Non-pupil days	0.3
Meetings	2.6
Professional reading	2.2
Other Activities (total)	*5.5*
Governing bodies	0.3
Extracurricular (sports, clubs, orchestras, etc.)	1.4
Miscellaneous	3.8

2.7 hours a week with about 1.75 hours of this time given over to transition. This amount of time, equivalent to 7 or 8 per cent of curriculum time, is technically available for instruction but 'evaporates' (ILEA, 1988) in the normal operation of a primary school. We do not take the view of Gump (1976) that time used in this way is 'wasted', but it reduces the time available to the teacher for teaching the curriculum, exacerbates the problem mentioned above of delivering the whole curriculum and has not been allowed for in the revision of the National Curriculum by Dearing (SCAA, 1993). Thirdly, the teachers spent approximately 6.8 hours a week on routines (displays, registration, transition, supervision) excluding any time on routines in the category of Other Activities. This is equivalent to one third of the time spent teaching pupils. Our interviews with Key Stage 1 teachers on this matter revealed that they thought lack of time in the school day was the main problem for them in managing the curriculum, and the data from the questionnaires for all primary teachers showed that 'lack of time' was the main obstacle to implementation of the National Curriculum for 80 per cent of teachers. There is something paradoxical in the way teachers' time is used if they see themselves as having not enough time available to realise the cognitive objectives of the curriculum, but spend nearly seven hours a week on low-level, time-consuming routines which do not obviously contribute to cognitive development of their pupils.

The use of secondary teachers' time

The overall pattern of secondary teachers' time is presented at Table 7.3 below. Six points about the use of secondary teachers' time need to be made at this stage. First, unlike the data on primary teachers, there was a considerable variation in the time spent teaching according to the salary status of the teachers; the higher up the salary scale the less teaching was done. This difference was statistically significant (linear trend, $p > .001$) but there was an obvious 'threshold' with teachers' senior posts (i.e. in 1991, incentive allowances D, E and Deputy Headships) having substantially less teaching than the other teachers to allow for their administrative and managerial responsibilities. The second point follows from the above. The higher up the salary scale the more time was spent on school administration. Again, these differences were linear and statistically highly significant ($p < .001$, linear trend). The fact that this is a somewhat obvious, even banal, point does not mean that it has no significance for management. Thirdly, teachers spent approximately two-and-a-half hours a week teaching subjects other than the main subject in which they were qualified. As might be expected, there was significantly more Other Subject teaching in smaller schools (linear trend, $p < .001$). Fourthly, there was a gender difference. Men and women worked similar overall hours and taught for similar amounts of time when salary status is allowed for. However, women teachers spent significantly more time teaching younger (Key Stage 3) pupils ($p < .01$, analysis of variance) and significantly less ($p < .05$, analysis of variance) teaching the older (post-16) students. For this reason women taught larger classes on average than men. Fifthly, there was a consistent and positive statistical association between time spent on main subject teaching and time spent on Preparation ($p < .001$, linear trend). It might be thought that more time would have to be spent planning lessons in subjects for which teachers lacked qualifications, but the opposite was true. This may mean that teachers spend more time planning in their 'own' subject because they themselves are interested in

Table 7.3 A profile of secondary teachers' work in 27 subcategories (time in hours per week)

Category	Hours per week
Teaching (total)	*16.9*
Main subject	13.9
Other subject	2.5
Assessment	0.4
Testing (not NC)	0.8
Preparation (total)	*12.9*
Preparation/planning	5.8
Marking	6.8
Organisation	1.2
Professional Development (total)	*5.3*
Courses	1.2
Travel to courses	0.7
Training days	0.2
Meetings	2.5
Reading	0.9
Administration (total)	*18.1*
School/department administration	5.7
Examination administration	1.7
Pastoral care	1.5
Parents	1.1
Displays	0.2
Supervision	0.8
Liaison	0.7
Worship	0.6
Real break	2.4
Working break	2.3
Registration	1.2
Non-contact time	0.4
Other Activities (total)	*4.1*
Governing bodies	0.2
Sports, clubs	1.5
Miscellaneous	2.4

it and are more committed to motivating pupils to learn it, but the finding may also be explained in part by the likelihood that some 'Other Teaching' simply involved 'covering' lessons for absent teachers, either at short notice or where the lesson material had already been prepared and would be marked by the absent teachers themselves. In either case, it raises issues of the quality of teaching in such classes.

A sixth point is the relatively low proportion of the working time (31 per cent and about 17 hours per week) spent teaching and the substantial time used for administration (nearly 9 hours per week) and school routines (nearly 3 hours per week). As with their primary colleagues, the question arises of how many of these activities might be able to be carried out by non-teaching staff.

MANAGEMENT ISSUES

Two points about the evidence above need to be made before the main management issues are discussed. The first is whether the evidence is of a temporary 'blip' in teacher workloads because it was collected during a period of unusually intense reform or whether it reflects a more permanent pattern. Without further evidence it is difficult to be entirely confident, but the data on the primary teachers, collected over a four-year period, showed a similar length of working week and patterning of work activities in the final year as in the first. (There was a 'blip' in 1991, but only then.) More importantly, systemic reform is becoming a permanent feature of education in most societies (OECD, 1990; Fullan, 1992) and a return to stasis in the UK seems improbable. A picture of workloads under the conditions of reform may for this reason be the most appropriate basis for generalisation.

The second point is more straightforward: time is money, with teachers' salaries typically accounting for at least 70 per cent of school budgets. On this basis alone an analysis of the way teachers' time is used must have substantial implications for the management of schools. It should be noted, therefore, that the discussion which follows is primarily evidence led, that is based on a consideration of how teachers' time was *used*, rather than more general theorising about how teachers' time should be *managed*. The discussion concentrates upon two broad issues, namely, teacher conscientiousness and the division of labour in schools. Although the former may be thought of as primarily a matter for individual control, and the latter for organisational control, our argument is that in both, the occupational culture of schools may be a source of resistance to change in the management of teachers' time.

The dilemma of conscientiousness

We have demonstrated the pervasive and positive association between 'conscientiousness' and long hours spent on work by individual teachers – the conscientiousness syndrome. Long hours spent on work of course do not inevitably imply professional virtue; they may equally reflect inefficient use of time, ambition, self-indulgent pleasure in work or an empty social life. Nor should they be read as a proxy for stress, necessarily. There was however a generally perceived problem with long hours. The teachers thought that about ten hours a week of their 'own' time in term time (on top of the 33 hours a week of statutorily directed work time) could reasonably be expected of them. This would give an overall working term-time week of approximately 43 hours. Yet they were working approximately ten hours a week longer than this, on average. This was, as we have shown earlier, out of a *personal* sense of obligation and did not arise specifically from, for example, extra responsibilities associated with high salary status.

We were able to explore this finding in interviews (with infant teachers only) reported fully in Evans *et al*. (1994). Here are two vignettes of teachers we interviewed. They represent two positions around which teachers may need to exercise personal choice.

One of the teachers, Tricia, had nursery and reception children, and argued that the heavy workload of implementing National Curriculum and assessment had adversely affected her relationships within her family. She thought she needed non-contact time to do all that was being expected of her in school but she would only accept non-contact time on conditions:

> *Even though I have talked about non-contact time, I don't want non-contact time unless the person in my class is me, or a clone of me, or someone who is going to be able to go in there and carry on or do something which will enhance those children who are learning for half-an-hour a day or one day a week, or whatever. I don't want someone going in there just doing a holding job, . . . suppose somebody was to say, 'You can have one day off a week to do record-keeping, to do administration work, that sort of thing, go on courses' . . . I would rather do it in my own time at home if I had to, because then I'd cram five days into four.*

We classified Tricia as 'overconscientious' because she seemed ready to give in to what she saw as unrealistic and inappropriate demands, and did so out of an obligation to do her best for her pupils.

The second teacher, Christine, we characterised as 'sane'. She was in a tiny minority. Christine had decided to limit her impulse towards overwork because she was anxious to protect her own time and her personal and family life. She discussed her strategy thus:

> *I frequently have to say, 'No, I can't do that', especially when other members of staff want my time for something, something that they are doing. I just haven't got the time. The headteacher doesn't get everything she wants either - if she asks me I say, 'Yes, I'll try', and if she comes back a couple of weeks later I have to say, 'Sorry, I haven't had any time'.*
> How do you feel about that?
> *I would like to have more time to help other members of the staff but I think, what it comes down to is, your own class has to come first. You have to do your best for your own class, you can't take your time out to do things for other people in school if you haven't done what you should for your own class. We are all experienced teachers, we haven't got any probationary teachers, so I don't feel that much of an obligation to do things for other members of staff.*

Christine had established a cool, no-nonsense approach to the new demands. If they took longer than people were expecting them to take, then people would have to put up with it or sack her.

It has been conventional to analyse teachers' attitudes to teaching according to Hoyle's (1974) concept of 'restricted' and 'extended' professionalism; the former defining their work as primarily teaching, the latter responding to a broader set of professional expectations, including theorising and working in the professional development activities. The polarisation is, of course, somewhat false, and in any case relative, but it is interesting to turn the value assumptions of Hoyle's analysis on their head. For teachers like Christine, restricted professionalism put a brake on otherwise unrealistic time demands and enabled them to obtain or regain a greater sense of control over their working time. For those like Tricia, an extended sense of professional obligation removed the brake and left the use of their time at the mercy of an uncoordinated and confused multiple set of national policy initiatives frequently poorly managed by LEAs or headteachers.

It is difficult to argue against conscientiousness in a profession largely concerned with children and young people but such motivation is problematic for two reasons. The first is that, under systemic reform, conscientiousness may create a trap for individual teachers because it has the power to render them victims of conflicting demands. This is particularly true in systems such as the UK where particular reforms turn out to be unworkable; or where multiple innovations, in addition to curriculum reform, are fed into the system simultaneously.

The pressures are not restricted to the UK. A report in 1991 from the International Labour Office (ILO, 1991), based on an analysis of teachers' work in more than forty countries, argued that the nature of teachers' work was changing in response to a range of new expectations being placed on the schools. Not only were curriculum reform programmes being put in place but there was also an accelerated trend for moral and social responsibilities, previously exercised by other agencies (e.g. the home and family, the church, the welfare agencies and local communities) to be transferred to schools. The reasons for this are obvious; school is the only universally experienced institution in societies that are morally and socially fractured or fragmented. The school thus becomes the prime site in which policies for the creation and reinforcement of a moral and social order can be implemented – the prime site, in which society attempts to create the identities of its future members. In some areas, schools are the only site for such policies to be enacted, and teachers are expected to take on the responsibility of ensuring that they work. The most obvious locations are in the 'underclass' areas where, for some pupils, school is the main locus of moral and social stability. But it is, none the less, a phenomenon common to all teachers, intensifying the pressure for high workloads. As a study of contemporary teaching (OECD, 1990, p. 99) commented: 'The broadening . . . of demands (on education) has its equivalent at the level of the individual teacher. What once would have been regarded as exceptional devotion to duty has now become viewed as normal practice.'

The second point is that no one, other than individuals themselves, is likely to limit demands on teachers' time. It is in the interest both of those whose objectives are systemic reform, and those whose responsibilities are managing the reforms at school level, to have a compliant and overconscientious workforce. As Fullan (1992) has argued, state-engendered reforms need 'the passive professional' if they are to succeed. In practice, however, individual teachers who exercise their right to say 'no' to what they perceive to be excessive workloads may conflict with the occupational culture of the school; they may be labelled uncooperative, unhelpful, uncollegial or, worst of all, a restricted professional. Nevertheless, the evidence from Evans *et al.* (1994) was that the overconscientious teachers found their personal and domestic lives adversely affected by their acceptance of term-time working weeks of between 50 and 60 hours. In such a situation, the management of teachers' time is primarily a responsibility that individuals can effectively exercise. As is argued elsewhere (Campbell, 1992), no one else can manage a teacher's time because no one else sees and experiences the time subjectively. The tension between individual needs and organisational pressures reflects the dilemma created for a profession socialised into conscientiousness. We would not wish to be apocalyptic, but where the dilemma remains unresolved the psychological stress on teachers may become intense. Acker (1987) attributed 'burnout' in American teachers to the vocationally driven nature of their training, especially associated with a workforce numerically dominated by women.

Division of labour or the multiplication of demands?

We have shown that, both for primary and secondary teachers, teaching occupied about 30 per cent of their working time, with about a further 25 per cent on associated preparation, planning and assessment. Of the remaining time, a substantial proportion was spent on low-level routines. In primary schools this amounted to between six and seven hours per week. In secondary schools, time on routines and administration amounted to about ten hours a week. It is not possible to distinguish precisely how much of this time was spent on intellectually demanding management activities requiring professional judgement and, therefore, requiring professional qualifications and experience. In the primary schools we could show that most of it did not, because most of it was coded specifically. In respect of secondary schools, other evidence, e.g. Torrington and Weightman's (1989), suggests that substantial amounts of time per week were spent by the highest-paid teachers on relatively low-level routine tasks, often of a clerical nature.

Torrington and Weightman distinguished between *technical* work (e.g.

marking, teaching, anything directly involving pupils), *administrative* work ('organisational maintenance' such as filling in forms and lists, arranging furniture, telephoning, photocopying, etc.) and *managerial* work (setting precedents, influencing others to assent to decisions, ensuring that agreed policies are put into practice, etc.). They provided evidence about seventy senior or middle managers, observed for a day or half a day. One conclusion they drew is particularly germane to our evidence. They say (*ibid.*, p. 102): 'Perhaps the most stunning figure is the average amount of time Deputies (31%), Senior teachers (27%), Heads of Pastoral (29%) and curriculum areas (24%) spend on low-grade clerical duties, that is administrative work.' They explained the attraction of such work to senior staff as the relative ease there was in getting it completed, and the conflation of administrative and managerial tasks in teachers' minds. They none the less drew the conclusion (*ibid.*, p. 103) that 'It is ridiculous to see well-paid professionals doing work that a properly trained administrator or clerk could do better'.

Torrington and Weightman's analysis predates the introduction of local management of schools (LMS), which created conditions for greater managerial flexibility. Nor is it clear how representative the days or half days observed were. Moreover their proportions of time refer to the *observed school day* (i.e. excluding work away from school). Their discussion of the work of senior staff in secondary schools is tinged with disapproval. They quote their project secretary, who had been typing up segments of the observation records of the deputies, as saying, 'Is that what they do? I could do that!' However, it could be argued, as Duffy (1993) does, that part of the problem was the unpredictable policy climate in which the schools had to operate in the late 1980s and early 1990s, which made long-term rational planning of staff time more difficult. Nevertheless it raises a significant policy issue for school management as a whole, especially for the headteacher and the governing body. It is worth their examining the current use of senior teachers' time to see if the provision of more support staff (to whom delegation of routine administration could be made) would enable both their managerial and their teaching skills to be exploited more effectively than is the case for many at present.

The same issue exists at the primary-school level despite the flatter structure of responsibilities. The use of teachers' time, in what are relatively small organisations, is fairly easy to monitor, should a management group including the governing body wish to do so. Under LMS, some activities currently undertaken by teachers, e.g. displays, registration, transition, supervision, clerical activities, might more sensibly be delegated to para-professionals. The amount of time that might be freed in this way is difficult to quantify, and it does not lend itself easily to direct translation into school policy. This is because much of it is scattered in short bursts throughout the day, and some of it occurs within teaching time, such as when the teacher moves the class from its normal room to the hall, for example, for music and movement. There is also, especially at Key Stage 1, some reluctance amongst teachers (see Goodyear, 1992) to divide labour between themselves and non-teaching assistants in ways that could be construed as divisive. This is a difficult problem in the 'collaborative cultures' of primary schools (Nias *et al.*, 1989). It has also been argued that the non-cognitive aspects of the teachers' work with very young children are very important influences upon social and moral development, in helping them become part of an institution larger than the family. On this argument, time spent by teachers in talking to children as they walk to the hall, in listening to them whilst helping them do up their coats, etc., feeds into the teacher's overall knowledge of the child, and helps the child understand that the teacher is concerned about more than teaching in a limited cognitive sense. Also important is the argument (Thomas, 1993) that activities that appear to an outsider to lack cognitive dimensions may, in fact, serve cognitive objectives and should not be seen as 'non-cognitive chores'.

None the less, we think our evidence should force a reconsideration of the use of non-teaching assistants and other para-professionals. Our argument for a more appropriate use of para-professionals is strengthened by the fact that we found that primary teachers who had most time with non-teaching assistants spent significantly *more*, not less, time than other teachers on display and supervision. It could be that in some schools the appointment of para-professionals, appropriately used, would provide teachers with more non-contact time than would be the case if the equivalent funding were used to appoint a part-time teacher. When Duthie (1972, p. 96) examined this issue in Scottish primary schools, he suggested, despite considerable methodological difficulties in obtaining reliable evidence, that there would be work for one para-professional for every two teachers, 'if maximum use is to be made of their services'.

The advantages of such an increased division of labour between teachers and para-professionals are that it is likely to lead to a greater sense of achievement by teachers, it would harmonise professional practice more closely to many of the teachers' colleagues in the rest of Europe (see Osborn, 1985), and it would reduce individual workloads. It might also improve, over time, the image of the profession, through increased concentration on the technical specialisation of teaching. However, as with conscientiousness, the changes proposed are likely to conflict with the existing practice and occupational culture, and may therefore be resisted within schools. In a more general way, however, the issue will have to be faced by all schools. At the level of primary schools there is now a considerable body of evidence, from reports on primary education in The Netherlands, France, Japan and Italy by HMI (DES, 1987; 1991; DfE, 1992; Ofsted, 1992; 1993a; 1994), that where teachers' work is more narrowly focused than it is in the UK, higher cognitive achievement by pupils is achieved, and teacher job satisfaction is improved (though the causal connection is not established). The implied transference of professional practice from one society to another is problematic, but at the very least these studies raise the issue for UK schools. It is an issue identified in a more broadly focused comparative study conducted for the OECD (1990). In this study, a major task requiring attention for the management of reform was 'the proper distribution of tasks between teachers as professionals with the principal responsibilities for instructional duties, and other personnel' (*ibid.*, p. 99).

These considerations raise two dilemmas for the senior management of schools under systemic reform. First, should they encourage, albeit tacitly, the overconscientiousness that characterised most of our teachers' approach to work? In an obvious sense teacher conscientiousness will contribute strongly to the realisation of the school's goals and may be assumed to be of direct benefit to the pupils, and from that point of view might be encouraged or even exploited. There are two arguments against this; one moral, the other pragmatic. Teachers, like other workers, are human beings with lives and identities outside work. A morally responsible headteacher would not wish to see teachers' work routinely intensified to the point where, as illustrated in the study by Evans *et. al.* (1994), teachers had given up reading novels or going to the theatre, and the quality of their domestic relationships was adversely affected. Moreover, there was no evidence in our research that working long hours led to more effective teaching – if anything the interview data (in Evans *et al.*, 1994) hinted at reduced effectiveness. Long hours may have a positive value loading in the professional culture, but heads might note that in other workplaces and other societies, the value loading is negative. In a study of finance managers, Neale and Mindel (1991) showed that Scandinavians interpreted long hours spent on work as a sign of incompetence, while British managers thought they revealed loyalty and enthusiasm.

Secondly, governing bodies and heads are charged with implementing statutory reforms, with several initiatives requiring simultaneous introduction. Knowing from common sense or from the research literature that not all the changes can reasonably be made to work, whatever their statutory force, should governors and heads intervene to limit the impact of multiple innovations on their teachers' work? The problem here is that management would need to show that it was taking its statutory responsibilities seriously, whilst attempting to render the reform process manageable both for the school as a whole and for the individual teacher.

Both dilemmas will be resolved differently according to the individual school context, but their general resolution will be found by establishing strategic priorities. To take the UK curriculum reforms as one example, the Dearing review (SCAA, 1993) gave official sanction to schools to decide which components of the National Curriculum to cover in depth and which 'with a lighter touch'. It is an interesting question about why official sanction should have been needed. In Italian primary schools (Ofsted, 1994, p. 7), the first task at the beginning of each school year is to plan which elements of the National Curriculum will be covered. The general message for managers is that they might seize more clearly the opportunity to prioritise, so as to realise the school's strategic objectives over time, and to protect their staff from the worst effects of a professional socialisation which inclines to overconscientiousness.

The culture of a school, as Woods argues, is the medium through which all reforms have to pass. 'Through their working practices, teachers shape, transform, adapt or resist educational innovations' (Woods, cited in Evetts, 1990, p. 43). Without recourse to generalised theories of management or of the reform process, we believe our evidence about how teachers' time is used raises significant questions about how it might be managed better for the individual teacher. However, the answers to these questions may conflict with the occupational culture in which they will have to be solved and, for this reason if no other, changes will have to be effected slowly and with sensitivity.

REFERENCES

Acker, S. (1987) Primary school teaching as an occupation, in Delamont, S. (ed.) *The Primary School Teacher*, Lewes, Falmer Press.

Alexander, R.J. (1992) *Policy and Practice in Primary Education*, London, Routledge.

Bassey, M. (1977) *Nine Hundred Primary Teachers*, Nottingham, Trent Polytechnic.

Bell, L. (1988) *Management Skills in Primary Schools*, London, Routledge.

Bennett, N., Andrae, J., Heggarty, P. and Wade, B. (1980) *Open Plan Schools*, Windsor, NFER/Nelson.

Campbell, R.J. (1992) *The Management of Teachers' Time in Primary Schools: Concepts, Evidence and Issues*, ASPE Paper, Stoke, Trentham Books.

Campbell, R.J. and Neill, S.R. St J. (1994a) *Primary Teachers at Work*, London, Routledge.

Campbell, R.J. and Neill, S.R. St J. (1994b) *Secondary Teachers at Work*, London, Routledge.

Campbell, R.J. and Neill, S.R. St J. (1994c) *Curriculum Reform at Key Stage 1: Teacher Commitment and Policy Failure*, London, Longman.

Coopers and Lybrand Deloitte (1991) *Costs of the National Curriculum in Primary Schools*, London, National Union of Teachers.

Department of Education and Science (1984) *Aspects of Primary Education in The Netherlands*, London, HMSO.

Department of Education and Science (1987) *Primary Staffing Survey*, London, HMSO.

Department of Education and Science (1991) *Aspects of Primary Education in France*, London, HMSO.

Department for Education (1992) *Teaching and Learning in Japanese Elementary Schools*, London, HMSO.

Duffy, M. (1993) article in *The Times Educational Supplement*, 16 July.

Duthie, J.H., (1972) A study of the teacher's day, in Morrison, A. and McIntyre, D. (eds) *Social Psychology of Teaching*, Harmondsworth, Penguin Books

Evans, L., Packwood, A., Neill, S.R. St J. and Campbell, R.J. (1994) *The Meaning of Infant Teachers' Work*, London, Routledge.

Evetts, J. (1990) *Women Teachers in Primary Education*, London, Methuen.

Fullan, M. (1992) Staff development, innovation and institutional development, in Joyce, B. (ed.) *Changing School Culture through Staff Development*, Virginia, ASCD.

Galton, M. and Simon, B. (1980) *Inside the Primary Classroom*, London, Routledge & Kegan Paul.

Goodyear, R. (1992) *The Use and Management of Infant Teachers' Time*, Warwick Papers on Education Policy, No. 3, Stoke, Trentham Books.

Gump, P.V. (1976) Operating environments in schools of open and traditional design, *School Review*, Vol. 8, No. 24, pp. 575–93.

Hargreaves, A. (1989) Teachers' work and the politics of time and space, paper given at the American Educational Research Association Annual Conference, San Francisco, March.

Hilsum, S. and Cane, B.S. (1971) *The Teacher's Day*, Windsor, NFER.

Hilsum, S. and Strong, C. (1978) *The Secondary Teacher's Day*, Windsor, NFER.

Hoyle, E. (1974) Professionality, professionalism and control in teaching, in Houghton, V., McHugh, R. and Morgan, C. (eds) *Management in Education*, London, Ward Lock.

Inner London Education Authority (1988) *National Curriculum Planning*, London, ILEA.

International Labour Office (1991) *Teachers: Challenges of the 1990s: Second Joint Meeting on Conditions of Work of Teachers (1991)*, Geneva, International Labour Office.

Keddie, N. (1971) Classroom knowledge, in Young, M. (ed.) *Knowledge and Control: New Directions for the Sociology of Education*, London, Collier-Macmillan.

Knight, B. (1989) *Managing School Time*, Harlow, Longman.

Lortie, D. (1969) The balance of control and autonomy in elementary school teaching, in Etzioni, A. (ed.) *The Semi-Professions and their Organization*, New York, Academic Press.

Lowe, B. (1991) *Activity Sampling*, Hull, Humberside County Council.

Meyer, J.W., Kamens, D.H. and Benavot, A. (1992) *School Knowledge for the Masses: World Models and National Primary Curricular Categories in the Twentieth Century*, Lewes, Falmer Press.

NAS/UWT (1991) *Teacher Workload Survey*, Birmingham, NAS/UWT.

National Curriculum Council (1993) *National Curriculum at Key Stages 1 and 2: Advice to the Secretary of State*, York, NCC.

Neale, S. and Mindel, G. (1991) Personnel management, cited in *The Independent*, 31 December.

Nias, J. (1989) *Primary Teachers Talking*, London, Routledge.

Nias, J., Southworth, G. and Yeomans, R. (1989) *Staff Relationships in the Primary School*, London, Cassell.

OECD (1990) *The Teacher Today: Tasks, Conditions, Policies*, Paris, OECD.

Ofsted (1992) *Aspects of Primary Education in France*, London, HMSO.

Ofsted, (1993a) *Aspects of Primary Education in Japan*, London, HMSO.

Ofsted (1993b) *Curriculum Organisation and Curriculum Practice in Primary Schools: A Follow-up Report*, London, HMSO.

Ofsted (1994) *Aspects of Primary Education in Italy*, London, HMSO.

Osborn, M. (1985) *Teachers' Conceptions of their Professional Responsibility in England and France*, Bristol, School of Education, University of Bristol.

Poppleton, P. and Riseborough, G. (1990) Teaching in the mid-1980s: the centrality of work in secondary teachers' lives', *British Educational Research Journal*, Vol. 16.2, pp. 105–22.

SCAA Report (1993) *The National Curriculum and its Assessment*, final report.

School Teachers' Review Body (1995) *Fourth Report* (Cm 2765), London, HMSO.

Thomas, N. (1993) Breadth, balance and the National Curriculum, in Campbell, R.J. (ed.) *Breadth and Balance in the National Curriculum*, Lewes, Falmer Press.

Tizard, B., Blatchford, P., Burke, J., Farquhar, C. and Plewis, I. (1988) *Young Children at School in the Inner City*, New York, Lawrence Erlbaum Associates.

Torrington, D. and Weightman, J. (1989) *The Reality of School Management*, Oxford, Blackwell.

8

MANAGING STRESS IN EDUCATION

Megan Crawford

INTRODUCTION

Jack Dunham (1992) recounts being asked to speak to a group of head-teachers on stress management. The letter of invitation concluded with the words: 'One of my colleagues has suggested that you might like to send us a tape so that we could try out the cure' (*ibid*.)! If only it were that simple. Stress and its effective management are high on the agenda of many schools and colleges today. Not only is stress identified as a major problem in nine out of ten workplaces (Warren and Towl, 1995), leading to rising absenteeism and low morale, but it is also seen by many educational managers to be unacceptable in an effective and well run organisation. This chapter examines the concept of stress, and its management, both on a personal and organisational level. It argues that those who manage people need skills on both these levels if they are to be effective. The beneficial effects of stress are also discussed as is the ability to know when stress becomes 'distress'. Finally, the strategies that educational managers can use to help maintain acceptable stress levels in their own particular organisation are examined.

Workplace stress is prevalent in many organisations, not just in educa-tion, and increasingly it is being seen as a subject for managers to take seriously. Outside education in 1994, John Walker, a social worker, argued successfully in court that the two nervous breakdowns he had suffered were caused by negligence on the part of his employers, Northumberland County Council. As this is written a similar case in nursing involving stress caused, it is claimed by poor staffing levels, is in the legal system. Although some people may still feel that the word 'stress' is used as a catch-all for various problems ranging from job dissatisfaction to moaning about employers, the current evidence seems to refute this. Stress or stress-related illnesses are often cited as a reason for teachers taking early retirement. Carvel and Macleod (1995) reported that recruitment to the profession is failing to keep pace with increasing stress-related early retirement.

Research carried out in the USA in the late 1970s showed that teacher life expectancy was four years lower than the national average (Truch, 1980). Other research carried out before the recent upsurge in incidents suggests that work stress has special meaning in relation to the teaching profession. Teachers are required to play many roles such as 'supportive parent, disciplining taskmaster, stimulating actor and information resource person . . . the special affective characteristics of the profession exert pressure towards presenting an understanding, supportive and optimistic appearance' (Smilansky, 1984, p. 85). A study by Anderson (1978) suggested that there is a higher amount of stress-related illness amongst groups of people who have responsibility for the well-being of others. Thus the environment in which people work can produce high stress levels: 'Until stress is recognised fully as a specific and detrimental influence on health, individuals will continue to hide the truth from themselves and their employers, going "off sick" and adopting poor and potentially fatal coping strategies' (Watts and Cooper, 1992, p. 101). The increasing impact of stress on retention levels in education means that those who manage the education service need to have an understanding of the theoretical background to stress management, and strategies for managing levels of stress in their organisations.

DEFINING THE PROBLEM: WHAT IS STRESS?

Trying to achieve a common understanding of stress is by no means an easy task. Before looking for a definition, it is as well to consider what happens when people *experience* stress. The stress reaction has its origins in the 'fight or flight' model that occurred when prehistoric humans were faced with a frightening situation. The physical hormones involved to make the body ready to fight for its existence in the wild are now being used to gear up for action in a different way. A person may not be able to attack someone physically who is causing them stress, but some of the signs will be the same – raised blood pressure, sickness in the stomach. If these 'attacks' continue then people collapse from stress-related illnesses. Even if there is a refusal to recognise the stress, eventually the body will begin to show unmistakable signs. There can be many visible responses when people are feeling stressed, e.g. anxiety, poor concentration and difficulty in decision-making. This increased adrenalin can be beneficial as one strives to finish a task on time.

Physical responses to perceived threats vary widely from individual to individual but, if left untreated, a pattern of frustration, anxiety and exhaustion – a downward spiral – develops. If this continues over too long a period the person becomes exhausted as all their personal and physical reserves are used up. Hans Selye (1956) described this as the General Adaptation Syndrome. He also developed a framework for describing the four basic variations of stress:

- Hyperstress or too much stress.
- Distress or bad stress.
- Hypostress or understress.
- Eustress or good stress.

Too much stress and there are the effects detailed above, too little and people don't produce their best. Most of this chapter is concerned with the negative forms of stress but Hebb (1972) highlights the fact that too few demands make for boredom, and that the individual must somehow balance demands to meet personal capacities and therefore achieve peak performance. This also applies to stress as a negative force.

Selye (1956) defines stress as 'the rate of all the wear and tear caused by life'. In their classic study of teachers, Kyriacou and Sutcliffe (1978) define stress as the experience by a teacher of unpleasant emotions such as tension, frustration, anxiety, anger and depression resulting from aspects of the work teachers do. They emphasise the role of the teacher's perception of the circumstances, and the degree of control he or she feels. This suggests that most stress comes from the way that the person thinks about it, and appraises it. In all these definitions, the individual's response to stress is seen as paramount. As there is patently no way to avoid stress, the emphasis needs to be on a person's reaction to it. Although stressors (any action or stimulus that causes the stress response) may be unavoidable, they are many and varied in education. Dunham (1992) suggests that a view of stress commonly held is to look at external pressures, e.g. governmental changes, and see stress as a reaction to these outside pressures. Change can be a stressor, especially if it is rapid and continual as in schools and colleges in the 1980s and 1990s. Many of the changes in this period were not sought by the people involved so ownership was lacking. An example of this was the transition to new contracts in colleges after incorporation. Research into the transition found that lecturers had a sense of powerlessness which managers did little to alleviate, exacerbating the stress (Hewitt and Crawford 1996). Many studies (Kyriacou and Sutcliffe, 1978; Cook, 1992; Dunham, 1992) look at the stressors that teachers identify as causing stress. Although all the writers emphasise that each must be placed within its own particular organisational context, several sources of stress emerge.

It is appropriate to note that teachers and lecturers are not the only staff members who experience stress. All staff who work in schools and colleges should note the Health and Safety Commission identification of work-related factors which contribute to stress. Apart from rapid change, these also include time pressures, poor student motivation, poor working conditions and low perceived status. The latter two could be particularly important for associate staff in schools and colleges. Budget cuts and job insecurity apply to teaching and lecturing staff, but in a climate of budget reduction, savings may be made through reduction of hours for teaching assistants and school administrative staff. As research (Crawford, 1995; Mortimore *et al.*, 1995) has shown that these groups are already vulnerable to low status, this may only confirm associate staff worries about their role in the organisation as a whole. All the strategies that are discussed in this chapter should be seen as applicable in theory to *all* staff who work in educational settings. The context within which associate staff work needs to be critically examined so that ways of managing their particular stressors will emerge.

Stress may cause problems in the workplace, but if people have well developed coping resources and strategies they can reduce these pressures. When they are unable to do this, mental and physical stress reactions follow. Selye's classic framework may be helpful in understanding how stress causes problems to so many. Watts and Cooper (1992, p. 57) suggest that we need to look at the overall balance between our stress levels and individual vulnerability, using a stress equation: 'Life stress + work stress + individual vulnerability = stress symptoms outcome.' This is actually much harder than it sounds, especially if the workplace is one where there is no culture of admitting to difficulties and it is seen as a sign of weakness. At a personal level, it may be necessary to accept feelings and admit that it is not always possible to cope. Individuals may be involved in an institution where management does not take the stress situation seriously. They can still mitigate the effects of stress on themselves by employing coping strategies. Understanding individual issues, how others work and the role of personality, may also help in managing stress levels.

THE INDIVIDUAL

Forbes (1979) examined the characteristics that might help identify a person prone to stress. Not every stressed person will have all these traits! Some of them include a tendency to overplan each day; the need to win; desire for recognition; inability to relax without feeling guilty; impatience with delay/interruptions; involvement in multiple projects with many deadlines; excessive competitive drive; and workaholism – people who feel uncomfortable if they don't have something work related to do, even at home (quoted in Greenberg, 1984, pp. 84–5).

Several sorts of individual 'coping patterns' or 'coping mechanisms' can be identified in individuals and groups. Oddly enough, the first strategy of many people is to deny the reality of the stressful situation for as long as possible. In order to do this successfully, palliative measures may be necessary. Palliative measures, e.g. smoking, drinking and overeating, are those short-term ones that give an immediate relief. They need to be replaced by a more effective overall response. Hughes (1990) suggests palliative responses as one of four measures that an individual might use to cope with stressors. Any individual can employ a combination of these at any one time. Direct mechanisms may include political action of some kind: trying to modify job demands by changing the system or possibly changing the culture of the organisation. Indirect action is when an individual may change responds to demands by using peer support groups, counselling and other strategies. Compensatory patterns may include developing outside interests, e.g. swimming, a more balanced lifestyle overall. Hughes' direct mechanisms are the ones that make for the best long-term positive outcomes. This is where the organisation plays an important part, and will be returned to later.

Personality will also decide how threats are assessed, which coping styles are taken up and the strategies chosen to moderate the pressures. A classic study was carried out by two cardiologists, Friedman and Rosenman (1974). Whilst looking at the cause of heart disease, they identified two types of personalities. Type 'A' were more likely to have heart problems and were identified as being ambitious, competitive, hypercritical, perfectionist, workaholics who were often anxious and insecure underneath. They often took on two or more tasks at the same time. Type 'B', on the other hand, were mostly able to give themselves time to reflect, were generally more laid back and yet still able to respond to situations effectively. They did not view work as the most important part of their existence, and adopted a more balanced approach. This should be viewed as a tool when looking at stress, for people may have mixed characteristics. Kelly (1988) discovered that headteachers scored higher than average type 'A' scores. Rees (1989) suggested that it would be more fruitful to regard it as a vicious circle of interaction between stress and certain personality traits, with one tending to exaggerate the other.

Another factor to be taken into account when discussing whether people can be more prone to stress is the concept of hardiness. This can be defined as having several important attributes. Watts and Cooper (1992) call these attributes commitment (belief in self), control (belief that one can influence events) and challenge (a positive attitude to change). Hardy personalities seem to perceive clearly where they are going in life, and know that they are in control and responsible for their behaviours. When new stressors arise these will be seen as opportunities rather than threats.

Closely linked to the concept of a hardy personality is the idea of 'locus of control'. This is the extent to which individuals see things that are happening to them as in or out of their control. It has two aspects: internal and external. Those who have an *internal* locus of control use their internal resources to control their environment. Those whose locus of control is *external* view life in a much more passive way with them playing no real part in how events turn out. Greenberg and Valletutti (1980) make the point that if people do not make time for themselves, and ignore stress warning signs, they are increasing their risk of severe stress-related disorders. Frogatt and Stamp (1991, p. 116) argue that most work-related stress can be turned into a positive experience, by ensuring that

1. Demands upon you, perceived or otherwise, should remain within your capability, and you must know where your limits lie.
2. You must build up resources/skills to deal effectively with the demands you have chosen to accept.
3. Be aware of life events . . . and do not underestimate their impact upon your coping skills.

These are useful points to remember, but the authors acknowledge that this is not possible if the stress you are already under is too great.

This is not the place to develop other personal coping strategies, but exercise, diet and relaxation should all play a part in a personal stress-management programme. It would appear that some people can tolerate a high level of stress, but even the most hardy may succumb eventually. This will vary depending on the context, the length of time the stress has been present and the way that person views its worth to him or her as an individual. Because the individual is so important in stress management, stress will affect different people doing the same task in the same setting in different ways. Individual constructions of reality are vital. Even the possibility of analysing stress will be seen by some as threatening because of the degree of self-searching that it requires. However, understanding one's own personal sense of stress is a necessary part of the process that will enable coping mechanisms to develop.

THE ORGANISATION: MANAGEMENT IMPLICATIONS

Although as an individual one may be able to maintain a happy balance by successful coping strategies, the organisation in which individuals work plays a vital part in sustaining this. A study by Phelps (1977) looked at the criminal justice system in America, and identified many organisational stressors that could be applied to working in schools and colleges. These include poor working relationships amongst staff, too much paperwork, a lack of training, poor job security and a lack of promotion opportunities. The latter two have been stressors that education has only recently begun to tackle. Taking an organisational focus helps managers to see that effective stress management must become part of the culture of the organisation. Stressful working conditions can create a climate of frustration and tension, often due to a long-term build-up of stress. This may lead to severe stress or 'burnout'. This concept is a useful one for highlighting some of the strategies we have already discussed. In a state of burnout, a person finds his or her emotional resources exhausted and he or she may feel undervalued or worthless. The only way for this individual to go is downward, and depression or other ill-health may be the result. It could be argued that the nature of educational organisations makes burnout a possibility at all times. The threat to self-esteem of admitting that one cannot cope is huge. Teachers and lecturers fear they may be seen as weak, and may recourse to some of the palliatives described earlier, which serve to exacerbate the situation. Blaming the individual is an easy way for an organisation to avoid tackling the real problem, but burnout happens to all kinds of individuals when a situation arises that they cannot resolve by their usual coping strategies. They can become overloaded with too much change, too many demands on their time and not enough time in which to do the core job effectively. Managers need to be able to identify the signs in others of severe stress. This can often be changes in that person's normal behaviour pattern, e.g. over-reactions to events, failing to complete tasks, memory lapses, mood swings, etc. Those in management positions need to evolve structures to listen, support and help staff avoid the vicious cycle of worthlessness, and perhaps long-term sick leave that may arise if it is ignored. Valuing individuals within an organisation may mitigate some of the external forces that are feeding the feelings of stress and inadequacy.

Hughes' (1990) direct strategy (see earlier) is particularly relevant to those involved in management as it focuses on what can be done to prevent or alleviate stress in the institution. Managers can build up the resources for tackling stress in their organisation, and at the same time strengthen the personal and interpersonal resources of their staff. This may imply long-term cultural change. Individuals' personal realities need to be examined in the context of both the home and the workplace, as such biographical details may give a clue to what may tip the balance for them from coping to distress. A change or significant event in someone's personal life must be seen as having the potential to do this. Managing events such as bereavement requires skill and the knowledge that it may be better for the staff member to have a longer time out in order to recover than perhaps seems necessary. Making individuals return to work before they have recovered from a major life event may cause more problems for the organisation in the longer term. Equally, those who are involved in HRM must realise that certain problems are beyond the scope of school or college-based help, and be prepared to make appropriate referrals.

Managers can also help in periods of organisational uncertainty and change by presenting relevant information to staff. Communication channels within the organisation need to be examined to make sure they are operating effectively. Open discussion and awareness of conflict management strategies are also areas where good application of skills can decrease stress levels. Knowing how to approach the stressed colleague is a skill in itself. We have already noted that denial may be present in many stressed individuals. An organisational culture that allows a channel for expressions of problems may help to prevent this problem becoming serious. There is much less written about understress, but it can be just as serious a challenge for a manager to motivate those who are underused or underachieving as it can to tackle the signs of distress.

Those who have formal leadership roles such as headteachers may suffer from particular kinds of stressors. Galloway *et al.* (1986) conducted a study of primary school headteachers in New Zealand to discover which aspects of the job the head found most stressful. The results showed how difficult it is to define stressors outside a particular context. The researchers felt that people in positions of authority are often reluctant to admit to stress because of its equation with professional inadequacy. However, they did note that stress seems to arise most frequently from the multiple roles that a headteacher has to adopt, and can be mitigated to some extent by support and co-operation from parents.

Leadership styles may also have an effect on the amount of stress in the organisation. This may not mean just one person in a leadership position, but the way leadership is performed through all levels of an organisation. The emphasis in an organisation may be on developing the team as a resource in handling stress.

In bureaucratical educational organisations there may be specific coping strategies adopted by the staff. Veninga and Spradley (1981) found that people tend to employ one of five strategies when faced with tasks that they view as secondary to their 'core' post: *loyal servants* cope by complying with the organisation's rules; *angry prisoners* employ passive resistance to the bureaucracy; *stress fugitives* tend to procrastinate and neglect their duties; *job reformers* cope by aiming to change the practice of the organisation; and *stress managers* try to express themselves openly and honestly, never pretending they have all the answers.

Cook (1992) suggests several positive management strategies for handling severe stress:

- Managers can help individuals set realistic goals taking account of limitations as well as their abilities.
- They can make suggestions for doing the same thing differently, especially if individuals have developed a habit which is particularly stress inducing.
- Organisations can make time for individuals to have 'emotional breathers', and allow staff to recharge their batteries.
- Take things less personally, perhaps by having a 'review partner' to discuss issues, or even a diary – both help put problems in perspective.

Using group support from colleagues can be very effective. It is important for managers to remember that some individuals will want to work things out on their own or with more one-to-one support. Not everybody is comfortable in groups. As a final stress-reducing move, Cook suggests that moving jobs shouldn't be seen as running away but rather as making a better choice. Of course, new organisational settings may prove to have even more potential stressors. Webster (1994) also suggests that there are clear issues for managers. Her list includes the following (adapted from *ibid.*, p. 14):

- Change perception of stress/problems as weakness.
- Involve staff in problem-solving.
- Agree on shared objectives.
- Ensure effective communication.
- Be supportive.
- Emphasise prevention rather than coping later.
- Treat or rehabilitate teachers who have stress-related problems.
- Evolve adequate training and career development possibilities.
- Create a pleasant working environment.
- Encourage group problem-solving to deal with problems and put forward suggestions for action.
- Be accessible and co-operative.

Managers need to have clear strategies, as they would for other management issues, that are clearly monitored to achieve success.

CONCLUSION

Selye (1956) called stress the 'spice of life', and this chapter does not deny the powerful positive effects of stress. What it does argue for is a coherent management strategy in educational organisations that recognises the importance of stress in human resource management, and addresses stress-related issues in a clearly strategic way. Stress management should be a defined part of the management of the effective educational organisation.

The chapter opened with the thought that there might be an instant solution to the stress that many have to manage in their workplaces today. It argues that effective management strategies, and greater awareness of the extent of the problem, are what is needed for the future. There may be no instant 'cure' for the high levels of stress in schools and colleges, but managers need to 'open up pathways of support in all directions in an organisation – upwards, sideways and downwards . . . an active participation by all members in the continuing development of . . . a healthy organisation' (Dunham, 1992, p. 184). The 'cure' may need to come from improved management strategies, and a growing awareness that time spent on stress management is management time well spent.

REFERENCES

Anderson, R.A. (1978) *Stress Power*, New York, Human Services Press.
Carvel, J. and Macleod, D. (1995) 'Ministers face teachers' shortage time bomb, *Guardian*, 12 December.
Cook, R. (1992) *The Prevention and Management of Stress*, Harlow, Longman.

Crawford, M. (1995) Service with a smile, *Management in Education*, Vol. 9, No. 4, pp. 21–23.

Dunham, J. (1992) *Stress in Teaching*, London, Routledge.

Forbes, R. (1979) *Life Stress* New York, Doubleday.

Friedman, M. and Rosenman, R. (1974) *Type A Behaviour and Your Heart*, London, Wildwood House.

Froggatt, H. and Stamp, P. (1991) *Managing Pressure at Work*, London, BBC Books.

Galloway, D., Panckhurst, F., Boswell, K., Boswell, C. and Green, K. (1986) Sources of stress for primary school headteachers in New Zealand, *British Educational Research Journal*, Vol. 12, No. 3.

Greenberg, S.F. (1984) *Stress and the Teaching Profession*, Baltimore, Md., Paul H. Brookes Publishing.

Greenberg, S.F. and Valletutti, P.J. (1980) *Stress and the Helping Professions*, Baltimore, Md, Paul H. Brookes Publishing.

Health and Safety Commission (1990) *Managing Occupational Stress*, London, HMSO.

Hebb, D. (1972) *Textbook of Psychology*, Philadelphia, Penn., Saunders.

Hewitt, P. and Crawford, M. (1996) *Introducing New Contracts: Managing Change within the Context of an Enterprise Culture*, FEDU.

Hughes, J. (1990) Stress scourge or stimulant?, *Nursing Standard*, Vol. 5 No. 4, pp. 30–3.

Kelly, M.J. (1988) *The Manchester Survey of Occupational Stress in Headteachers and Principals in the UK*, Manchester, Manchester Polytechnic.

Kyriacou, C. and Sutcliffe, J. (1978) Teacher stress: prevalence, sources and symptoms, *Educational Psychology*, Vol. 48 pp. 159–67.

Mortimore, P. and Mortimore, J. (with Thomas, H.) (1995) *Managing Associate Staff*, London, Paul Chapman.

Phelps, L. (1977) *Police Tasks and Related Stress Factors; from an Organizational Perspective*, Reno, University of Nevada Press.

Rees, F. (1989) *Teacher Stress: An Exploratory Study*, Slough, NFER.

Selye, H. (1956) *The Stress of Life*, New York, Macgraw-Hill.

Smilansky, J. (1984) External and internal correlates of teachers' satisfaction and willingness to report stress, *Educational Psychology*, Vol. 54, pp. 84–92.

Truch, S. (1980) *Teacher Burnout*, Novato, Calif., Therapy Publications.

Veninga, R.L. and Spradley, J.P. (1981) *The Work–Stress Connection: How to Cope with Job Burnout*, New York, Ballantine Books.

Warren, E. and Towl, C. (1995) *The Stress Workbook*, London, The Industrial Society.

Watts, M. and Cooper, S. (1992) *Relax: Dealing with Stress*, London, BBC Books.

Webster, P. (1994) *Your Coping Strategies in Teaching*, London, New Education Press.

9

MANAGING FOR EQUAL OPPORTUNITIES: THE GENDER ISSUE

Marianne Coleman

THE NEED FOR EQUAL OPPORTUNITIES

An understanding of equal opportunities is of particular concern to managers of people. Managers in the UK must take account of the law, which seeks to protect employees against discrimination on the grounds of sex, marital status, race, nationality or ethnic origin and disability. In the USA, age is added to this list. In the UK, age may also be cited as a cause of indirect discrimination, where it can be shown that women may be more adversely affected than men by an age-related ruling (Acker, 1994, p. 140). It is common practice for educational employers such as local education authorities or further and higher education institutions to announce in their recruitment advertising that they are 'equal opportunities employers', or, that they are 'committed to' or 'working for' equality.

Statutory provision, and the publication of intentions, go some way to providing an equal opportunities context for the management of people. However, the protection of the law is rarely invoked, and proving dis-crimination through an industrial tribunal is difficult, and may take its toll both personally and professionally (Chadwick, 1989). In addition, both managers, and the people they manage, may be influenced by stereotypes and assumptions regarding gender, race or disability in the choices and decisions that they make. The law cannot permeate all decisions relating to selection procedures and other aspects of professional development, such as appraisal, all of which may be influenced by stereotypical thinking. In the chapters in this book on recruitment and selection and on appraisal, David Middlewood considers the management implications of these matters.

In this chapter we are focusing on the implications of equal opportunities for managers of people, in particular, how research findings on gender issues may inform human resource management. These mostly relate to a lack of equity for women, particularly in relation to promotion. However, men also face problems associated with gender stereotypes, for example, if they wish to build a career in early years teaching. Issues relating to family responsibilities tend to be associated with women, and, as a result, the role of the father in the family may be underemphasised (Moss, 1995). Both men and women may benefit from working in an organisation where the importance of child care and family responsibilities is recognised and understood.

This chapter starts with a particular focus on barriers to progress experienced by women. This is particularly appropriate in the context of education, since women are so heavily represented amongst the ranks of teachers employed in schools, and also have a significant presence as lecturers in colleges. Many women are also employed as associate staff in education, often in part-time work and in areas traditionally regarded as 'women's work', such as secretarial, cleaning, catering and the care of young children.

SETTING THE SCENE: THE EXTENT OF THE PROBLEM

In primary schools, women constitute 81 per cent of the teaching force, whilst in secondary schools, men and women teachers are roughly equal in number (DfEE, 1995). In the case studies undertaken by Mortimore *et al.* (1994), women held 83 per cent of the associate staff posts in primary schools and 71 per cent in secondary schools. However, male associate staff are more likely than women to be 'in senior positions of responsibility with higher status and pay' (*ibid.*, p. 181) and men teachers and lecturers are much more likely than women to hold positions of senior management, except in schools where the youngest children are taught. For example, nearly half the headteachers in the primary sector are women, but this statistic masks the fact that males tend to hold the junior and middle school headships. Of nursery headteachers, 98.6 per cent are women, as are 96.5 per cent of infant headteachers, but women only account for the headships of 29 per cent of junior schools and 27 per cent of middle schools deemed primary (DfEE 1995).

In primary schools in England and Wales, women are well represented at all levels, but the proportion of women holding senior posts is much lower than the percentage of women in primary teaching overall (see Table 9.1). In secondary education, the distribution of senior posts is markedly different for women and men, although the total number of male and female teachers employed in this phase of education is very similar. Whilst women predominate in the lower levels of posts of responsibility, in the more senior

Table 9.1 Male and female teachers, deputy headteachers and headteachers in nursery and primary schools in England and Wales, 31 March 1993 (%)

	Men	Women
All teachers	18.5	81.5
Deputy headteachers	32.2	67.8
Headteachers	49.7	50.3

Source: DfEE, 1995.

Table 9.2 Distribution of male and female teachers in secondary schools, 31 March 1993 (%)

	Men	Women
All teachers	50.4	49.6
Deputy head	66.4	33.6
Headteacher	78.1	21.9

Source: DfEE, 1995.

posts, the discrepancy between the numbers of men and women is most marked (see Table 9.2). There is some research evidence to confirm the supposition that women have to out-perform men in order to achieve promotion. For example, women holding allowances appear to carry more responsibility than their male equivalents, particularly at middle management levels (Weightman, 1989; McMullan, 1993). In addition, the curricular areas where men tend to predominate (maths, science, technology and humanities) are those where promotions are most likely to occur, whereas the areas of female predominance (languages, arts and special needs) are less likely to include posts with higher allowances (McMullan, 1993).

In further and higher education, men out-number women by nearly three to one (DfE, 1993) and only a small number of women hold senior management positions (see Table 9.3). The change in status of colleges of further and higher education in England and Wales has led to a delay in the publication of national statistics. However, the last nationally collected records of LEA further education colleges indicate the predominance of men in senior positions.

The proportion of women employed in higher education, particularly those who hold senior posts, is also very small. In the academic year 1993–4, women held only 5.5 per cent of professorial chairs in the 'old' universities and they represented 12 per cent of all senior lecturers and

Table 9.3 Male and female academic staff employed in FE establishments, 31 March 1990 (%)

	Men	Women
Principals	86.4	13.6
Vice-principals	86.3	13.7
Heads of department	83.1	16.9
Principal lecturer	84.1	15.9
Senior lecturer	78.8	21.2
Lecturers	62.1	37.9

Source: DfE, 1993.

readers and 27 per cent of lecturers (USR, 1994). In 1990 four out of the 34 polytechnics were headed by women (DfEE, 1995).

This chapter is concerned with equal opportunities. Those concerned with human resource management should therefore be aware of the various barriers to women's progress. These may be analysed as overt and covert discrimination, socialisation and constraints that are culturally defined and relate to work and to responsibilities in the home (Coleman, 1994). The implications of these barriers for managers of people in education are extensive and concern both the ethos of the school or college and the structures that are put into place. Such structures include policies for recruitment and selection of staff, the induction of staff and every aspect of professional development.

Instances of overt discrimination are rare, but subtle pressures and pervasive stereotypes may act to produce constraints on the position and progress of women within schools and colleges. We turn now to consider the extent to which gender stereotypes, both female and male, are connected with certain roles in education, and the resulting constraints that occur in the workplace.

GENDER AND ROLES IN EDUCATION

The identification of women with supportive roles and of men with leadership roles is a stereotype that may be linked with processes of socialisation. Theories of the socialisation of women are sometimes used to explain why women are relatively rarely in positions of power. Schmuck (1986) criticises this linkage by pointing out that it implies that the male image of leadership is the norm, and that women are the 'deficit model'; it would then follow that women should be trained to make up this deficit and adopt a 'male' leadership mode, thus devaluing a range of qualities that are identified with women and with the more collaborative and empowering style of leadership. We may rationally accept that there is a range of successful leadership styles, but the stereotype of the male leader persists; the head of a secondary school, the professor in a university department and the chief education officer of an LEA are 'expected' to be male. Darking (1991, p. 18) reports Dr Kathryn Riley sitting down at an LEA meeting to be told by a man at the meeting: '"Only chief officers sit here." "Yes I know", she said, and stayed put. "Only chief officers sit here," the man repeated. "Yes I know," she said. "I am one."'

Senior women managers in secondary schools tend to be identified with certain types of roles. There has been an assumption that 'every [secondary] school had three deputies: one female, with a pastoral/girls' responsibility, and two male, in charge of the timetable, the curriculum, examinations, administration, boys' discipline etc.' (Roach, 1993, p. 63). Female senior and middle managers have tended to be identified with the pastoral role which is less likely to provide an automatic route to headship. The study on secondary school headship carried out by Weindling and Earley (1987) showed that most heads had specialised in academic rather than pastoral roles.

Research shows that women are becoming aware of the danger of being stereotyped as pastoral managers. The women secondary school deputies interviewed by McBurney and Hough (1989) had a wide range of experience. The findings of Coleman (1996a) also indicated an awareness and avoidance of stereotyping in the career of female headteachers. The headteachers interviewed all had a variety of experience as deputies. They regarded curriculum responsibilities as particularly desirable, and the rotation of duties within the senior management team had also provided the opportunity of gaining experience in premises management, discipline and the management of staff. The traditional role of senior mistress – 'making sure the school looked nice, floral display' (*ibid.*, p. 7) – was recognised and had been deliberately avoided.

Gender stereotyping may be particularly prevalent in FE colleges, where subject specialities tend to be more gender specific. Joanna Tait, Principal of Bishop Auckland College, is quoted as saying: 'Colleges were set up as male institutions, training engineers and miners with may be a few typing classes' (Ward, 1995). The existence of female role models in areas where they are rare may have particular impact. Carter and Kirkup (1992, p. 243) refer to a woman engineer as a 'living contradiction in the male working world of engineering'.

Indeed the position of role model may be a difficult and isolating experience, not least for black women who may find themselves in especially demanding circumstances. McKellar, (1989) writing under the apposite title 'Only the fittest of the fittest will survive', estimated that she was one of only 27 black teacher educators in higher education in England, Scotland and Wales, representing 0.6 per cent of the total. She does not state how many of the 27 were women.

Men and women are both limited by role stereotyping. It was recognised by one female secondary head that: '[Men] are socialized into having to be hard-nosed . . . I think it's considered more acceptable for women to be reflective, for women to talk about what might look more like the softer side of educational thought' (quoted in Coleman, 1996b, p. 172). Another of the same group of female heads pointed out the particular sensitivities that men may face in trying to break out of a stereotype: 'Men and women have the same qualities, but women are expected to be caring so they can be. Men can be just as caring. As a woman you can put your hand on someone's shoulder to reassure them, for a man that might be misinterpreted' (*ibid.*).

This automatic identification of males with a certain type of managerialism may be an advantage to males in gaining promotion, but establishes expectations that they will behave in a 'masculine' way. The changes experienced in the 1980s and 1990s, and the resulting uncertainty in FE colleges, are linked with the perception that a male manager will suit the difficult climate of the times. In one case a new male manager, succeeding a female, was identified as suitable because he is: '"more businesslike", "wanting action", "less approachable" and "not a listener". At the same time, . . . this new Principal [was seen as] a "strong man" who would take "hard decisions" and possibly enable the college to survive' (Whitehead, 1995, p. 13).

Men who wish to teach in primary education, particularly in early years, experience some difficulty. The care of very small children and babies is generally seen as a female prerogative. Acker (1994, p. 88) suggests several contributory factors:

> stereotypes are such that men who choose this route run the risk of being regarded as sexually deviant,
> women provide a cheap source of labour that is capable of flexibility through part-time work and can be responsive to demographic and political change,
> women may contribute to maintaining early years education as female, since they wish to hold on to one of the few areas where they are powerful.

Research with a group of students engaged in teacher training identified that 'young men are actively socializing themselves out' of teaching young children (Aspinwall and Drummond, 1989, p. 14). The young male students perceived themselves as not having the right qualities of patience and gentleness whilst assuming that women 'quite naturally and effortlessly, do have these qualities' (*ibid*).

The stereotyping of roles as male or female narrows the career choices available to teachers and managers in education. Managers should be aware that the positive role model of a male infant teacher, or a female secondary school head or FE principal, may help to diminish the stereotypes and widen choices and possibilities for others. Research undertaken by Wild (1994) identified the importance of the existence of positive role models for women aspiring to management in FE colleges. Professional development, including appraisal, should be informed by an awareness of the pervasiveness of gender stereotypes. In addition, managers of people in education may give more extensive consideration to the use of mentoring, both formal and informal, and general support and networking for marginalised groups. These may be important ways of countering discrimination and promoting equal opportunities.

MENTORING AND SUPPORT: POSITIVE CONTRIBUTIONS TO EQUAL OPPORTUNITIES

Mentoring of young and aspiring teachers and lecturers is generally a part of the induction process. However, mentoring of those in middle and senior management is less well established (see Chapter 11). A formal mentoring programme is likely to apply to all new teachers and lecturers, but there are some quite subtle barriers to progress that may be built into the culture of a school or college. For example there is some evidence to show that young male teachers are more likely to be informally mentored than young female teachers, and that opportunities for development may be given to them rather than females (Schmuck, 1986; Shakeshaft, 1989). The value of the more informal mentoring and networking in higher education was recognised by Cullen and Luna (1993). Their conclusion was, that in addition to the valuable formal mentoring relationships, it was important to create institutionalised opportunities for networking for women.

In some situations, possibly those areas most strongly identified as male, the efficacy of mentoring may be related to the perceived status of the mentor. It may therefore be more helpful to women in some circumstances to be mentored by a male senior colleague. Carter and Kirkup (1992, p. 247), working in the male environment of engineering, found that 'promotion prospects are enhanced for people who are mentored', and that 'we searched to uncover key [female] role models and we found few. Instead we found important relationships with helpful men'.

Female secondary headteachers also identified the importance of support in their progress to headship (Coleman, 1996a). They mentioned schools where the culture and ethos was one of encouragement and staff development; and instances where senior personnel in schools gave practical help such as mock interviews, and acted as mentors: 'she [the head] encouraged me to go for headship and probably more than any other person in my career, has been a mentor in that respect. She certainly was very instrumental in helping me think about headship and obviously in preparing me for it' (headteacher, quoted in Coleman, *ibid.*, p. 7–8).

Female managers in education value the support of other women. Several secondary headteachers stated that they gained professional support through other female heads (Coleman, 1996a). A female director of a former polytechnic indicated the importance of female support: 'I remain convinced that networks are an essential support for women as they move into posts where responsibilities and painful isolation may undermine their confidence' (Perry, 1993, p. 94).

However, not all women automatically support others. Research by Matthews (1995) identifies four types amongst women managers:

- *Activists* who seek to promote women within education.
- *Advocates* who support other women.
- *Isolates* who deny that discrimination exists.
- *Individualists* who take the view that it is the individual who matters, not his or her gender.

The last category tend to model themselves on male colleagues and to be rather judgemental about other women in senior management. Similarly, Wild (1994, p. 92) refers to women managers who 'pull the ladder up behind them'.

Managers should note that the general level of support, both informal and formal, that women receive is a key factor in encouraging career progress. However, in considering the barriers to progress encountered by women, a key area controlled by managers of people is that relating to recruitment.

PROMOTION AND SELECTION

Women are less likely than men to persist with applications for promotion (Grant, 1989; Shakeshaft, 1989). There is some evidence that many women are lacking in confidence in comparison to their male equivalents (Shakeshaft, 1989). Men are more likely to take a risk and apply for jobs where they have relatively few of the required qualifications, whereas women more often expect to be able to fill the full brief. They tend to be 'scrupulous in self-evaluation and therefore more critical and selective about career moves than many men teachers' (Al Khalifa, 1992, p. 96).

A review of the literature on gender bias in selection led Alimo-Metcalfe (1994, p. 97) to the conclusion that no matter what the training of the selector 'Male applicants were still preferred for the traditionally male job, and female applicants were favoured for the traditionally female job'. In addition, it is easy for bias on the part of selectors to be masked and for choices to be 'couched in terms of merit and explained as gender neutral' (Evetts, 1994, p. 90). It is therefore not surprising that, where women do apply for promotion, there are instances of covert, and even occasionally overt, discrimination in education. One female secondary headteacher recalled how her application for a deputy headship was turned down in a letter stating that although her application was excellent, 'in this case I have to interview men only' (Coleman, 1996a, p. 4).

There is some evidence to show that the role of the LEA was one of guarding equal opportunities in the selection procedure (Morgan *et al.*,

1983), and that women candidates for senior positions in schools may now be somewhat penalised by the responsibility for appointment passing to governors. Waring (1992, p. 15) suggests that governors may regard equal opportunities as a 'luxury' and quotes one governor on the selection process: 'Once we've really got the job sussed, then maybe we'll be looking at the wider issues, but at the moment I think we're struggling just to fulfil our legal obligations.'

For managers of people in education, there are implications with regard to the composition of selection panels, and sound reasons for ensuring that governors as well as education professionals have access to, and awareness of, equal opportunities policies and training. In addition, managers may specifically consider how best to support women in being realistic in recognising and evaluating their own abilities.

CAREER BREAKS

Career breaks are taken for many reasons, but for women taking a career break associated with maternity leave and the care of children there may be particular problems, including practical difficulties associated with child-care arrangements. The return to work is seen in terms of her 'choice' and as such the onus is on her to manage the combination of roles. Managers of people in education do not always take into account the difficulties faced by the parents of very young children.

Women who have been successful in educational management may have minimised or avoided career breaks, thus following a career pattern similar to that expected of males. Four of the five secondary headteachers interviewed by Coleman (1996a) had taken no career break. Two had no children and two had taken the basic maternity leave when they had their one child.

However, the normal effect of a break in service is to have a 'dramatic impact on the teaching career' (Evetts, 1990, p. 93). In particular, this is likely to occur for those who return to full-time work seeking promotion after either a career break or part-time work. In addition, the effect of LMS on primary schools has meant that many older and experienced teachers returning to work after a break to care for children are too expensive to be employed. There is evidence that some women may re-enter the profession at a lower status than they had previously held (Morgan *et al.*, 1983), whereas 'Men rarely experienced demotion after absence from teaching, even when they had worked outside the educational system' (Weindling and Earley, 1987, p. 25).

Women may recognise the value of the additional skills accrued through looking after their young children, but the value of such a career break is generally perceived to be less than that taken for study, long-term industrial placement or secondment to the advisory service.

Women wishing to return to teaching or lecturing after a career break, particularly when they have responsibility for the care of young children, may have little choice but to accept the teaching opportunities that are made available. Mortimore *et al.* (1994) point out that taking a post as a member of the associate staff may offer women other than teachers, who may have taken a career break, a route back into the job market, but also identify that the rates of pay are poor and that women recruited thus are likely to find themselves in a situation that is 'unjust', and that part-time contracts may mask demands to 'work beyond the limits of their jobs' (*ibid.*, p. 193).

Managers may wish to consider how best to minimise the difficulties that are faced by women returning to work after maternity leave, or a more extended career break associated with looking after a family. Managers may also consider the wealth of experience that women bring to their jobs as teachers and lecturers at the point when they return to a full-time career.

WORK AND HOME

Some of the problems that are faced by women who have taken a career break for child care may lie in the identification of domestic responsibilities with women, enhanced by the fact that Britain is now the only country in the European Union not to offer any paternity leave. In addition, British fathers work the longest hours in Europe, on average 47 hours a week in 1993 (Moss, 1995).

The twin demands of career and family affect both men and women, but it is women who most often carry the major responsibility within the home. Even where a couple set out consciously to be a dual career family, the woman is likely to carry the greater load of household responsibility: 'The household management role is a gender boundary which remains contentious and difficult to dismantle' (Lewis, 1994, p. 231). The difficulties of managing a domestic role with a career are greatly increased when the couple have children. Acker (1994) refers to this as the 'triple shift'. For both parents there is likely to be role conflict and stress (Lewis, 1994).

The dual career was typical of the female secondary headteachers interviewed by the author (Coleman, 1996a) where there was evidence of joint decisions about career moves and of 'taking it in turns' over promotion and geographical moves. This approach is noted by Evetts (1994, p. 58), in what she terms a 'balancing strategy'. However, she also identifies the strength of the 'two person single career' (*ibid.*, p. 50) which allows the man to have the full support of his wife in pursuing his career, and allows him to work at a pace difficult to equal by women bearing domestic responsibilities, or by individuals from dual career families.

The removal of barriers to the progress of women that arise from domestic constraints will depend on changes in the wider society. Such changes would include better child care, maternity and paternity (parental) rights

(Adler *et al.*, 1993), and could also include more flexible work patterns. Moss (1995, p. xxii) identifies the importance of changes in public policy, but also points out that 'workplace policies from employers and trades unions . . . can contribute to cultural change'.

Social attitudes, cultural influences and stereotyping are pervasive, in their effects on equal opportunities. However, research data do help us to establish an idea of the barriers faced by women working in education. In the final section of this chapter, we consider some of the recommendations for change that have emerged from research findings on gender issues that are relevant to managers of people in schools and colleges.

IMPLICATIONS FOR MANAGERS

Addressing organisational factors

Schmuck (1986, p. 178) identified the factors that tend to differentiate male and female promotion within schools:

the grooming and recruitment of male teachers, sex-biased preparatory programmes in institutions of higher education, the preference for males in sponsoring and mentoring future administrators, the lack of female role models for women teachers, differential opportunities for males and females to exhibit leadership, and male domination on selection committee which leads to discrimination on hiring.

Her summary is that 'At each step of administrative preparation, job seeking and selection, there are organizational processes which clearly indicate a preference for males' (*ibid.*).

Managers in schools, colleges and institutions of higher education can take some responsibility to address these organisational processes by ensuring that the culture of the organisation is imbued with the concept of equal opportunities, and by considering practical issues, such as the gender composition of selection panels and influential committees, the creation of mentoring schemes and the development of role models for both aspiring teachers and their students.

A change in the ethos of the organisation

Research commissioned by Business in the Community examined 150 international examples of successful organisational change for women (Hammond, 1994). The critical success factors identified included the long-term support of top management and a clear understanding that a change in the culture towards women made good business sense. These lessons can be applied to education, where the support of senior managers is generally needed for any initiative to succeed, and where there is at present a potential loss to schools and colleges of many able women managers as a result of the skewed distribution of senior posts between men and women.

Many of the research findings outlined in this chapter have indicated ways in which the culture of schools and colleges can be changed so that women may play an equal part. Legislation provides the context for equal opportunity, and it would be possible to add to this a programme of affirmative action, as in the USA. On a smaller scale individual schools and colleges could operate an informal quota system to be taken into consideration when appointing for promoted posts. In addition, managers of people may also look at ways in which to encourage and assist equal opportunities for women and men in taking their role in family life, for example by encouraging the sharing of leave for the care of sick children.

Mentoring and role models

Research findings indicate the importance of mentoring, both formal and informal, and managers could do much to encourage a culture that fosters informal mentoring and support, and to provide a structure which ensures that women receive encouragement in seeking promotion. Although stereotypes are hard to shake off, role models, mentoring and support through networking may help younger women to aspire and achieve. The success of women-only management courses (Al Khalifa, 1992; Gold, 1993) may be considered in planning professional development. Role stereotypes may be diminished by increased awareness and resulting action on the part of managers.

Training for appraisal and selection

Stereotypes may particularly impinge on the effectiveness of appraisal. Thompson (1992) identifies the importance of awareness training for appraisers. She quotes research findings that show underassessment of women by male line managers who may identify stereotypical male characteristics with leadership potential, and who, consciously or unconsciously, see men as having 'more right to promotion because they are the main bread-winners' (*ibid.*, p. 259). The diffidence of women and their tendency to be more self-critical than men may lead to misunderstanding in the appraisal process, which may also be affected by the different communication styles of men and women (Shakeshaft, 1989; Schick-Case, 1994). For associate staff, appraisal and staff development are particularly important. Without them 'women may be trapped in the post' (Mortimore *et al.*, 1994, p. 179). Awareness training may also be appropriate for those responsible for selection and promotion of staff, including governors. The tendency for selectors to choose a candidate who resembles themselves argues for the equal representation of men and women on selection panels.

The wider aspects of equal opportunities for women and men may lie outside the power of individual managers, in the realms of social change. However, in seeking to promote equality, managers of people in education may need to question the appropriateness of the structures and processes of their school or college and consider how best to promote change in its culture and ethos.

REFERENCES

Acker, S. (1994) *Gendered Education: Sociological Reflections on Women, Teaching and Feminism*, Buckingham, Open University Press.

Adler, S., Laney, J. and Packer, M. (1993) *Managing Women*, Buckingham, Open University Press.

Alimo-Metcalfe, B. (1994) Gender bias in the selection and assessment of women in management, in Davidson, M.J. and Burke, R.J. (eds) *Women in Management: Current Research Issues*, London, Paul Chapman.

Al Khalifa, E. (1992) Management by halves: women teachers and school management, in Bennett, N., Crawford, M. and Riches, C. (eds) *Managing Change in Education: Individual and Organizational Perspectives*, London, Paul Chapman.

Aspinwall, K. and Drummond, M. (1989) Socialized into primary teaching, in De Lyon, H. and Widdowson Migniuolo, F. (eds) *Women Teachers: Issues and Experiences*, Milton Keynes, Open University Press.

Carter, R. and Kirkup, G. (1992) Why do we still have so few women engineers in Europe and the USA? In *Volume II Contributions to GASAT Conference*, published for GASAT by the Eindhoven University of Technology.

Chadwick, V. (1989) Equal opportunities in the teaching profession – the myth and the reality, in De Lyon, H. and Widdowson Migniuolo, F. (eds) *Women Teachers: Issues and Experiences*, Milton Keynes, Open University Press.

Coleman, M. (1994) Women in educational management, in Bush, T. and West-Burnham, J. (eds) *The Principles of Educational Management*, Harlow, Longman.

Coleman, M. (1996a) Barriers to career progress for women in education: the perceptions of female headteachers, *Educational Research*, Vol. 38, No 3, pp. 1–13.

Coleman, M. (1996b) The management style of female headteachers, in *Educational Management and Administration*, Vol. 24, No 2, pp. 163–74.

Cullen, D. and Luna, G. (1993) Women mentoring in academe: addressing the gender gap in higher education, *Gender and Education*, Vol. 5, No 2, pp. 125–7.

Darking, L. (1991) The Equalizers, *The Times Educational Supplement*, 3 May.

DfE (1993) *Statistics of Education: Teachers England and Wales 1990*, London, HMSO.

DfEE (1995) *Statistics of Education: Teachers England and Wales 1993*, London, HMSO.

Evetts, J. (1990) *Women in Primary Teaching: Career Contexts and Strategies*, London, Unwin Hyman.

Evetts, J. (1994) *Becoming a Secondary Headteacher*, London, Cassell.

Gold, A. (1993) 'Women-friendly' management development programmes, in Ouston, J. (ed.) *Women in Education Management*, Harlow, Longman.

Grant, R. (1989) Women teachers' career pathways: towards an alternative model of 'career', in Acker, S. (ed.) *Teachers' Gender and Careers*, Lewes, Falmer Press.

Hammond, V. (1994) Opportunity 2000: good practice in UK organizations, in Davidson, M.J. and Burke, R.J. (eds) *Women in Management: Current Research Issues*, London, Paul Chapman.

Lewis, S. (1994) Role tensions and dual-career couples, in Davidson, M.J. and Burke, R.J. (eds) *Women in Management: Current Research Issues*, London, Paul Chapman.

Matthews, E. (1995) Women principals' views on sex equity: exploring issues of integration and information, in Dunlap, D. and Schmuck, P. (eds) *Women Leading in Education*, Albany, NY, State University of New York Press.

McBurney, E. and Hough, J. (1989) Role perceptions of female deputy heads, *Educational Management and Administration*, Vol. 17, pp. 115–18.

McKellar, B. (1989) Only the fittest of the fittest will survive: black women and education, in Acker, S. (ed.) *Teachers' Gender and Careers*, Lewes, Falmer Press.

Morgan, C., Hall, V. and Mackay, H. (1983) *The Selection of Secondary School Headteachers*, Milton Keynes, Open University Press.

Mortimore, P. and Mortimore, J. (with Thomas, H.) (1994) *Managing Associate Staff: Innovation in Primary and Secondary Schools*, London, Paul Chapman.

Moss, P. (ed.) (1995) *Father Figures: Fathers in the Families of the 1990s*, Edinburgh, HMSO.

Perry, P. (1993) From HMI to polytechnic director, in Ozga, J. (ed.) *Women in Educational Management*, Buckingham, Open University Press.

Roach, M. (1993) The secondary deputy, in Ozga, J. (ed.) *Women in Educational Management*, Buckingham, Open University Press.

Schick-Case, S. (1994) Gender differences in communication and behaviour in organizations, in Davidson, M.J. and Burke, R.J. (eds) *Women in Management: Current Research Issues*, London, Paul Chapman.

Schmuck, P.A. (1986) School management and administration: an analysis by gender, in Hoyle, E. and McMahon, A. (eds) *The Management of Schools, World Yearbook of Education 1986*, London, Kogan Page.

Shakeshaft, C. (1989) *Women in Educational Administration*, Newbury Park, Calif., Sage.

Thompson, M. (1992) Appraisal and equal opportunities, in Bennett, N., Crawford, M. and Riches, C. (eds) *Managing Change in Education*, London, Paul Chapman.

Universities' Statistical Record (1994) *University Statistics 1993–1994, Vol. 1*, Cheltenham, University Grants Committee.

Ward, L. (1995) Women who surf the gender network, *The Times Educational Supplement*, 1 December.

Waring, S. (1992) Women teachers' careers: do governors hold the key?, *Management in Education*, Vol. 6, No. 4, pp. 13–16.

Weightman, J. (1989) Women in management, *Educational Management and Administration*, Vol. 17, pp. 119–22.

Weindling, D. and Earley, P. (1987) *Secondary Headship: The First Years*, Windsor, NFER/Nelson.

Whitehead, S. (1995) Men managers: the gendered/gendering subject, conference paper presented at the University of Huddersfield, July.

Wild, R. (1994) Barriers to women's promotion in FE, *Journal of Further and Higher Education*, Vol. 18, No. 3, pp. 83–95.

Section D: the management of key processes

In the final section, the focus is on the direct application of management to those processes which are a central part of the way in which schools and colleges operate. It is through these processes that managers are able to make changes that are the most visible indicators of a particular approach to managing people. Effective recruitment and selection is the crucial starting point, as David Middlewood's Chapter 10 emphasises. Emphasis on performance increases the need for appropriate appointments, whilst the uniqueness of each organisation may work against consistency in practice across organisations. Both here and in Marianne Coleman's Chapter 11 on induction and mentoring, significant variations in practice are described. She suggests that mentoring may be an important tool for change and that an organisation committed to its use demonstrates some of the most effective management of its people.

In Chapter 12, David Middlewood draws attention to significant developments in the appraisal of performance and relates these to the context of individual and organisational improvement. He argues that appraisal can be central to performance management if it is used for development *and* evaluation and is integrated into management processes. In Chapter 13 on staff development, he argues that there is a need for all staff to be involved in policies which affect their training. Real change cannot be effected without ownership by staff, and their individual needs, including career aspirations, must be acknowledged. The aim is to develop a culture in which the many diverse needs at all levels in an organisation are recognised, and that a range of opportunities to meet them are offered. Keith Foreman's final chapter discusses performance management. He describes approaches to assessing performance and also tackles the difficult issue of *under*performance. In the context of self-management, the problem of people who are not contributing adequately to school or college performance cannot be ignored. He concludes, however, with an emphasis on the positive by stressing the need to recognise that effective motivation of people needs to value them as individuals if performance is to be enhanced.

10

MANAGING RECRUITMENT AND SELECTION

David Middlewood

THE IMPORTANCE OF EFFECTIVE RECRUITMENT AND SELECTION

Given that people are the most important resource in educational organis-ations, it is a truism to say that appointing such people is the most important task that managers undertake. As Drucker (1988, p. 17) has pointed out, no organisation can depend on genius: 'the supply is always scarce and unreliable.' In the task of recruitment and selection, managers may be described as encouraging the best people to apply and then as choosing the best people for the jobs or tasks.

Recruitment and selection procedures, especially interviews, have received constant attention in the worlds of social and occupational psychology, and personnel management, in the past seventy years. Norris (1993) reports that by the late 1970s there was a reasonable consistency of findings that structured processes, including the training of interviewers, were likely to increase validity of selections. Research work in the 1980s has reinforced the need for structure and formality to reduce discrimination against applicants, on grounds of gender, race, age or disability. Legislation is common now, in many countries, which places a responsibility on managers to avoid this discrimination, although the legislative emphasis will vary. For example, the UK does not specifically legislate against age discrimination; the USA does. The fact that much of this research tends to focus more on selection than recruitment is hardly surprising given that selection is the part of the process which is more visible. Most people in education are able to describe something wrong with a particular selection but as Hill (1989, p. 144) points out, 'Such evidence is, of course, anecdotal and may be unreliable, exaggerated or out of date'.

Several changes in the environment of educational organisations recently have added impetus to the need to manage recruitment and selection more effectively:

1) The first of these is the movement, in several countries, to schools and colleges becoming more autonomous. This greater self-governance means, for example, that the responsibility for ensuring that the legislation is adhered to is that of the governing body or directorate. The consequences of failing in this responsibility, such as complaints and industrial tribunals, fall upon the organisation's representatives.

2) A further consequence of self-governance, arising from the school or college managing its own budget, is the financial implication of ineffective appointments. The opportunity for schools and colleges to manage their own resources has inevitably sharpened awareness of the financial significance of making the right appointments of the people who will work in the organisation and who are the most expensive resource. A poor appointment will prove extremely costly, both in financial and human terms.

3) In the 1990s, a greater emphasis upon the visible outputs of schools, colleges and educational services has focused attention upon the need for ways of assessing performance. This assessment, with its related interest in targets and competences, can inevitably be seen as beginning at the time when a person is to be recruited to fulfil a particular function. Hence, the relevance of effective assessment at the selection stage.

CONTEXTS OF RECRUITMENT AND SELECTION

Most of the research into effective recruitment and selection is of a generic nature and there has been little research specific to the educational context. Much of what does exist relates to headteacher or principal appointments. In some countries, principals of schools and colleges complete an appropriate qualification and training process and are *allocated* by regional boards to a particular organisation for a fixed period of tenure, before being moved to another (e.g. Canada). In a second model, principals qualify and then have to be *selected* in a competitive situation (e.g. Australia). In the UK, there is a 'free market' in head/principal appointments. There are no regional boards to advise and indeed no formal process for passing on information about appropriate candidates for headship, although undoubtedly informal networks exist. Each individual school, no matter how small, is responsible for its own processes in appointing a new headteacher. From 1997, a new National Professional Qualification for Headteachers (NPQH) will be in place, indicating a minimum requirement for governing bodies in this process.

Each of these different contexts for appointments has its own issues concerning their most effective management. The free market approach

> can be bewildering and frustrating for headship applicants, since they may be close to being appointed at School A, only to find that they must begin again on equal terms with all other applicants for School B. Since the pressure is on for schools to achieve 'success' in a highly visible way (e.g. league tables), it is not surprising that those responsible for the school's progress will wish to stress its individuality. Unfortunately for headship applicants, this individuality can show itself in a variety of approaches to the selection of a new head.
>
> (Middlewood, 1995, p. 22)

In Australia the local school councils have become responsible for setting goals and priorities at the individual school level and are demanding that principals be selected to suit *their* schools. 'Local selection of principals has become an increasingly important issue' (Donovan, 1995, p. 10). Another view is that local *participation* in the decision-making, as distinct from local selection, provides the appropriate balance (Brierley, 1995).

In summary, whatever the context, the balance to be managed in effective recruitment and selection is that between impartial and efficient assessment methods, which are fair to the system and all applicants, and what Morgan (1989, p. 169) has described as the need 'to satisfy the demand for a visible democratic accountability, a social legitimation by the local community'. The argument for the individuality of schools and colleges requiring the appointment of the persons best fitted for a post in a particular school or college, whatever the post, ought not to extend to excessive variation or inconsistency in the methods used to select those persons.

ARGUMENTS FOR STRUCTURED APPROACHES

Two principal pieces of evidence in this field were both related to heads/principals in secondary education. Apart from the occasional case study (e.g. Southworth, 1987), little evidence exists in the primary field. Baltzell and Dentler (1983, p. 112) found a lack of clear definition of what was sought in USA school principals by the selectors:

> Every district had a deeply held image of a 'good' principal ... This image appeared to be widely shared by central administrators, parents and principals themselves. However, time and time again, this fit seemed to rest on personal perceptions of a candidate's physical presence, projections of a certain self-confidence, and assertiveness, and embodiment of community values and methods of operation.

In England and Wales, the team that investigated the appointment of secondary school headteachers (the POST project) found that the selection

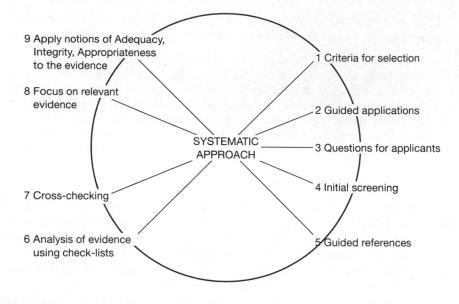

Figure 10.1 A recruitment and selection model
Source: Southworth, 1990, p. 117

procedures constituted a 'lottery' and that, specifically, they had four main shortcomings:

(a) selectors had a meagre knowledge of the job and used undeclared criteria;
(b) the roles of the different groups of selectors were ambiguous;
(c) the selectors used a restricted selection technology;
(d) (of most significance) non job-related factors dominated the decision.

(Morgan, 1986, p. 153)

Meyer (1995) used the same 'lottery' analogy to describe the 1995 selection process in Victoria, Australia: 'lottery outcomes still exist – keep buying a ticket and you may win one day' (quoted in Van Halen, 1995, p. 14). Interestingly, Meyer relates the element of chance to the applicants whereas Morgan *et al.* (1984) were commenting on the likelihood of managed procedures finding the best candidate.

There are therefore strong arguments for a rational and structured selection process to be managed in recruiting and selecting people. Southworth (1990) offers such a rational model (see Figure 10.1).

The initial steps are as follows (adapted from Hill, 1989):

- Define the job to be filled (job specification).
- Identify the skills, knowledge, attitudes and values necessary to do the job (person specification).
- Decide upon what will count as evidence of the possession of those competencies and attributes.

MANAGING RECRUITMENT

In the modern context, outlined in Chapter 1, managers cannot assume either that labour market conditions of yesterday apply today or that the wider employment context is not relevant to the particular or local situation. It has been suggested that there are five contexts for recruitment management:

Growth and survival — issues arising from e.g. expansion or retrenchment
Succession planning — issues related to e.g. staff age profile
Labour market — who is available for recruitment e.g. more international possibilities
Legislation — e.g. equal opportunities
Local conditions — e.g. competing schools or colleges.

(O'Neill *et al.*, 1994, p. 46)

The actual field from which organisations recruit staff, and the factors affecting decisions about appointments, are changing constantly. Examples include the following:

- *Re-entrants* to the teaching profession, which increased dramatically in the early 1980s in England and Wales (see Fidler, 1993 pp. 9–10).
- A general increase in the number of *entry routes* into teaching and lecturing.
- A greater focus upon the role of *associate staff vis-à-vis* teaching staff (see Mortimore *et al.*, 1994).
- The existence of the *pool of inactive teachers* (PIT), qualified but not active: 'Over 400,000 teachers are currently employed in the maintained sector in England and Wales. Part-time employment accounts for less than 5 per cent of the total. There are over 350,000 people with teaching qualifications currently not employed in the maintained sector, over half of whom (200,000) are female, aged 30–49' (Buchan *et al.*, 1988, p. 1).
- *High staff turnover,* particularly in urban and inner-city areas (NCE, 1993).
- The increase in *part-time* staff, especially in further education (Fagg, 1991), and *fixed-term* contracts.
- The movement to negotiate, especially in further and higher education, on the basis of individual contracts wherever possible (Fagg, 1991; O'Neill *et al.*, 1994).

Defining the job

Clearly the focus in devising the job specification needs to be on the job to be done not on the person who used to do it. The needs of the organisation's clients (pupils and students), reflected in the institutional development plan, should shape this. As Taylor and Hemmingway (1990) point out, the 'team' responsible for this plan need to reach decisions on what is being sought. Most employees in educational organisations have job descriptions but these need to be more than a set of tasks. In some instances, they may include elements of a person specification which is necessary for the post.

Person specification

The task for the managers here is to identify the skills, knowledge, attitudes and values necessary to do the job. The perceptions of stakeholders other than professionals as to what constitutes effectiveness in a person to fill a post become important. Governors of schools and colleges, for example, may seek qualities which take more account of external accountability than some professionals who wish to focus solely on 'job performance'. Hinds (1992) offers an interesting model of the different 'layers' of governors' expectations of a teacher, i.e. teaching a particular group, taking a wider responsibility, educating, working as part of a team, relating to some other part of school or college community, and offering leadership in something else (see Figure 10.2). Hinds (*ibid.*, p. 125) suggests that in recruitment one of the weaknesses often is that the governors and senior professionals

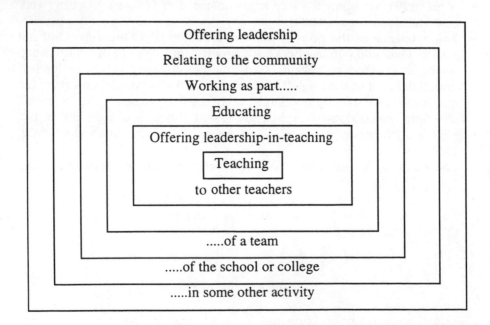

Figure 10.2   Governors' expectations of a teacher
Source: Hinds, 1992, p. 126

'in setting a contract, do not actually make the terms and expectations explicit'.

A further aspect of a person specification may be a consideration of potential for development. Only indicators can be anticipated. The demands of the future cannot be precisely known which might therefore be an argument for managers to stress qualities as much as skills in the requirements of the person. Equally, the mesh between the person to be appointed and the organisation's culture is very important and, as Belbin (1981) identified, also the mesh between members of the new team.

Management issues in recruitment

This chapter deals with 'recruitment and selection' and it seems clear that integrating these processes is good practice, to enable key principles to operate throughout. It can be argued that this integration should also include induction (Bell, 1988; O'Neill *et al.*, 1994). Indeed, induction might be considered as beginning as soon as the advertisement for a post is studied by the person who eventually will be appointed. Certainly, the advertisement and subsequent information materials provide an opportunity for unsuitable candidates to deselect themselves.

A vital issue for managers of recruitment is undoubtedly that of equal opportunities. All stages of the process need to be checked against criteria for ensuring that no potential applicants are discriminated against on unacceptable – and unlawful – criteria. Posts involving part-time staff may be particularly vulnerable. In a case study of the appointment of a part-time assistant, Parker-Jenkins (1994) describes how, among other factors, the following were paid careful attention:

- To ensure as wide a field for recruitment as possible, advertisements were placed in locations outside those which only people in the 'normal' educational circles would reach.
- References were not required since those who have been absent from the labour market – or never in it – might feel reluctant to apply because of the lack of 'appropriate' referees.
- Candidates who did not necessarily follow the conventional format of application were still considered if their suitability matched the job criteria.
- Each interviewee was asked the same questions based on the agreed criteria for the post as advertised.
- Debriefing, immediate or later, was offered to all unsuccessful interviewees.
- All interviewees were asked for their perception of the interview process.

As Parker-Jenkins points out, it can be a time-consuming, lengthy and potentially difficult procedure for what might be *merely* the recruitment and selection of part-time, temporary staff. However, these are precisely the posts which may often be filled through informal contacts. It could well be argued that in education, in particular, these are the very posts which offer opportunities for managers to recruit from unconventional backgrounds, thus widening the students' access to a range of staff, as well as fulfilling in practice the equal opportunity principle. 'If access to opportunity is to become universal, it must reach out beyond the nepotism of educational circles' (*ibid.*, p. 3).

Issues of equal opportunities, and ensuring structured approaches throughout recruitment and selection procedures, are important also because of the sensitivity of *internal appointments* and *promotion*. When organisations are contracting, the option of appointing an existing member of staff is attractive for financial reasons (see Chapter 1). Apart from the importance of ensuring credibility in the procedure and thereby of the person appointed, managers have to consider also the need for new blood. An inward-looking culture which perpetuates stereotyped models of men or women company workers is in danger of what has been described as 'organisational incest' (Hunt, 1986, p. 211).

MANAGING SELECTION

Who should be involved?

The movement to self-governance in schools and colleges, described by Tony Bush in Chapter 1, has affected the management of selection in terms of the *personnel* involved. Each school or college may be keen to establish its uniqueness and this will be particularly evident in the selection of the leading professional, i.e. headteacher/principal. However, as stated earlier, this uniqueness should not result in 'excessive variation or inconsistency in the method used to select that person' (Middlewood, 1995, p. 23).

The main influence, alongside that of the professionals, is that of lay governors representing community, business and other interests. Some of these may have experience as selectors outside education. In schools, the issue of parent involvement, for example, is clearly important. In Australia, there is much debate concerning parents' role in the appointment of principals. Van Halen (1995, p. 15) argues that training in selection is essential for parents:

> Parents on selection panels fall into one of three categories: those who leave the decisions to the professionals; a group that have their minds made up beforehand and do not come clean about the hidden agendas; and finally, the minority who are trained in the selection processes or who are open about the process and stay with the assessment criteria all along.

Representation of staff interests is seen to be far more significant at other levels, including that of assistant principal. In 1995 in Victoria, 63 per cent of selections of assistant principals involved a staff member, none in principals' selections. There are strong arguments for involving staff in the selection processes of a new member. First, the job description is likely to be more comprehensive and realistic and, secondly, as the new person will be part of a team (Southworth, 1987; Hinds, 1992) it would be 'strange, to say the least, not to involve that team in the selection of its new member' (Hill, 1989, p. 147).

Clearly, the involvement of lay personnel is intended to bring a valuable, different perspective from that of the professionals working within the organisation. However, it should not be assumed that training should be restricted to the lay personnel since senior managers in education often reach their positions without such training or indeed much experience of managing selection – except of course as recipients of the process. Van Halen (1995) claims that it has taken him ten years as a principal, with 'significant' training, to feel confident about selecting teachers and middle managers. Norris (1993, p. 27) indicates that, by the end of the 1970s, through research studies outside education, 'interviewer bias was also found to be significantly reduced by using trained interviewers'.

How are candidates to be assessed?

The three main issues to be considered are the *criteria* (the standards against which candidates are assessed), the *weighting* (the relative importance of the different criteria) and the *instruments* (the methods by which assessment is made).

The *criteria* relate closely to the job and person specifications and will include biographical data, skills and knowledge. Attitudes and values are also crucial, perhaps especially in education, both on a personal level and also the extent to which the individual's beliefs and ambitions, for example, fit with the values of the organisation. Similarly, the technical (or specialist) competence of a candidate may be reasonably clear but the functional aspects of the role of a new team member, for example, are much less so. Belbin's work (1981) has shown why selection needs to take account of the ability of the individual to contribute effectively to a team. Belbin's typology of team members, for example, can provide a guide to selectors in terms of what they may be seeking to complement existing staff but inconsistent behaviour and organisational micropolitics would ensure that it could be no more than a guide.

The *weighting* of the various criteria cannot by its very nature be precise but it does enable the criteria to be used consistently. It is easy to say that one task is more important than another but rather more difficult to give it a value. Weighting, however, is one way of reducing inconsistencies in the selection process and Bell (1988) has demonstrated how it can be applied by giving, for example, a score out of ten for a criterion considered very important and out of five for one less so. In the POST research project, mentioned earlier, it was found that selectors of secondary school headteachers gave a low weighting to job-related skills and knowledge and also to quality of experience and performance to date. The decisive weighting was given to personality/personal qualities. 'This weighting given in headteacher selection to hunt the right personality is wholly consistent with all major research on interviewing' (Morgan, 1986, p. 149). The establishment of weightings of criteria at the outset, while not excluding bias in any one area, can ensure that any such bias is not disproportionate in the consideration of all the criteria.

Since the assessment of one human being by others inevitably contains subjectivity, the concern for managers of selection in education is to bring as much objectivity as possible into the process. For this reason, the issue of *how* to carry out the assessment deserves a fuller examination.

Competency approaches

The competency approach focuses on assessment under conditions as near as possible to those in which they are normally displayed. At senior level in particular, as Black and Wolf (1990) indicated, some of the most effective management actions may be almost invisible: 'An effective manager can be seen to deal effectively with a crisis; a more effective manager doesn't have crises to survive' (Ouston, 1993, p. 217).

Although competency approaches to selection should be seen as merely one source of information to be considered by selectors, Ouston (1993) expressed a concern that governors, for example, might be tempted to give competence-based assessment more significance than other approaches, perhaps because it looked 'scientific'. One of the critical aspects of competency assessment in selection is that it is manifestly not possible to see someone actually performing the role for which he or she is applying. Ouston points out that we need both indicators that predict future good performance and also a view of future demands. 'If the model is very skills based, rather than qualities based, it is likely to reflect the present rather than the future' (*ibid.*, p. 218).

One of the devices through which competency approaches have been developed is the use of *assessment centres*. Widely used in business, industry and the military, their use in education in the USA was widespread by the end of the 1980s (McCleary and Ogawa, 1989). In England and Wales some centres were established in the early 1990s. Proponents of assessment centres (Joiner, 1984; Green, 1991; Lyons *et al.*, 1993) all made strong claims for the effectiveness of such centres, based on independent evaluation and research. Their ability to predict job success ('predictive validity') is seen to be high, proven and therefore of great value to school or college selectors. The final stage of the assessment centre process would be 'the production of a report on each shortlisted candidate upon which an informed selection decision could be made by governors' (Lyons *et al.*, 1993, p. 246). Green (1991) usefully summarises the four elements in an educational assessment centre:

1) Identifying the management competencies required for success.
2) Designing job-related exercises to test the competencies.
3) Training assessors to assess the performance of participants on the job-related exercises.
4) Producing a personal report about each EAC participant.

The major argument against the use of assessment centres is that of expense, in terms of money and time and of the contexts within which they assess becoming out of date. As Lyons *et al.* (1993, p. 248) stress, 'research and development into the practice of Assessment and Development Centres to look at how one can make the process more accurate, resource and cost-effective, user friendly and up-to-date, is thus of crucial importance'. However, Jirasinghe and Lyons (1996, p. 111) also point out the attraction of assessment centres for affirmative action in equal opportunities issues.

New initiatives by the Teacher Training Agency (TTA) in England and Wales, such as the Headteachers Leadership and Management project (HEADLAMP), have focused attention on the processes for identifying the needs of senior staff and thereby the ways of assessing relevant abilities or competencies. A National Professional Qualification for Headteachers, for implementation in autumn 1997, is an attempt to establish assessable minimum requirements which governors may set in balance with their decision to determine who is the best individual for their particular school.

Tests used through assessment centres, which are essentially processes *not* places, include exercises such as sifting and prioritising documents (in-tray), role play simulations, leaderless group discussions, oral and visual presentations, and written reports. An assessment centre will offer these with trained assessors present and in standardised conditions, but selection managers are able to make use of such devices independently and the use of oral presentation, for example, appears to be quite common in middle and senior management selection in education. However, consistency and validity of criteria in using such presentations are by no means clear. 'Some are prepared, some unprepared; some topics are given, some unseen; sometimes the presentation is followed by questions, sometimes not. This variability makes it clear that the criteria used by those assessing the presentation must in themselves be varied . . . the criteria used . . . are also less than explicit . . .' (Middlewood, 1995, p. 23).

Interviewing

A face-to-face interview plays a significant part in any selection process. The interview has been widely studied and, since the findings consistently point up the unreliability of the interview as a predictor of future performance, it is important that it plays only one part in any selection procedure. Some of the findings have been summarised by Hill (1989):

- Physically attractive candidates are more likely to be appointed (Gilmore, 1986).
- Most interviewers do not take notes (Morgan *et al.*, 1983).
- An average candidate who follows several poor candidates is seen as particularly good (Carlson, 1971).
- Interviewers reach their decision about each candidate very early in the interview, under four minutes in one study (Hackett, 1992).
- Even in highly structured selection procedures the interview is used to justify and explain the decision rather than guide it (Salaman and Thompson, 1974).

Norris (1993) offers a model of a fair and valid selection process in which the interview remains important but other processes place it in perspective and into which assessment centre information can be fed (see Figure 10.3). However, in his case study at a further education college, despite emphasis on the structured rational elements, 'the information used in the decision-making process was largely restricted to an assessment of candidates' performance during the interview with little weight given to the results of the work sample tests' (*ibid.*, p. 30).

Much examination has been done of the complex processes involved in the communications (Riches, 1992) and interpersonal perceptions (Hinton, 1993) of interviews. Studies by Funder (1987) have shown that people are susceptible to a whole range of illusions and other errors of perception. There are difficulties in assessing, say, 'creativity' compared with 'courtesy'. An interview is an artificial situation and interviewers may be subject to 'logical error' (by which the assumption is made that anyone with one characteristic, e.g. politeness, must automatically have another, e.g. intelligence) or the 'halo' effect (by which an interviewer being impressed by one characteristic will attribute positive features to all the interviewee's other characteristics). However, as Kenny and Albright (1987) point out, even though a person (e.g. a selector) makes errors, it does not mean he or she is unskilled or even inaccurate. Hinton (1993, p. 134) summarises that 'the massive amount of work on errors should not necessarily be taken as evidence for human inaccuracy' and concludes, reassuringly, that a selection panel is significantly better than one person and 'despite differences in their judgements they could well perform their function successfully and select a suitable candidate for the job' (*ibid.*, p. 137).

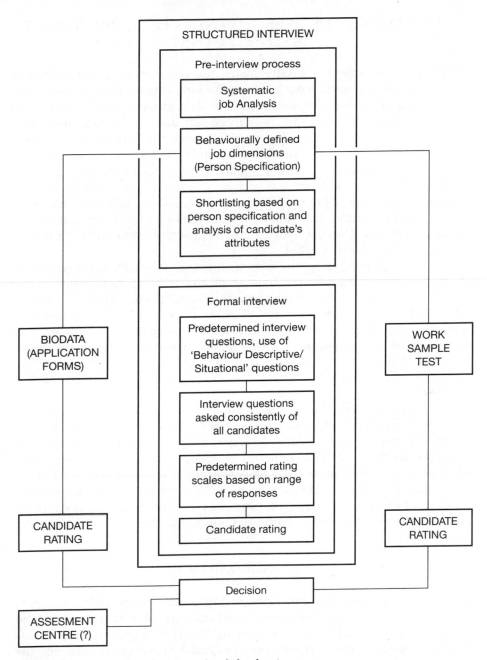

Figure 10.3   A model of a fair and valid selection process
Source: Norris, 1993, p. 28

EVALUATING THE EFFECTIVENESS OF RECRUITMENT AND SELECTION

When an appointment is finally made, the selectors will inevitably feel that the process is complete. However, the satisfaction of a selection panel in reaching an agreed decision is not at all a measure of the success of the appointment. Funder (1987) pointed out that, if an interview panel agree on the characteristics of a candidate, then they are likely to believe themselves accurate. Agreement may simply be seen as indicating that people are accepting a common standard of judgement. Any accuracy in terms of future performance is what Hinton (1993) calls 'pragmatic accuracy': 'One never knows whether unsuccessful candidates could do the job better because they don't get the chance to try. From the panel's point of view that does not really matter if they have done their job as well as they need to.' (*ibid.*, p. 136).

One way of monitoring the effectiveness of selection management is to make predictions of performance at the time of appointment and record this against the actual performance of those appointed over a period of time. If those appointed were consistently giving low performance, for example, the actual selection management would need to be examined. An adaptation of Gellerman's Grid of Performance evaluation, used in some civil service departments and some armed services, could give a simple monitoring device, such as that shown in Figure 10.4.

By allocating a number to each appointee and placing it in one of the prediction boxes, the number is then allocated an 'actual' box on every performance review. Although there might be other factors affecting underperformance, managers should be concerned at any entries in box (f). However, they might equally be concerned if someone allocated (a) on appointment is in (e) on review. Such a simple monitoring device enables managers to look at the selection processes and the variables, such as the actual personnel involved in particular appointments.

CONCLUSION

Recruitment and selection processes in education remain critical issues in the effective management of schools and colleges. Whilst there is greater awareness of the importance of making the right appointments in the search for institutional improvement, the growth of self-governance and the influence of lay personnel suggest that it will remain an area of controversy at times. More interest in competences and rational approaches to selection, and the introduction of the NPQH in England and Wales, for example, are evidence of a more effective approach to management. However, the figures discussed in Marianne Coleman's chapter on gender are a

Predicted performance (by selectors at performance)

		High	Good	Satisfactory
	High	(a)	(b)	(c)
Actual performance (through review)	**Good**	(b)		
	Satisfactory	(c)		
	Low	(d)		

Figure 10.4 Performance evaluation

clear indication that complying with legislation on equal opportunities is inadequate without further development of the attitudes and understanding of managers of recruitment and selection.

REFERENCES

Baltzell, C. and Dentler, R. (1983) *Selecting American School Principals: A Research Report*, Cambridge, Mass., Abt Associates.

Belbin, M. (1981) *Management Teams: Why They Succeed or Fail*, London, Routledge.

Bell, L. (1988) *Management Skills in Primary Schools*, London, Routledge.

Black, H. and Wolf, A. (1990) *Knowledge and Competence: Current Issues in Training and Education*, Sheffield, Department of Employment COIC.

Brierley, T. (1995) Principal selection: who decides?, *Principal Matters*, Vol. 7, No. 3, pp. 10.

Buchan, J., Pearson, R. and Pike, G. (1988) *Supply and Demand for Teachers in the 1990s, IMS Paper* 151, Brighton, Institute of Manpower Studies.

Carlson, R. (1971) Effect of interview information in altering valid impressions, *Journal of Applied Psychology*, Vol. 55, No. 1, pp. 66–72.

Donovan, B. (1995) Principal selection: a major issues, *Principal Matters*, Vol. 7, No. 3, p. 10.

Drucker, P. (1988) *Management*, London, Pan Books.

Fagg, V. (1991) Personnel management implications – pay and conditions of service, paper presented to conference of the Association of Colleges of Further and Higher Education, Glasgow.

Fidler, B. (1993) Balancing the supply and demand for school teachers, in Fidler, B., Fugl, B. and Esp, D. (eds) *The Supply and Recruitment of School Teachers*, Harlow, Longman.

Funder, D.C. (1987) Errors and mistakes: evaluating the accuracy of social judgement, *Psychological Review*, Vol. 101, pp. 75–90.

Gilmore, D.C. (1986) Effects of applicant attractiveness, *Journal of Occupational Psychology*, Vol. 59, No. 10, pp. 103–9.

Green, H. (1991) Strategies for management development: towards coherence, in Bennett, N., Crawford, M. and Riches, C. (eds) *Managing Change in Education*, Milton Keynes, Open University Press.

Hackett, P. (1992) *Success in Management: Personnel* (3rd edn), London, John Murray.

Hill, T. (1989) *Studies in Primary Education*, London, David Fulton.

Hinds, T. (1992) What can be the governors' contribution in staff appraisal?, *Educational Management and Administration*, Vol. 20, No. 2, pp. 123–128.

Hinton, P.R. (1993) *The Psychology of Inter-personal Perception*, London, Routledge.

Hunt, J. (1986) *Managing People at Work*, Maidenhead, McGraw-Hill.

Jirasinghe, D. and Lyons, G. (1996) *The Competent Head*, Lewes, Falmer Press.

Joiner, D.A. (1984) Assessment centres in the public sector: a practical approach, in Riches, C. and Morgan, C. (eds) *Human Resource Management in Education*, Milton Keynes, Open University Press.

Kenny, D. and Albright, L. (1987) Accuracy in interpersonal perception, *Psychological Bulletin*, Vol. 102, pp. 390–402.

Lyons, G., Jirasinghe, D., Ewers, C. and Edwards, S. (1993) The development of a headteachers' assessment centre, *Educational Management and Administration*, Vol. 21, No. 4, pp. 245–248.

McCleary, L. and Ogawa, R. (1989) The assessment centre process for selecting school leaders, *School Organisation*, Vol. 9, No. 1, pp. 103–13.

Meyer, B. (1995) Selecting principals: the chance factor, *Principal Matters*, vol. 7, no. 2.

Middlewood, D. (1995) All shapes and sizes: aspiring headteachers in the UK, *Principal Matters*, Vol. 7, No. 3, pp. 22–23.

Morgan, C. (1986) The selection and appointment of heads, in Hoyle, E. and McMahon, A. (eds) *World Yearbook of Education 1986: The Management of Schools*, London, Kogan Page.

Morgan, C. (1989) Inside the interview black box, in Riches, C. and Morgan, C. (eds) *Human Resource Management in Education*, Milton Keynes, Open University Press.

Morgan, C., Hall, V. and Mackay, A. (1983) *The Selection of Secondary School Headteachers*, Milton Keynes, Open University Press.

Mortimore, P. and Mortimore, J. (with Thomas, H.) (1994) *Managing Associate Staff*, London, Paul Chapman.

NCE (National Commission on Education) (1993) *Learning to Succeed*, London, Heinemann.

Norris, K. (1993) Avoidable inequalities?, *Management in Education*, Vol. 7, No. 2, pp. 27–30.

O'Neill, J., Middlewood, D. and Glover, D. (1994) *Managing Human Resources in Schools and Colleges*, Harlow, Longman.

Ouston, J. (1993) Management competences, school effectiveness and education management, *Educational Management and Administration*, Vol. 21, No. 4, pp. 212–221.

Parker-Jenkins, M. (1994) Part-time staff recruitment: an equal opportunities dilemma, *Management in Education*, Vol. 8, No. 2, pp. 3–4.

Riches, C. (1992) Developing communication skills in interviewing, in Bennett, N., Crawford, M. and Riches, C. (eds) *Managing Change in Education*, Milton Keynes, Open University Press.

Salaman, G. and Thompson, K. (1974) *The Sociology of Interviews*, Milton Keynes, Open University Press.

Southworth, G. (1987) Staff selection or by appointment?, in Southworth, G. (ed.) *Readings in Primary School Management*, Lewes, Falmer Press.

Southworth, G. (1990) *Staff Selection in the Primary School*, London, Blackwell.

Taylor, F. and Hemmingway, J. (1990) *Picking the Team*, London, Video Arts from DES.

Van Halen, B. (1995) We can do it better, *Principal Matters*, Vol. 7, No. 3, pp. 14–15.

11

MANAGING INDUCTION AND MENTORING

Marianne Coleman

INTRODUCTION

An entrant to any new job goes through an induction process of learning about the job, about his or her new colleagues and about the 'culture' of the place of work. The process is likely to be assisted by a degree of formal or informal mentoring by one or more people who are given, or take, the responsibility for such initiation. The extent to which teachers and lecturers have a formal and comprehensive induction programme, the nature of the programme, and the provision and use of mentors have varied according to changes in educational policy and funding, and with no consistent pattern operating between individual schools and colleges.

Whilst induction and mentoring may frequently be associated with young, newly qualified entrants to the profession, all new recruits to a school or college may expect some brief, general programme of induction. For example, a college of further education includes 'a checklist of topics, some practical and others more general, to ensure that new postholders receive as much support as possible' (Gilchrist, 1994, p. 67).

Colleges may also wish to explain procedures such as appraisal and policies such as that for equality of opportunity. The University of Leicester runs an 'Introduction to the university' training session and also provides guidelines and a checklist for the provision of induction programmes within each department. Most schools and colleges provide a handbook for staff in addition to introductory sessions.

Mentoring is often used in association with induction, but the impact of mentoring may go beyond an induction process to become embedded in wider professional development. In this way mentoring can 'extend the use of . . . effective feedback, dialogue and target-setting skills through a system of continuous professional development and support' (Smith, 1996, p. 11).

In this chapter we are considering the management of induction and mentoring, in relation to the needs of all staff, both those who are new to the profession and those who are new to an institution. Although mentoring may be most commonly associated with the induction of new teachers, it is also used for both the induction and professional development of middle and senior managers, most notably in the programmes developed for headteachers (Bolam *et al.*, 1995; Bush *et al.*, 1996). We turn now to consider the nature and purpose of induction.

WHAT DO WE MEAN BY INDUCTION?

For all new recruits the process of induction includes practical elements of information giving, but may go beyond 'introduction', and encompass support for development: 'Without doubt, effective induction practices mean "never having to say you're sorry you got the damned job", but, most importantly, they also provide a proper foundation for a career where learning and development are considered to be on-going' (Earley and Kinder, 1994, p. 143).

Trethowan and Smith (1984, p. 1) identify induction as a process: 'which enables a newcomer to become a fully effective member of an organisation as quickly and as easily as possible'. In order for this to occur the new recruit will need basic information about the school or college, the people in it and routines and procedures. They will need to develop their skills and competencies in the job and they should grow in their understanding of the ethos and culture of the institution. Research carried out by Gartside *et al.* (1988) showed that new lecturers in colleges of further education needed three areas of induction:

* to know more about the administrative working of the college;
* to adjust to FE culture; and
* to cope with difficulties in teaching.

Similarly, O'Neill *et al.* (1994, p. 68) sum up the purposes of induction in schools and colleges as 'socialisation; achieving competence; and exposure to institutional culture'.

Socialisation must include the activities which enable a new recruit to function as effectively as others within the school or college. Schein (1978) identified five elements in the process of socialisation:

1) Accepting the reality of the organisation (i.e. constraints on the individual).
2) Dealing with resistance to change (in trying to introduce new ideas to the place of work).

3) Learning how to cope with the amount of organisation and job definition available.
4) Dealing with the boss and understanding what is valued and rewarded in the institution.
5) Locating your own place in the organisation and developing an identity.

This final aspect may be most akin to the more informal processes of induction, and likely to be achieved through the mentoring processes, discussed later in this chapter.

Induction has a particular importance for newly qualified teachers (NQTs), for whom achieving competence in the job may encompass a wide range of skills. Tickle (1994, p. 43) refers to the Council for the Accreditation of Teacher Education (CATE) criteria of personal qualities, professional skills and academic subject expertise but stresses that competences should not mean the acquisition of 'the minimum technical skills of moderately good teachers' but should lead to continuing progress and improvement: the idea of the teacher as learner.

Whether it is the achievement of competence or the continuing development of the new recruit, some of the more practical aspects of the 'rights' of the NQT may be relevant. For example, Earley and Kinder (1994) discuss a reduced timetable; opportunities for structured observation of the NQT by a mentor; observation of experienced teachers by the new teacher; and limiting the responsibilities of NQTs, e.g. not being a form tutor in secondary schools or not being subject co-ordinator in primary schools.

Such 'rights' apply equally in further education. However, Gartside *et al.* (1988) found that observation was not undertaken systematically in the FE colleges they researched. It tended to occur when there was a perceived problem, rather than being used for formative and developmental purposes. The two-year research programme conducted by Tickle (1994, p. 187) found that 'the state of affairs with regard to the observation of teaching, and discussions about it, were mostly unsatisfactory'. It was felt that there should be more stress on the professional development of new teachers, and that the focus of the observation should be agreed in advance. The observation itself should be followed by formative feedback.

A practical support framework may also help the inductee to absorb some of the institutional culture that is identified as the third major purpose of induction. The research findings on induction led Tickle (1994) to suggest the following framework to support an induction programme, in addition to the provision of a handbook or the equivalent:

• Opportunities to meet teaching and support staff to understand their roles.
• An introduction to the provision of resources.
• Opportunities for observation and to be observed.
• Knowledge of the locality including the link schools.

- Knowledge of the community aspect of the school including the pastoral system, links with parents and support services.
- Understanding of the core values of the school and the arrangements for pupil learning, e.g. assessment and record keeping.
- Appreciation of the quality of teaching, including planning, preparation, classroom management and evaluation.

With the exception of the opportunities for observation and to be observed, this list could provide the basis for an induction programme for all those new to a school, including associate staff.

A further aspect of induction leading to an understanding of the culture and ethos of the institution, and the beginning of the socialisation process, could include visits to the school or college before appointment. Research reported by Tickle (*ibid.*) identifies the contrast in the experience between appointees who have made few, if any, preparatory visits before taking up their post, and student teachers who often have extended in-school preparation for a professional placement. It was felt that a school might take the initiative in ensuring that visits take place: 'clear invitations were needed from the school, with commitment of staff time, to ensure that new appointees felt welcome' (*ibid.*, p. 175).

WHO IS INVOLVED IN INDUCTION?

The induction process may involve a variety of personnel. Four main models of induction support emerged from the Earley and Kinder (1994) research. Whilst these models were derived from research on the induction of NQTs, they could equally well apply to an experienced new recruit to a school or college:

1) Mono-support, the support of a single person, usually a member of the SMT.
2) Bi-support, usually from a mentor (middle management) in addition to a central induction programme usually organised by senior management.
3) Tri-support systems, offering a combination of central meetings, middle or senior management mentor support and another officially designated mentor in the role of 'buddy' or 'critical friend' who was of similar status to the inductee.
4) Multi-support systems where support was offered at a number of levels and in addition there was evidence of co-ordination between the levels, e.g. the training of mentors in the schools.

The research of Gartside *et al.* (1988) in Scottish colleges of further education showed that it was the heads of department who were mainly responsible for arranging induction programmes, often taking the responsibility of teaching classes themselves to allow new lecturers to attend induction sessions. Research with NQTs in secondary schools showed that the provision of induction programmes was not necessarily consistent across the departments of the school, and that it was certainly not co-ordinated with mentors who had no input into the induction sessions: 'I'm not even aware of what happens in the generalised induction programme' (mentor quoted in Bush *et al.*, 1996, p. 124). The resulting lack of coherence is unlikely to assist in promoting the general professional development of new teachers.

WHO NEEDS INDUCTION?

Whilst induction is often associated with new entrants into the profession, it also applies to experienced staff new to the institution. The recommen-dations of the School Management Task Force (DfE, 1990) included the induction and mentoring of new headteachers and other senior staff. However, the induction needs of experienced and senior staff will be different from those of the new recruit. Indeed, the background and experience of all those new to the school or college are likely to affect their particular needs as inductees. The implication is that programmes of induction should be individualised to take into account the needs of new teachers and lecturers.

In particular, lecturers in FE colleges tend to come from a range of professional and industrial backgrounds, to have had no compulsory preservice training course and in addition many of them may be part-time appointments (Gartside *et al.*, 1988). Part-time employees, who have the same needs for induction as their full-time colleagues, may miss out on induction for a variety of reasons. They may not be paid for attending induction sessions, they may miss out on informal induction because they spend so little non-teaching time in the college and they may not feel that they have the right to induction: 'Many part-time staff did not see themselves as being worthy of help' (*ibid.*, p. 26).

Trethowan and Smith (1984, p. 3) make the point that associate staff should be included in any induction programme: 'Anyone who doubts the necessity for such a programme should consider the economic cost of operating with a caretaker, technician or secretary whose knowledge, skills, or philosophy do not allow them to contribute effectively to their school.'

Mortimore *et al.* (1994) suggest that associate staff may need specific guidelines within the induction process on their relations with pupils, teachers and parents, and clear indications of support on discipline prob-lems. Similarly, Emerson and Goddard (1993) make a particular case for the induction of supply teachers, commenting on the challenges faced by teach-ers who are less familiar with the school, and who may need support with pupils who are faced with disruption to their normal classroom routine.

CHARACTERISTICS OF EFFECTIVE INDUCTION

The variety of induction needs indicates that flexibility in the induction process is required if it is to be effective. In concluding the report on their research on induction practice, Earley and Kinder (1994) identify flexibility and add that induction should

- meet teachers' needs (training, development, social and psychological);
- be part of a school-wide approach to supporting all staff;
- be systematic and planned, including links to specific individuals, observation and feedback;
- include reflection on practice (with a mentor);
- enable staff to become active and valued members who can contribute to the school; and
- lay the foundation for a life-long professional career.

Induction is often linked to mentoring, and we turn now to consider the nature of mentoring and the ways in which mentors may contribute to the development of staff and to school or college professional development.

WHAT IS MEANT BY MENTORING?

The archetypal mentor relationship identified by Kram (1983) is that of an experienced adult in mid-life giving both career and psychosocial support to a young person entering the adult world, specifically the world of work. However, mentoring is not limited to new entrants to the profession; it is increasingly being recognised as being of benefit to mature adults who are entering a new phase of their life or a new job, particularly where promotion and increased responsibilities are concerned. Mentors have the role of supporting and training new headteachers, and mentoring is also being used for both the induction and support of middle managers. In the case of the mentoring of new headteachers, the role has been likened to that of a 'counsellor', and a 'coach' although, in England, it is more generally seen as 'peer support' (Bush *et al.*, 1996). The notion of a mentor is not necessarily limited to a relatively brief induction process, but may be seen as an ongoing part of professional development.

In schools, the role of the mentor has taken on a new focus with the move towards school-based initial teacher education and a reduction in the role of higher education. Teachers and managers in schools have been faced with a new set of demands whereby they take on much of the responsibility for the training of new teachers. Similarly, the reduction in the role of the LEA, and the abolition of the probationary year, has increased the need for the NQT to be mentored by a teacher in the school. Within schools and colleges, the importance of mentoring for student teachers and NQTs may be focused on the subject mentor and the increase in professional competence, or it may be focused on a wider role, stressing the functions of socialisation and acculturation. In some cases there may be a blurring of the distinction between mentoring and line management or appraisal. Certainly there may be a tension for mentors if their role includes observation of the mentee, where an element of judgement may be implicit.

Mentoring is now being used in so many contexts that it is not surprising to find a lack of consistency in how the term is understood, and how the role of the mentor is developed. Research in secondary schools identified: 'fragmented and inconsistent practices across departments, where effective mentoring was dependent on the value placed on it by individual mentors,' (Bush *et al.*, 1996, p. 124). Problems with mentoring in further education colleges also include inconsistency in practice: 'inevitable disparities in the quality of oversight and help provided by individual mentors' (Cantor *et al.*, 1995, p. 118).

Certain issues arise with regard to the management of mentoring, including the desirability of establishing a common understanding of what is meant by mentoring for those participating in the process, a decision on who will be mentored, the responsibility of matching mentor to mentee and the arrangement of training for mentors. There may be considerable differences as well as similarities in the different forms of mentoring now being experienced in schools. These include mentoring of student teachers, mentoring of NQTs, mentoring of headteachers and mentoring as a key part of whole-school (or college) development, which could involve mentoring of all staff new to post, including associate staff.

MENTORING IN INITIAL TEACHER EDUCATION

The partnership model of initial teacher education, with the higher education institution (HEI) and the school sharing the role of educating the new teacher, has enhanced awareness of mentoring. The model of mentoring that initially developed was based on secondary school practice and, as a result, may have stressed the importance of subject mentoring. However, as more of the training period is being spent in the school than the HEI, the school takes on a responsibility for training in the wider aspects of the teaching role. The potential responsibility may mean that the mentoring process cannot be isolated within the school, but should become part of mentoring 'culture'. Whilst this idea is appealing, the practice of mentoring is variable, both in quality and in style. Maynard and Furlong (1994) have identified models of mentoring which exemplify some of the possible styles, and which echo the three main strands running through induction identified elsewhere (Tickle, 1994):

- The apprenticeship model, where learning to teach is through emulating the example of experienced teachers (mentors);

- The competency based approach, where the mentor becomes a systematic trainer, coaching the trainee in specified competences;
- The reflective model, where the mentor takes on the role of stimulating critical reflection and becomes a 'co-enquirer'.

(Maynard and Furlong, 1994, p. 82)

The differences in these models raise the issue of the relationship between mentor and mentee and the need for a common understanding of the functions implicit in that relationship. The apprenticeship and competency-based models may imply a more formal, instructional and assessing role, whereas the reflective model implies a relationship that is between equals.

Elliott and Calderhead (1995, p. 177) identified a range of mentor approaches in their research in primary schools which supports the existence of the three models, although there was little evidence for the reflective model, except where things were not going well: 'It was as if breakdown in class management or other teaching routines were needed in order to generate reflection.' The recommendation that primary schools play a greater part in the subject training for initial teacher education (ITE) (DfE, 1993) stresses the aspect of mentoring that relates to competency. However, research on mentoring in primary schools (Campbell and Kane, 1996; Maynard, 1996) has indicated the reluctance of teachers and students to see primary school teachers as anything other than whole-class teachers.

The reliance on teacher mentors in schools as part of ITE is relatively new. However, research reviewing the experience of mentors in the Oxford Internship Scheme, which was first established in 1987, allows some reflection on the implications for school managers of the in-school mentoring of students. The issues raised by the mentors were

- the importance of the subject teachers as well as the official mentors, in informally mentoring students or 'interns' and the implications for managing this;
- difficulties in meeting the mentoring needs of both interns and NQTs, and understanding that whilst there may be opportunities for collaboration between students and NQTs, their needs are different;
- the effect on pupils: 'the more appropriate the provision made for student teachers' learning, the more certain one can be that pupils will benefit' (Carney and Hagger, 1996, p. 113); and
- the impact in terms of professional benefits for teachers.

MENTORING OF NEWLY QUALIFIED TEACHERS

As Carney and Hagger (1996, p. 107) point out, despite similarities between students and NQTs 'student teachers are learners, and need support for their learning; NQTs . . . are teachers'. However, it is generally recognised that a mentor is valuable to an NQT and may be an important element of the induction process (NCE, 1993; Earley and Kinder, 1994). In a study of 13 NQTs in a range of schools, 'Mentoring was highly valued by new teachers and their mentors' (Bush *et al.*, 1996, p. 129). One of the NQTs elaborated:

> The benefit is that there is someone there who you can talk to: who has been at the school more than a couple of years; who hopefully can give you realistic guidelines as to what you might be achieving; who knows many of the pupils; who knows the school's strategies and routines. That clearly is helpful.
>
> (*Ibid.*, p. 127)

Benefits of mentoring reported by the NQTs relate to the purposes of induction, socialisation, the growth of competence and the understanding of the school culture:

- having a 'sounding board' who was an experienced member of staff, but who was non-judgmental;
- being offered guidance and reassurance;
- receiving constructive feedback on progress;
- the opportunity to be observed whilst teaching.

> (*Ibid.*)

The benefits of mentoring are experienced by mentors as well as those who are mentored. The mentors see it as an opportunity for professional development. The benefits included 'the opportunity to reflect on and question their own subconscious practice' (*ibid.*, p. 128); to learn about new developments from the NQTs; and to add to their range of professional skills, thus improving career prospects.

Earley and Kinder (1994, pp. 70–6) differentiate types of mentor activity associated with the induction of NQTs:

- Mentor as classroom support (generally found in primary schools, where the mentor acts as an additional teacher).
- Mentor as classroom analyst; the mentor observes and comments on NQT practice.
- Mentor as collaborative planner, where the mentor and NQT have joint curriculum planning sessions.
- Mentor as informationalist, an inevitable part of the work of most mentors.
- Mentor as welfare monitor, again an element of almost all relationships, but for some the relationship may come to no more than this.

The implications that emerge for the schools from these studies include the need for the recognition by senior management of the time that is involved in mentoring NQTs to ensure that mentoring is developmental as well as instrumental:

> I really do think that if the induction of NQTs is being done properly, it's

got to be timetabled. There's got to be time set aside which is yours with that particular person. That has got to be built in from the start and if it's not built in you end up with a situation where the thing has just drifted.

(Mentor, head of department, quoted in Bush *et al.*, 1996, p. 127)

Other problems included the lack of co-ordination within the schools, indicated above, and the difficulties of matching NQT to mentor, in particular, the potential difficulty of being mentored by a senior member of staff who may be somewhat unapproachable. The lack of time officially afforded to mentoring and the inconsistent practice revealed by the research may indicate that the induction and mentoring processes may be somewhat superficial and not fully embedded in professional development practice.

MENTORING HEADTEACHERS

Mentoring of principals in the USA and in Singapore predates any for-malised British experience. A review of research relating to mentoring of principals in the USA led Daresh and Playko (1992, p. 146) to conclude: 'We believe that the use of mentors to assist leaders is a powerful tool that may be used to bring about more effective practice in schools. Structured mentor programs are effective strategies to help individuals move into leadership roles more smoothly.'

In Britain, the School Management Task Force (DES, 1990) recommended the development of a programme of mentoring of new headteachers by experienced heads. In the absence of specific training for aspiring headteachers, mentoring was particularly important, and could be regarded as 'a substitute for training rather than forming part of it' (Bush, 1995, p. 3). In contrast to the in-service British programme, the mentoring of principals in Singapore and in the USA forms part of a preservice training programme and qualification (Bush, 1995). Thus the mentoring of aspiring principals in Singapore is identified chiefly as a learning process, whilst for British headteachers the main benefit is seen as the provision of a sounding board (Coleman *et al.*, 1996). The development of the Headteachers Leadership and Management Programme (Headlamp) and the National Professional Qualification for Headship (NPQH) in England and Wales, extends the concepts of training and learning for new headteachers and may involve a programme of mentoring, but need not necessarily do so.

An evaluation of the pilot scheme for mentoring new headteachers in England and Wales (Bolam *et al.*, 1995, p. 37) found that the benefits of mentoring were

- the opportunity to talk through problems;
- being able to reflect on what it means to be a headteacher;
- reducing the sense of isolation;
- obtaining another perspective;
- improving self-confidence.

The mentors also identified benefits from the process, including an opportunity for their own professional development. The research of Bush *et al.* (1996) endorsed the benefits for both mentor and mentee as well as pointing to the potential impact on the school. The initial focus of the mentoring process was clearly linked to personal qualities and issues, but later in the first year of headship, there was recognition of the impact on school management: 'Directly and indirectly he has had an impact on decisions made within the school. I had to be comfortable they were my decisions even though they were a product of joint discussion' (new head quoted in Bush *et al.*, *ibid.*, p. 137).

The mentoring of new headteachers or principals differs from the mentoring of other new recruits, since the socialisation and acculturation processes of the induction element relate to the role rather than the institution. The new headteacher, given the opportunity of regular meeting with a mentor, may then be able to use the mentoring process more extensively for reflection on both his or her role and the development of the school.

TRAINING FOR MENTORS

Training has been found to be important for the successful mentoring of new or aspiring principals. In Singapore, research on the learning of protégés concluded that 'For mentoring to be successful, both mentors and protégés should be prepared (Low, 1995, p. 25). Lessons learned from a review of mentoring schemes in the USA led to the conclusion that 'even when individuals want to serve as mentors and possess all the desirable characteristics of effective mentors, they still need additional training to carry out this important role' (Daresh and Playko, 1992, p. 149).

In England and Wales, the mentor qualities that were valued most by new headteachers were the ability to listen and personal qualities of openness and approachability (Bolam *et al.*, 1995; Coleman *et al.*, 1996). The headteacher mentors had benefited from training, as funding had been made available for the initial project. As a result there appeared to be a consistent view of the nature of mentoring amongst the trained mentor heads. However, training is not systematically available for mentors of NQTs or in ITE, which may account for the inconsistency in practice and understanding of the concept of mentoring. The desirability of mentor training is recognised in further education, where the demands on mentors are termed 'particularly severe' (Cantor *et al.*, 1995, p. 118). One area identified as important in training is the area of interpersonal skills, which appears to be the quality that counts most in mentoring in ITE. The survey of 150 secondary school ITE mentors found that this was true, even where the mentor was subject specific (Brooks, 1996).

Whilst admitting that some teachers may be naturally equipped with the skills of mentoring, Sampson and Yeomans (1994, p. 207) point out that we cannot rely on this stock of natural talent. In relation to mentors in primary schools involved in ITE, they suggest 'that there is a need for training which can build skills, knowledge and qualities which are additional to those needed for an effective teacher, but which may enhance teacher effectiveness'.

THE WHOLE-SCHOOL IMPACT OF MENTORING

Mentoring is typically regarded as part of the induction process for student teachers, NQTs and new entrants to a school or college, both experienced and inexperienced. It may also be used as a management strategy to bring about change within a school. Research on mentoring of middle managers (Bush *et al.*, 1996) identified two such examples. One was a primary school where mentoring was used with three team leaders following the decision not to appoint a deputy head. In the other, a secondary school, mentoring of middle management took place to encourage: 'the movement away from an hierarchical, dependency culture in which the headteacher was perceived as the sole arbiter to one of high levels of delegation of responsibility and the encouragement of interdependent working' (*ibid.*, p. 130).

The success of this mentoring was dependent on the strength of the interpersonal relationships, the availability of the mentor and the informality of the process. Mentoring, both formal and informal, can be very powerful in encouraging a climate of equal opportunities and in the professional development of women (see Chapter 9). There is potentially a very strong link between mentoring and staff development activity: 'mentoring offers [that] support by providing individuals with someone who can give feedback, question, share, discuss, challenge, confront and guide one through the learning cycle' (Kelly *et al.*, 1992, pp. 173–4). The reflection that is part of the 'learning stance' identified by Tickle (1994) is enhanced by the opportunity for discussion and critical feedback.

However, the encouragement of mentoring and induction implies the development of a whole-school policy relating to all staff, both teachers and associate staff, commitment within the school or college and the resulting application of resources. In such an institution 'a school-wide climate of mentoring must be established, so that mentoring becomes a general principle which is central to the operation of the school as a community, an activity which will be of benefit to all' (Wilkin, 1992, p. 21).

Glover and Mardle (1996, p. 94) refer to a whole-school approach to mentoring ITE students: 'The most successful training environment appears to be one where the senior staff of the school has developed a policy for associate [student] training as part of a total staff development policy, . . . and where the concept of the training school has become part of the culture.' The induction of new staff into a school or college is likely to have repercussions for the remainder of their career, certainly for their span within that institution.

Mentoring in association with induction, or as a means of bringing about change, is a powerful and effective tool, when sufficiently resourced. It is no surprise that the research undertaken by Earley and Kinder (1994) showed that good practice with regard to induction and mentoring is likely to be found in schools with a strong commitment to staff development.

REFERENCES

Bolam, R., McMahon, A., Pocklingon, K. and Weindling, D. (1995) Mentoring for new headteachers: recent British experience, *Journal of Educational Administration*, Vol. 33, No. 5, pp. 29–44.

Brooks, V. (1996) Mentoring: the interpersonal dimension, *Teacher Development*, February, pp. 5–10.

Bush, T. (1995) Mentoring for principals: pre-service and in-service models, *Singapore Journal of Education*, Vol. 15, No. 1, pp. 1–13.

Bush, T., Coleman, M., Wall, D. and West-Burnham, J. (1996) Mentoring and continuing professional development, in McIntyre, D. and Hagger, H. (eds) *Developing the Profession of Teaching*, London, David Fulton.

Campbell, A. and Kane, I. (1996) Mentoring and primary school culture, in McIntype, D. and Hagger, H. (eds) *Mentors in Schools: Developing the Profession of Teaching*, London, David Fulton.

Cantor, L., Roberts, I. and Pratley, B. (1995) *A Guide to Further Education in England and Wales*, London, Cassell.

Carney, S. and Hagger, H. (1996) Working with beginning teachers: the impact on schools, in McIntype, D. and Hagger, H. (eds) *Mentors in Schools: Developing the Profession of Teaching*, London, David Fulton.

Coleman, M., Low, G.T., Bush T. and Chew, J. (1996) Re-thinking training for principals: the role of mentoring, paper given at the AERA Conference, New York, April.

Daresh, J. and Playko, M. (1992) Mentoring for headteachers: a review of major issues, *School Organisation*, Vol. 12, No 2, pp. 145–152.

DES (1990) *Developing School Management: The Way Forward*, London, School Management Task Force/HMSO.

DfE (1993) *Initial Training of Primary School Teachers: New Criteria for Courses* (Circular 14/93), London, HMSO.

Earley, P. and Kinder, K. (1994) *Initiation Rights: Effective Induction Practices for New Teachers*, Windsor, NFER.

Elliott, B. and Calderhead, J. (1995) Mentoring for teacher developments: possibilities and caveats, in Kerry, T. and Shelton Mayes, A. (eds) *Issues in Mentoring*, London, Routledge.

Emerson, C. and Goddard, I. (1993) *Managing Staff in Schools*, Oxford, Heinemann Educational.

Gartside, P., Allan, J. and Munn, P. (1988) *In at the Deep End? Induction in Colleges of Further Education*, Edinburgh, SCRE.

Gilchrist, H. (1995) Recruitment and selection – the heart of the college, in Brain, G. (ed.) *Managing and Developing People*, Bristol, The Staff College.

Glover, D. and Mardle, G. (1996) Issues in the management of mentoring, in McIntyre, D. and Hagger, H. (eds) *Mentors in Schools: Developing the Profession of Teaching*, London, David Fulton.

Kelly, M., Beck, T. and ap Thomas, J. (1992) Mentoring as a staff development activity, in Wilkin, M. (ed.) *Mentoring in Schools*, London, Kogan Page.

Kram, K. (1983) Phases of the mentor relationship, *Academy of Management Journal*, Vol. 26, No. 4, pp. 608–25.

Low, G.T. (1995) Mentoring in Singapore: what and how do protégés learn? *International Studies in Educational Administration*, Vol. 23, No. 2, pp. 19–27.

Maynard, T. (1996) Mentoring subject knowledge in the primary school, in McIntyre, D. and Hagger, H. (eds) *Mentors in Schools: Developing the Profession of Teaching*, London, David Fulton.

Maynard, T. and Furlong, J. (1994) Teachers' expertise and models of mentoring, in McIntyre, D., Hagger, H. and Wilkin, M. (eds) *Perspectives on School-Based Teacher Education*, London, Kogan Page.

Mortimore, P. and Mortimore, J. (with Thomas, H.) (1994) *Managing Associate Staff: Innovation in Primary and Secondary Schools*, London, Paul Chapman.

National Commission on Education (1993) *Learning to Succeed: Report of the Paul Hamlyn Foundation*, London, Heinemann.

O'Neill, J., Middlewood, D. and Glover, D. (1994*) Managing Human Resources in Schools and Colleges*, Harlow, Longman.

Sampson, J. and Yeomans, R. (1994) Implications for primary school-based teacher education', in Yeomans, R. and Sampson, J. (eds) *Mentorship in the Primary School*, Lewes, Falmer Press.

Schein, E.H. (1978) *Career Dynamics*, New York, Addison-Wesley.

Smith, P. (1996) Mentoring in middle management, *Management in Education*, Vol. 10, No 1, pp. 10–11.

Tickle, L. (1994) *The Induction of New Teachers: Reflective Professional Practice*, London, Cassell.

Trethowan, D. and Smith, D. (1984) *Induction*, London, The Industrial Society.

Wilkin, M. (ed.) (1992) *Mentoring in Schools*, London, Kogan Page.

12

MANAGING APPRAISAL

David Middlewood

PURPOSES OF APPRAISAL

In the context of the effective managing of people, some form of feedback about performance is widely accepted as central both inside and outside education. If appraisal is seen in this light, then the way in which it is managed becomes fundamental to staff management in any organisation (Hunt, 1986; Fidler, 1992). The implementation of formal schemes of appraisal of performance in educational organisations is relatively recent; in the UK schemes were introduced in schools, further education and higher education in the late 1980s and have only been fully implemented in the early 1990s. This chapter is primarily focused upon appraisal in the UK, where, by 1996, major evaluations and reviews indicate significant shifts in appraisal management.

The purposes of appraisal relate both to improving individual performance and to greater organisational effectiveness, the latter ultimately being in the organisation's key purpose, i.e. pupil or student learning. Kedney and Saunders (1993, p. 5) point out that a college cannot be taken seriously which claims to 'have concerns for people and educational standards if it does not apply to itself a proper consideration of its performance. To do so must demand the setting of adequate benchmarks for staff.' In the national evaluation of the Teacher Appraisal Scheme, Barber *et al.* (1995, p. 61) concluded that appraisal contributes to eight of the eleven factors identified by Ofsted as characteristics of effective schools:

- enhancing *professional leadership*
- promoting *a shared vision and goals*
- increasing *the concentration on teaching and learning*
- establishing *explicit high expectations* of staff

- ensuring *positive reinforcement* through acknowledging the contributions of staff
- *monitoring progress* and the career development of staff
- providing opportunities to develop more *purposeful teaching*
- enhancing the sense of a school being *a learning organisation*.

DUAL FUNCTION OF APPRAISAL

The 'Aims of appraisal in England and Wales', set out in *The School Teacher Regulations* (1991), placed emphasis on recognition of achievement, career development, professional development, and where there were those 'having difficulty', providing 'guidance, counselling and training'. Only one of the six stated aims directly refers to school benefits: 'to improve the management of schools.'

At the heart of appraisal is a possible tension between its *developmental* purpose and its *evaluation* purpose (see Beer, 1986). The individual needs to be motivated personally to continue to improve through the process, and evaluation or assessment needs to occur so that the accountability of that individual to the organisation is ensured. Sheen (1995) argues that teachers as public servants must face scrutiny of 'differentiation of performance' (i.e. they must accept that appraisal will make it clear that some teachers perform better than others). He takes what may be described as the 'classic' personnel management view that 'Performance management is a process that starts with the setting of targets and provides for regular monitoring and coaching . . .' (*ibid.*, p. 13). However, several factors need to be taken into account in managing appraisal in education, not least the professional autonomy of teachers and lecturers, the confusion over what rewards or benefits accrue and the attribution of key 'results' (O'Neill *et al.*, 1994, p. 82).

These factors relate to the issue of whether teaching can be measured in quantifiable terms and thus be recorded in an objective way, or whether qualitative terms should be preferred, with the risk of accusations of a purely subjective assessment. It is interesting to note the movement, outside education, away from the purely quantifiable approach. Longenecker's (1989) study indicated the dangers of seeing appraisal merely as a 'tool', leading to longer-term effects such as cynicism and suspect data. Above all, the approach was subject to manager manipulation (see Figure 12.1). If a manager is able to view appraisal as a device merely to reinforce already-formed opinions about the worth of an employee, then it will be open to exploitation for the purposes that the manager may already have. For example, a manager might be tempted to 'transfer' or promote an employee to another department. The avoidance of the manipulation indicated here seems to be an argument for finding a balance between support for the individual and the hard-edged requirements of the organisation.

Eccles (1991) sees as essential the need for 'qualitative as well as

		INFLATED EVALUATIVE APPRAISAL	DEFLATED EVALUATIVE APPRAISAL
RATER'S MOTIVE	**POSITIVE**	• Keep an employee motivated • Avoid creating a permanent record that might damage the employee's career • Reward good recent performance • Assist an employee with a personal problem • Reward effort • Liking the subordinate personally	• Scare better performance out of an employee to prevent eventual termination • Build a stronger case against an employee who is destined to be terminated
	DEVIANT	• Avoid hanging dirty laundry in public • Make themselves look good • Avoid conflict/confrontation with a subordinate • Promote a problem employee up and out	• Punish an employee • Encourage an employee to quit • Minimise merit pay increase • Comply with an organisational edict

Figure 12.1 A typology of motives and manipulative rating behaviour
Source: Adapted from Longenecker and Ludwig, 1990

quantitative' data and describes this as 'radical rethinking' in the business world. In education, the emphasis prior to and during the introduction of statutory appraisal schemes was heavily upon growth and development (Day *et al.*, 1987; West-Burnham, 1993). Pennington (1993) stresses the need to reassure teachers of modern languages, for example, that appraisal is not 'assessment' although it does include the need for 'judgements' to be made.

THE INTRODUCTION AND IMPLEMENTATION OF APPRAISAL SCHEMES

Appraisal of teachers and lecturers is well established in schools, colleges and universities in the UK, USA, Canada and Australia, although other terms such as 'assessment' and 'review' are used. The emphases have been undoubtedly on the developmental aspects in the various schemes that have been in operation. Research established the need for professionals to feel ownership of the scheme for it to be likely to succeed (e.g. Montgomery and Hadfield, 1989; Fox, 1994; Smith, 1995). Montgomery and Hadfield (1989) were clear that a 'positive approach' was essential and established that the conditions necessary in a school where appraisal was likely to be introduced successfully included

- consensus of values;
- ethos of trust;
- positive self-image; and
- people open to learning.

Similarly, in appraisal in primary schools, the essence of the actual observation of teaching is 'to be supportive and constructive. Instead of a list of criticisms and negative comments . . .' (*ibid.*, p. 14). Research at Kingston Polytechnic, 1988–9, concluded that supportive appraisal '. . . increases motivation . . . can help identify and share expertise and enhance job satisfaction in situations where there are limited chances of promotion' (*ibid.*, p. 113).

The benefits of the developmental approach to appraisal seem clear from the various evaluations to date. Figure 12.2 links the components of actual

Benefit	Scheme's component
Recognition of individual achievement, leading to increased self-confidence	Collecting information
Opportunity to share ideas and issues through discussions with senior staff, leading to improved professional dialogue, communication and co-operation	Appraisal dialogue or interviews
Increased ability to think critically and reflectively about own practice	Experience and development in self-appraisal
Opportunity to improve actual practice and also communication and co-operation	Observation
Clarification of educational goals	Setting targets
Increase in motivation to improve performance	Agreed statement

Figure 12.2 Benefits of developmental appraisal and relationship to appraisal scheme's components

schemes of appraisal to these benefits. Although the equation is not as simplistic as this illustration, it is helpful to recognise that the components of any appraisal scheme, whether developmental or evaluative, are likely to be very similar to those shown above. Managers are also likely to agree that the benefits listed are desirable. The difference in outcomes therefore would seem likely to depend heavily upon *how* the schemes are managed.

At the introduction and implementation of appraisal schemes in England and Wales, the main threads of perceived effective management of appraisal were as follows:

1) A focus upon the growth and development of the *individual* teacher or lecturer. This development was to be supported through a process in which appraiser and appraisee operate as a professional partnership, driven by the appraisee's needs. This is shown through the *negotiated* focus for classroom observation, the *agreed* targets and agreed statement.

2) The accountability of the process was in most cases operated through the line management structure, with the person responsible for the performance of the appraisee carrying out the appraisal. Other models, such as peer appraisal, were hardly considered in higher education (Fox, 1994; Smith, 1995) and only in a minority of schools (Barber *et al.*, 1995). In two typical LEAs, the surveys found that 82 per cent of appraisals in Northamptonshire had been carried out on a line management basis (Middlewood *et al.*, 1995) and 70 per cent in Norfolk (Pennington, 1996).

3) The impact upon the organisation was seen as occurring through the aggregation of individual targets, leading to staff development policy which reflects identified needs and is incorporated into the institutional development plan. West-Burnham (1993), whilst supporting this principle, and offering a model for this (see Figure 12.3), points out that it can operate only under certain management conditions, including clear and public mission statements and development plans, clear needs and priorities for INSET and 'actual learning outcomes'.

4) To enable successful implementation of this model, a number of features of managing appraisal effectively on a whole-school or college basis have been identified, such as those listed below (adapted from Middlewood 1994):

   a) *Consistency of application* Whatever the actual form of appraisal (e.g. line manager, peer, etc.), it is important that appraisees are aware that all are being treated in a similar way. This means that resources (including time) should be distributed equitably, that venues are equally appropriate, that documentation is broadly similar, that procedures, such as note-taking, are agreed.

   b) *Objectivity of the process* Given that the process involves one person 'evaluating' another, some subjectivity is inevitable. However, the manager's task is to make the process as objective as possible, so

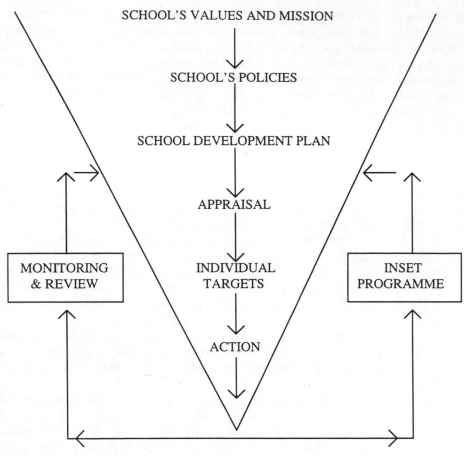

Figure 12.3　An appraisal scheme model
Source: West-Burnham, 1993, p. 21

that trust is developed, suspicions of personal bias are allayed and a
professional approach is assured.

c) *Process is as important as the outcome*　Only in a 'control model'
can the appraisal statement be viewed as the point of the whole
process. The learning involved in the sharing of appraiser and
appraisee experience will usually be one of the most significant
aspects of appraisal for the manager. Not all of this learning can be
acknowledged in the statement; indeed, some of the learning may
not be appreciated until later.

d) *Recognition that appraisal involves particular skills*　Understanding
the skills involved in appraisal clearly has implications for the
management of the selection and training of appraisers and the
allocation of appraisers to particular appraisees.

e) *Process is driven by the appraisee's needs* These needs may need to be elicited through negotiation and careful relating of them to school or college plans. Hence, the place of *self-appraisal* is fundamental to the success of this process.

f) *Maintain balance between confidentiality and sharing* Regulations require confidentiality of documentation, but appraisal cannot be fully 'private' because there needs to be a commitment to linking the appraisal learning and targets to the institution's development plans to which all staff contribute.

g) *Evaluation and review* Clearly, evaluation and reviewing the process is fundamental to the effectiveness of any managerial practice.

DEVELOPMENTS IN APPRAISAL MANAGEMENT

There is much evidence from the evaluations at national level (Barber *et al.*, 1995) and local level (Hopkins and West, 1994; Middlewood *et al.*, 1995) that all the elements from Middlewood (1994) remain relevant and therefore provide sound practical advice for those responsible for managing appraisal in education. However, experience, formal evaluations and changed circumstances suggest that appraisal in education will continue to evolve: 'Appraisal is at a crossroads; the enthusiasm generated in the first round of appraisals is beginning to wane' (Nixon, 1995, p. 14). Lessons have been learned from early implementation and the issues for managers of appraisal to take into account when developing their practice may be seen as follows.

The need to ensure a 'harder edge' to appraisal

A 'harder edge' to appraisal increases its evaluative and accountability aspects, whilst maintaining a developmental and supportive approach. Even at the commencement of formal appraisal schemes, writers such as Morris (1991, p. 168) pointed to the danger of a 'preciousness' about the process: 'the preciousness inheres in representing appraisal as totally non-threatening and (absurdly) non-judgmental.' Kedney and Saunders (1993) suggest that 'basing staff appraisal solely on the soft option of developmental outcomes is akin to regarding the appraisal process as the college equivalent of the confessional'! As Fidler (1995, p. 4) states, 'it is difficult to defend an appraisal scheme which leaves poor teachers untouched'. He goes on to describe as 'disingenuous' the notion that appraisal does not have an evaluative dimension, pointing out the lack of any alternative systematic procedure which checks on the performance of teachers. A review of evidence (TTA, 1996) emphasises the need for greater governor involvement, thus increasing accountability.

'Visible output' of organisations

The more public focus in the 1990s on the 'visible output' of educational organisations as a means of focusing on their accountability has continued to draw attention to the importance of the effective performance of *all* those who work in them, not merely academic staff. Interest in quality assurance schemes such as Investors In People (IIP) and BS ISO EN 9000 have reinforced the importance of staff other than academic employees and therefore the need for training and improvement. Mortimore *et al.*'s (1994) research on associate staff in primary and secondary schools found very few examples of formal appraisal of such staff but pointed out that 'if appraisal is seen as a right, the lack of it emphasises the status difference between teachers and other staff' (p. 190). Where a school, college or university is committed to valuing people and their performance equally, then management of appraisal must aim to include *all* employees. An example of a whole-school approach giving direct benefit is given by Rowan (1995, p. 7) when a mid-day assistant 'revealed a desire to develop her skills in the school office and now, following training, she is available to replace the school secretary should the need arise'.

Another group largely ignored, and potentially more difficult to include, especially in further education, is that of part-time staff. As the workforce of schools and colleges has become more fragmented, with more fixed-term contracts, supply contracts and part-time work, a significant number of employees are excluded at present, with the inevitable risk of their seeing appraisal of their contribution to student performance as irrelevant. The solution to this may lie in managing feedback on performance, not through any kind of formal system and certainly not a 'top-down' version, but in developing an appropriate culture for self-review and development. There are those such as Henry (1994) who see the notion of formal appraisal systems which focus on assessing individuals' performance as increasingly irrelevant; instead, culture is all important and this notion is all embracing, including part-time staff. In this context, it may be worth recalling that 'getting rid of appraisal' was in effect one of Deming's fourteen tenets of management, as he claimed that performance appraisal had 'devastated' western industry.

Appraisal incorporated into institutional planning

There is a need to incorporate appraisal of individual performance much more clearly into institutional development planning and staff development policies and programmes. Hopkins and West (1994, p. 13), in their evaluation of teacher and headteacher appraisal in Kent, found that 'in many schools there appeared to be no relationship between appraisal and wider school issues. Only in quite exceptional schools was appraisal having whole school impact as a result of the first cycle of appraisal'. Similarly, in Northamptonshire, the evaluators concluded that 'there appears to have been an extremely limited impact upon the formal management processes of development planning and staff development policies' (Middlewood *et al.*, 1995). It is interesting to note that the national evaluation placed much more emphasis on the perspectives of headteachers than did local ones. At the national level, there was a recognition of the need for an 'extra dimension' in order to relate appraisal to the school development plan (Barber *et al.*, 1995). The Northamptonshire survey offered an interesting insight into differing perspectives upon individual appraisal and its relationship to whole-school planning, through a divergence. Fifty per cent of the heads, deputies and appraisal co-ordinators said that appraisal had a positive impact upon the planning of staff development to a 'reasonable' or 'considerable' degree. On the other hand, 'virtually no' classroom teachers felt there had been any influence on such plans (Middlewood *et al.*, 1995, p. 13). This divergence may lead managers of appraisal to reflect on the 'ownership' factor, referred to earlier, with regard to the actuality of practice as opposed to rhetorical or written policies and plans. The Ofsted Chief Inspector's report of 1996 said that appraisal 'does not . . . often determine staff development policies' and 'Overall, appraisal has had little effect so far on the quality of teaching and it is unlikely to do so until it is focused more sharply on the essential features of the teacher's performance' (HMCI, 1996, p. 25).

However, as the national evaluation made clear, there was no clear linkage between appraisal and school inspection; indeed some schools suspended 'appraisal activity during the preparations for OFSTED inspection' (Barber *et al.*, 1995, p. 64)! One of the firm recommendations of this evaluation group was to examine links between the inspection framework and appraisal, particularly the link via school *self-review*.

EFFECTIVE APPRAISAL MANAGEMENT

In 1996, the Teacher Training Agency (TTA) and Ofsted jointly undertook a review of appraisal 'to help realise the potential of appraisal as a systematic means of improving teachers' practice' (TTA, 1996, p. 1), relating it to performance management and school improvement. Appraisal was seen in instrumental terms with a clear focus on individual and organisational performance. The scheme components which are specifically mentioned in the review are evidence collection, observation and target-setting. These have clear accountability aspects, and relate to some of the issues discussed above.

Hopkins and West (1994, p. 12) suggested in the evaluation of the Kent scheme that there was evidence of target-setting, for example, improving in the second and subsequent rounds of appraisal 'because the individual realises that he/she is in control'. It could be argued that this supports the arguments of those who suggest that the introduction of an appraisal scheme has its first impact upon attitudes and views in an organisation, and changes in practice occur subsequently. In one LEA, the impact upon the management cultures of schools was seen as 'considerable', with 'an increased emphasis on collegiality in school cultures, through sharing and openness' (Middlewood *et al.*, 1995, p. 13).

However, managers of schools, colleges and other organisations may well feel that the pressure for 'results' in education today does not allow what might be seen as a 'wait and hope' approach. For appraisal of any kind to be effective, in both its developmental and evaluative aspects, it needs to be *embedded* within the culture of the organisation. The establishment of this culture, within which performance is monitored and feedback given, remains perhaps the key task of senior managers. As Barber *et al.* (1995, p. 62) point out, 'from a management perspective, it is difficult to see how managers can have confidence that policies are being effectively put into practice without there being a culture which involves . . . observation and a sharing of . . . practice'. If appraisal also becomes perceived as 'the establishment of an entitlement', its relevance to the overall staff development policy and thereby institutional development plan becomes more readily accepted. Perhaps the third critical area is that of target-setting whereby the individual's aspirations and the goals of the organisation are combined and turned into practical objectives. 'While the other aspects of appraisal can contribute to an improved professional climate and raised morale, it is target-setting that decides whether it will lead to hard, practical action and therefore to school improvement' (*ibid.*, p. 62). This statement is equally applicable to all employees in all educational organisations.

Effective management of appraisal in education is therefore likely to involve setting the climate, establishing procedures, taking action, ensuring links with development plans, monitoring and evaluating appraisal.

Setting the climate

Organisations clearly already have a particular ethos. Are communications two-way? Is there an ethos of trust and respect? USA studies (e.g. Salaman, 1991) found that improvement will only occur when both trust and respect are present. Fidler (1995) offers an illustration of the relevance of this (see Figure 12.4).

If the organisational climate is less than ideal, then, as described earlier, the very experience of appraisal can open up communications, promote dialogue and develop openness. However, there are specific things that can be done. Pennington (1993, p. 4), for example, provides a helpful example of what can be done simply through ensuring that the terminology is appropriate for a particular organisation:

- Make sure that no-one ever refers to *assessment* – an exercise requiring

trust	no	does not admit difficulties but listens to advice	no improvement
	yes	improvement possible	admits difficulties but does not value advice
		yes	no
		respect	

Figure 12.4 Trust and respect in classroom monitoring
Source: Fidler, 1995, p. 3

measurement, and having too many connotations with assessment for grading or ranking to reflect the nature of appraisal . . .

- The professional discussion or conference is not an *interview*. The reciprocal nature of professional support as exemplified by the discussion and follow-up cannot be conveyed by people's concept of a one-way activity.
- Some people react anxiously to the use of the word *evidence* for the information gathered during the appraisal process. Even the word *data* can be a source of unease among those who have had no previous research experience.
- An agreed statement is what it says, not a *report*.
- Many people feel uncomfortable with the idea of targets. If objectives, goals or priorities are more helpful, use one of these instead. Action points are strategies or tasks which help the achievement of targets.

A second step, which many educational organisations have undertaken, is the establishment of a set of principles. This needs to be set out in a written statement, giving all appraisers and appraisees the knowledge that they have a point of mutual reference. Examples of what might be included in these principles are as follows:

1) A firm clarification of whether or not appraisal is linked in any way to determining pay, promotion or demotion. There is not sufficient space in this chapter to debate the whole issue of performance-related pay (PRP). For a fuller consideration, see Keith Foreman's chapter on managing performance. For a variety of reasons, including those listed earlier, it is particularly complex in a process such as education, and the views of Cracknell (1992, pp. 325–6) summarise the issues:

Linking pay to performance has the advantage of showing that the organisation really does recognise good performance and that it sees performance generally as important but it runs the risk of creating unnecessary tensions . . . PRP may be, for some organisations, a valuable step along the road to making PM [performance management] stick but it is by no means evident that it is a necessary step. That conclusion is relevant to appraisal systems in schools and colleges as well as in local government departments.

2) A commitment to equal opportunities. Some of the issues involved (gender, race, part-time workers) are addressed by Tony Bush (Chapter 1) and Marianne Coleman (Chapter 9). An intriguing example of gender issues in appraisal is noted by Wragg *et al.* (1996, p. 188) when finding that male–male observations pairs were more at ease than female–female pairs.

3) A commitment to appraisal for *everyone*, even if the form differs for individuals. Principals', headteachers' and chief education officers' appraisals differ in form from other employees' but the understanding that all are appraised is vital.

4) An assurance about the extent of confidentiality. How much will be shared? Who will have access to targets and statements? This principle is an important one for managers. Initial apprehensions about confidentiality were shown by evaluations to have been unfounded. However, a reluctance to share some aspects of the process has undoubtedly contributed to the failure of individual appraisals to improve staff development programmes. This is aptly shown in the comment of one Inset co-ordinator in a case-study school in Northamptonshire: 'It was difficult to plan for training when he was not privy to the individual targets' (Middlewood *et al.*, 1995, p. 15).

Establishing procedures for appraisal of all individuals and teams

One of the main issues of relevance here is the choice of appraisers. It can be argued that any educational organisation 'that does not use its management structure as the basis for appraisal relationships calls into question the role and functions of its so-called managers. If managers . . . are not responsible for the development of their colleagues then they could be seen as overpaid teachers and highly overpaid administrators' (West-Burnham, 1994, p. 29). Arguments for the appraiser being a line manager include:

the appraiser should:
a) be accountable for the appraisee's performance and hence have a direct interest in its improvement;
b) have a responsibility to ensure the appraisee's development;
c) have a wider view of school needs and possibilities and be able to help the appraisee prioritise conflicting demands on his or her time;
d) control resources which support and improve his or her performance;
e) be able to facilitate a change of job both within and between sections of the school.

(Fidler, 1995 p. 4)

An opposing view is that where appraisees select their own appraiser, they can be more than passive participants and are more likely to engage in a stimulating exchange of ideas and mutual learning. An example of this across three schools is described by Bennett *et al.* (1995, p. 16):

a primary, secondary and special school were involved in this experiment. Appraisees nominated members of staff whom they considered appropriate to act as their appraisers. The majority of the teachers involved were both appraisers and appraisees. Co-ordinators sensitively paired staff on the basis of their preferences; these preferences were found to have been made on the basis of respect, empathy and competence. As one participant observed:

the fact that we gave several names meant that there was nothing personal in the choices ... we were given diagrams of people who might be more helpful to us ... but you did have the opportunity to leave out someone who you saw ... that perhaps you weren't sympathetic with.

The question of who actually appraises remains therefore open. Relevant factors include practical ones such as the size of the organisation: 'There are small school issues of the perceived status of would-be appraisers, and of balancing the professional needs of colleagues to gain experience as appraisers with the demands of continuity and choice' (Middlewood *et al.*, 1995, p. 17). Some of the advantages and disadvantages of the two main forms are summarised in Figure 12.5.

Other models exist, such as upward appraisal, where employees appraise their own managers (e.g. Henry, 1994). However, line manager and peer appraisal undoubtedly predominate. Peer appraisal is seen as a 'softer' model in a review of evidence (TTA, 1996, p. 7, emphasis added), where 'structured discussion with the *line manager*' is seen as essential.

Other issues relating to the management of the actual procedures for appraisal include those of how confidentiality is to be managed, what documentation is required and which venues should be used for the appraisal interview.

Line management appraisal	Peer appraisal
• Ensures appraiser is better informed about the appraisee at interview • Keeps the process streamlined • May be seen as threatening • Line manager may not have experience of all the areas of work of the appraisee	• Appraiser could be someone with a proven expertise in an area of interest to the appraisee • Can be less threatening than observation by line manager • Can result in appraiser not having as good a picture of the appraisee when the interview takes place • Peer may not be in a position to facilitate any actions suggested by the appraisal

Figure 12.5 Advantages and disadvantages of forms of appraisal
Source: Adapted from Jones, 1993, p. 24

Taking action

Most research on appraisal before the introduction of schemes (e.g. Haslam *et al.*, 1993; Fox, 1994) concluded that it would be time-consuming and costly. Evaluation of appraisal in schools after the initial round of appraisal (Barber *et al.*, 1995; Middlewood *et al.*, 1995; Pennington, 1996; Wragg *et al.*, 1996) confirms fears about lack of resources and time available for second and subsequent appraisals. Since this research also indicated a fear that appraisal was slipping down the list of priorities, the issue of resources is significant. When resources, including time, are limited, those spent on appraisal will appear justified only if they are seen to bring tangible results. Managers therefore need to be aware of this critical issue since it affects attitudes towards appraisal and thereby its effectiveness.

Ensuring linkage with staff and organisational development plans

The critical area here is probably that of target-setting, identified by Barber *et al* (1995). The personal *ownership* of the targets is important – for the individual needs to regard them as an incentive to improvement; at the same time, the *sharing* of them is essential to enable overall planning and evaluation of organisational development to occur. Under the current regulations for teachers' targets in schools, governors have certain rights of access, yet the Northamptonshire survey showed nearly 40 per cent of schools where this had not been thought necessary or had been avoided. The national evaluation report firmly recommended that any future guidelines 'should set out clearly that the annex of an appraisal statement (i.e. targets) is not a confidential document and that those with a "need to know" should have access to it' (*ibid.*, p. 67).

What the national evaluation showed was that target-setting for a majority had not been accompanied either by action plans or success criteria, and in many cases no timetabling or prioritising (*ibid.*, p. 36). In addition to ensuring ownership and sharing of targets, therefore, managers need to ensure these tools for implementation of targets are routinely established.

Monitoring and evaluating the process and outcomes

Managing the monitoring and evaluation of the appraisal process is easier than evaluating the outcome. West-Burnham (1993, p. 76) suggests the purposes of process evaluation are

 – checking on the consistency of appraisees' experience
 – ensuring conformity to the (organisation's) strategy
 – identifying training needs (of managers and appraisers).

Evaluating the ultimate outcome of appraisal is obviously difficult, since its central aim is to improve the quality of learning in the educational organisation. Smith (1995, p. 203) noted that in general, in higher education for example, 'Researchers who examined the *introduction* of appraisal systems were, on the whole, more positive regarding its potential benefits than were those researchers who examined appraisal after periods of its operation'. It is possible that some of this difference relates to appraisees' disappointed expectations in terms of immediate benefits whereas, as Smith (*ibid.*) points out, appraisal of performance 'is intended to generate benefits many of which are of a long-term nature'.

The TTA review of appraisal in schools (1996) places emphasis on appraisal having an obvious and relatively short-term impact upon aspects of perfor-mance. Appraisal schemes can have, as evaluations show, some impact upon the incremental parts of a teacher's performance, e.g. improving a particular classroom skill. The research of Wragg *et al.* (1996, p. 188) found that, while over 70 per cent of teachers said they had derived personal benefit from appraisal, 'under half claimed they had actually changed their practice as a result of being appraised'. The report of Her Majesty's Chief Inspector of Schools states that appraisal is not sufficiently 'improving teachers' level of performance' (HMCI, 1996, p. 25). This comment and the context for the consequent review makes clear a perception of appraisal as being a means to visible improvement in classroom practice. If this actual regular interaction between teacher and student is seen as the 'transactional' element of teaching, there needs to be a recognition that education of people is essentially a more long-term 'transformational' process. It is clear also that impact of appraisal of performance of all those who work in educational organisations is certain to be more long term, indirect and difficult to assess. In other words, managing appraisal of performance has to be concerned with both the 'transactional'and the 'transformational' elements of organisational development and improve-ment. The integrating of appraisal, whether through a formal scheme or not, into a whole organisation approach to managing its people seems a prerequisite to its effectiveness in achieving both these elements.

REFERENCES

Barber, M., Evans, A, and Johnson, M. (1995) *An Evaluation of the National Scheme of School Teacher Appraisal*, London, DfEE.

Beer, M. (1986) Performance appraisal, in Lorsch, J.W. (ed.) *Handbook of Organiz-ational Behavior*, Englewood Cliffs, NJ, Prentice-Hall.

Bennett, H., Grunter, H. and Reed, S. (1995) Choose your own, *Management in Education*, Vol. 9, No. 4, pp. 15–16.

Cracknell, D. (1992) Experience of performance-related pay in an education department, in Fidler, B. and Cooper, R., op. cit.

Day, C., Johnston, D. and Whitaker, P. (1987) *Appraisal and Professional Develop-ment in Primary Schools*, Milton Keynes, Open University Press.

DfEE (1996) *Report of Her Majesty's Chief Inspector of Education*, London, DfEE.

Eccles, R. (1991) The performance measurement manifesto, in Holloway, J., Lewis, J.

and Mallory, G. (eds) *Performance Measurement and Evaluation*, Milton Keynes, Open University Press.

Fidler, B. (1995) Taking stock after the first round, *Management in Education*, Vol. 9. No. 4.

Fox, C. (1994) Management of the introduction of a staff appraisal scheme in HE, MBA dissertation, Leicester University.

Haslam, C., Bryman, A. and Webb, A. (1993) The impact of staff appraisal in universities, *Higher Education Management*, Vol. 5, No. 2, pp. 213–321.

Henry, T. (1994) Changing college culture, in Gorringe, R. and Toogood, P. (eds) *Changing the Culture of a College*, Bristol, The Staff College.

HMCI (1996) *The Appraisal of Teachers – a Report from the Office of Her Majesty's Chief Inspector of Schools*, London, Ofsted Publications.

Hopkins, D. and West, M. (1994) *Evaluation of Teacher and Head Teacher Appraisal*, Maidstone, Kent County Council.

Hunt, J. (1986) *Managing People at Work*, Maidenhead, McGraw-Hill.

Jones, J. (1993) *Appraisal and Staff Development in Schools*, London, David Fulton.

Kedney, B. and Saunders, B. (1993) *Coping with Incapability, Mendip Paper* 51, Bristol, The Staff College.

Longenecker, G. (1989) Truth or consequence: politics and performance appraisal, *Business Horizons*, December, pp. 1–7.

Longenecker, G. and Ludwig, D. (1990) Ethical dilemmas in performance appraisal revisited, in Holloway, J., Lewis, J. and Mallory, G. (1995) *Performance Measurement and Evaluation*, London, Sage.

Middlewood, D. (1994) *Managing Appraisal*, Leicester, University of Leicester.

Middlewood, D., Blount, J., Sharman, M. and Fay, C. (1995) *Evaluation of Teacher Appraisal in Northamptonshire*, Northampton, Northants County Council.

Montgomery, D. (1991) Positive appraisal: a critical review of ten years' work, *Management in Education*, Vol. 5, No. 3, pp. 41–5.

Montgomery, D. and Hadfield, N. (1989a) *Appraisal in Primary Schools*, London, Scholastic Press.

Montgomery, D. and Hadfield, N. (1989b) *Practical Teacher Appraisal*, London, Kogan Page.

Morris, B. (1991) Schoolteacher appraisal: reflections on recent history, *Educational Management and Administration*, Vol. 19, No. 13, pp. 166–71.

Mortimore, P. and Mortimore, J. (with Thomas, H.) (1994) *Managing Associate Staff*, London, Paul Chapman.

Nixon, J. (1995) Appraisal at the crossroads, *Management in Education*, Vol. 5, No. 3, pp. 41–45.

O'Neill, J., Middlewood, D. and Glover, D. (1994) *Managing Human Resources in Schools and Colleges*, Harlow, Longman.

Pennington, M. (1993) *Appraisal for Language Teachers*, London, Mary Glasgow.

Pennington, M. (1996) *Norfolk Appraisal 1991–1995*, Norwich, Norfolk County Council.

Rowan, D. (1995) The round of the year, *Management in Education*, Vol. 9, No. 4, pp. 7–10.

Salaman, L. (1991) *The Odyssey of Teacher Assessment*, Stanford, Stanford University.

Sheen, L. (1995) The new professionals, *Education*, Vol. 186, No. 24, p. 13.

Smith, R. (1995) Staff appraisal in higher education, *Higher Education*, Vol. 30, pp. 69–77.

TTA/Ofsted (1996) *Joint Review of Headteacher and Teacher Appraisal. Summary of Evidence*, London, TTA.

West-Burnham, J. (1993) *Appraisal Training Resource Manual*, Harlow, Longman.

West-Burnham, J. (1994) Appraisal as investment, *Education Today*, Vol. 44, pp. 1–5.

Wragg, E., Wikeley, F., Wragg, C. and Haynes, G. (1996) *Teacher Appraisal Observed*, London, Routledge.

13

MANAGING STAFF DEVELOPMENT

David Middlewood

INTRODUCTION

This chapter deals with the management of the development and training of all those who work in a school or college. It assumes a culture of development, therefore, which is *inclusive* rather than *exclusive*. The staff have development needs which may relate to various levels, the national, the institutional, the departmental or sectional as well as the individual. As schools and colleges have become responsible for their own resources, staff development policies and programmes are increasingly managed at the institutional level. In 1988, Hewton wrote that school-focused staff development would either be seen as 'a positive step towards greater professional autonomy' or 'as a management strategy to increase control and accountability' (Hewton, 1988, p. 142). In attempting effective management of staff development, inevitable tensions emerge, most notably between individual and organisational demands. For example, funding for staff development may be 'directed' to some extent into areas identified as national priorities. Managers of staff development need to be clear about the purposes of staff development, and the extent to which it can be used to sustain both institutional and individual development. For programmes to be effective in meeting purposes, managers need to understand what is involved in managing adults as learners, and to be able to plan and implement strategies and programmes. As with all effective management, there is a need to evaluate the outcomes of education and training to assess how they contribute to improving the performance of individuals *and* the organisation, for the benefit of the students.

STAFF DEVELOPMENT: IDENTIFYING AND PRIORITISING NEEDS

Managers should be able to articulate a concept of staff development, so that they are able to plan and implement programmes to meet the needs of their institution. As Jacky Lumby's chapter on the learning organisation emphasises, a school or college which neglects its adult learners will reduce its potential to be effective for the people who attend it.

One of the key factors in the management of staff development is identification of its aims and purposes. Woodward (1991) provides a useful review of research and literature related to managing staff development in further education. While her target audience is specific, important issues are raised that are applicable across phases. She refers to the report of the Association of Colleges of Further and Higher Education and the Association of Principals of Technical Institutions (1973, p. 2):

> The report put forward four aims for staff development:
>
> (1) to improve current performance and remedy existing weaknesses.
> (2) to prepare staff for changing duties and responsibilities and to encourage them to use new methods and techniques in their present posts.
> (3) to prepare teachers for advancement either in their own college or in the education service generally.
> (4) to enhance job satisfaction.

This view, which essentially proposes staff development as being for organisational improvement, is contrasted by Woodward (1991, p. 114) with what may be described as a 'partnership' approach, i.e. harmonising the needs of individuals and the organisation:

> Warren-Piper and Glatter (1977) view staff development as a 'systematic attempt to harmonise individuals' interests and wishes, and their carefully assessed requirements for furthering their careers with the forthcoming requirements of the organisation within which they work' (p. 26). Williams (1981) and Billing (1982) broaden out this partnership model: Williams by including pupils, ancillary staff and governors in the partnership, and Billing by pointing out that not only present but the future needs and objectives of all parties have to be satisfied.

These two views may be seen as a tension between those who see staff development as a means to an end, e.g. a changed teaching programme or a problem solved (Vaughan, 1983), and those who see it as 'sometimes being an end in itself in so far as it is a goal for managers and policymakers who are responsible for the development of the people in their charge as well as curricula' (Bradley, 1987, p. 191). Thus, from one perspective, the institution has a new situation to deal with so staff need to be trained to do this; from another, the training of staff is a necessary requirement for an institution so that people may develop whatever changes occur. In effect, individual development will lead to institutional development, whilst the improving conditions within a school or college will become the catalyst for further individual development.

This tension between individual and organisational development occurs because of the school's or college's need to improve performance and the recognition that the teacher or lecturer is at the centre of any improvement drive. The ability to identify needs which staff development must address is crucial to managers of staff development. Bush (1995) goes further by identifying four levels of need within larger organisations. He argues that a concentration solely on individual and institutional needs ignores the influence of 'subunits' (such as faculties, departments or divisions) and of groups in the external environment. The 'collective objectives' of these subunits, which are likely to be concerned with subject development, 'may or may not coalesce with individual needs' (Bush, 1995, p. 4). A simple illustration of this would be of a faculty, embracing separate subject disciplines, focusing upon development within one of these disciplines. Individual specialists in the other disciplines may feel their individual needs are being ignored at the expense of the whole faculty.

The influence of the external environment often relates to perceived needs at national level. In England and Wales, funds have been available for needs identified as priorities by national bodies. For example, following the introduction of the National Curriculum, training funds were 'targeted' at preparing teachers to teach the new schemes of work. Since these involved the actual daily work of teachers in schools, there could be little sense of ownership (Foreman, 1996). Another example involves the development of heads or principals. Schools may feel reluctant to commit resources to the training of headteachers; indeed headteachers may feel 'guilty' about spending scarce resources upon what staff may perceive as head's individual needs. The Teacher Training Agency (TTA) designated funds *specifically* for new headteachers which it saw as a means of enhancing quality management in school, through the Headteacher Leadership and Management Programme (Headlamp).

Even Bush's model of four levels may not exhaust the complexity of competing needs. The needs of support staff and of governors in schools and colleges have also to be met. Managers have to consider whether support staff should be seen as a 'subunit' or whether their needs are best met, in the interests of both individual support staff and the institution, through including, say, a science technician within the needs of a science department. Governors are not of course 'staff', but if they are to fulfil the role in the school's or college's development which institutional improvement requires, then their own training and development cannot be ignored. Esp (1991, p. 182) argues strongly that 'the pattern of training provided in the school for staff and governors will need to bring everyone along together as innovations are introduced and implemented'.

Any programme of staff development has to be devised in the context of attempting to meet the varying and sometimes conflicting needs within the institution. Whatever the programme, the effectiveness of its components depends, in part, upon the extent to which there is a recognition of those factors which affect the learning of adults. Southworth (1984) saw the whole process of staff development as essentially adult education and Wideen (1987, p. 5) is scornful of the notion that any changes in schools will occur through a view of staff development which assumes 'teachers and school principals can be manipulated through fiat and exhortation'. Managers need to have an understanding of:

1) what conditions facilitate effective adult learning; and
2) how particular training and development activities may be related to specific required outcomes.

CONDITIONS AFFECTING ADULT LEARNING

Whilst there are a range of theories about how learning occurs and while adults may require some of the same conceptual experiences as children (Kolb, 1993), the recognition of factors specific to adults is critical for managers of staff development (adapted from Brookfield, 1986):

- Adults learn when the goals and objectives are considered realistic and important.
- Adult learners need to see the results of their efforts and have accurate feedback.
- Learning a new skill, technique or concept, may produce anxiety and fear of external judgement.
- Adults come to the learning stage with a wide range of previous experience, knowledge, skills, interests and competence.
- Adults want to be involved in the selection of content, activities and assessment of INSET.
- Adults will resist learning situations which they believe to be an attack on their competence.
- Adults prefer to learn in an informal learning situation.
- Adult learning is enhanced by in-service activities that demonstrate respect, trust and concern for the learner.

The assumptions which managers may draw are as follows:

1) Adult learners need to have some measure of control over their experiences; this could include some choice of goals, resources or training method(s).
2) They possess a fund of experience and will wish to construct new learning (e.g. from training activities) around this experience. Adults who value their experience will not dismiss it just to accommodate new ideas (or at least they will not in *practice* although they may articulate dismissal). New learning will be measured against experience and there

may be conflict. As Taylor and Bishop (1994) point out, 'unlearning' is extremely difficult!

3) Nevertheless, capacity to learn is not restricted by age and is unimpaired by it (except through any physical decline).
4) Effective adult learning is most likely when relevance and short-term application are clear to the person concerned.

SPECIFIC ACTIVITIES AND THEIR RELATION TO REQUIRED OUTCOMES

Joyce and Showers (1980) claim that the outcomes of training can be classified into several levels of impact:

- *Awareness* – at the awareness level the importance of an area is realised and focus begins.
- *Conceptual underpinning* – concepts provide intellectual control over relevant content.
- *Principles and skills* – principles and skills are tools for action.
- *Application and problem-solving* – finally, the concepts, principles and skills are transferred to the classroom and into the teaching repertoire.

They also distinguish between five principal training methods (or 'components'):

- Presentation/description, e.g. by means of lecture/discussion.
- Modelling the new skills, e.g. by demonstration or video.
- Practising the new skills in simulated and controlled conditions, e.g. with peers or with small groups of students.
- Feedback on performance in simulated and/or real settings.
- Coaching/assistance on-the-job.

> If any of these components are left out, the impact of training will be weakened in the sense that fewer numbers of people will progress to the transfer level (which is the only level that has significant meaning for school improvement). The most effective training activities, then, will be those that combine theory, modelling, practice, feedback and coaching to application.
>
> (Joyce and Showers, 1980, p. 380)

Kinder *et al.* (1991) also found, in researching the impact of the in-service education of teachers (INSET) on actual classroom practice, that there was a 'hierarchy' of outcomes. Their typology of nine outcomes of INSET ranged from simply a recognition of the issue involved through to significant impact upon practice. 'Higher order' outcomes were seen as those which involved an emotional ownership by those receiving INSET. These outcomes were reflected in increased motivation and greater enthusiasm of the teacher. Enhanced knowledge and skills were also critical but substantial impact on practice was most likely to occur when these were linked through 'interdependency or knock-on' involvement with the emotional outcomes (*ibid.*, pp. 58–9). These findings have significance for managers of programmes since they suggest, as with Joyce and Showers, a link between the method and content of the activities.

Finally, there may need to be a recognition in the provision of programmes that the recipients will themselves reflect a range of learning *styles*, e.g. activist, reflector, theorist and pragmatist (Honey and Mumford, 1986). An activist type of learner may be an enthusiast for experimenting with new techniques and enjoy interactive experiences. Activities such as competitive team situations, role play and discussion are meaningful to the activist but lectures, research and theory are much less so. The theorist or logical learner may well operate in the opposite mode, disliking unstructured situations and preferring detail and planning, with discussion after reflection. The reflector prefers seeing the range of options and opportunities to observe or review but dislikes pressure to produce the solution. The pragmatist wants results, works well alone and prefers to solve problems in his or her own way; training therefore needs to have a clear purpose and be practical, preferably led by someone with practical experience.

Of course, people do not fall neatly into any one category but staff development managers must be aware that the *form* of any particular activity will be a significant factor for a number of the recipients, however sympathetic they are to the content. If the form is alien to a recipient, he or she may resist the content.

PLANNING STAFF DEVELOPMENT

Definitions of staff development stress its structured nature: 'a *planned* programme' (Oldroyd and Hall, 1991) and 'a *deliberate* and continuous process' (Billing, 1982). Gough and Hewett (1995) suggest that a staff development plan might consist of four sections:

1) Rationale: Why is it needed?
   What do we mean by staff development?
2) Guidelines (preparation): Needs identification.
   Matching of needs to provision.
3) Management: Implementing and monitoring the provision.
4) Evaluation: Why? What? Who? How?

An example of a rationale is as follows:

> In order that the pupils in this school are given the best possible opportunities to learn and develop, our staff – our most important resource – need to be well-motivated, up-to-date in their subject knowledge and educational thinking, and committed to the school mission.
>
> The management of this school, therefore, gives high priority to staff development, seeking – through this policy – to ensure that it is properly resourced and managed so as to meet the complementary needs of the individual and the school.
>
> (Gough and Hewett, 1995, p. 4)

Devising a staff development plan is crucial to the task of managing staff development. Priorities should be closely linked to the institutional development plan. A critical consideration is the allocation of financial resources. A model worked out by Ryan (1991), when a staff development co-ordinator in a primary school, is based upon the importance of staff development categories against collaboratively defined criteria. The model is hierarchical and allows for some degree of overlap between criteria. The prioritised hierarchy for allocation of staff development funds is as follows:

1) Does the development meet with the school/college development plan priorities?
2) Does the development meet with identified areas of professional development?
3) Does the development meet with perceived individual development?

Staff development funds are allocated if managers determine that the budget is sufficient to accommodate all areas. However, if funds are limited managers are required to prioritise in line with the published and agreed hierarchy; number one rates as the highest priority and number three the lowest. The relationship between the categories can be expressed in diagrammatic form (see Figure 13.1).

The planning of the programme needs to take account of the stages of career of each member of staff (e.g. induction, consolidation, new challenges, plateau, preparation for retirement) and also their career aspirations and perceptions of career. Bennet's (1985) research into the career perceptions of art teachers in secondary schools identified attitudes which are significant in determining which components of a programme might be

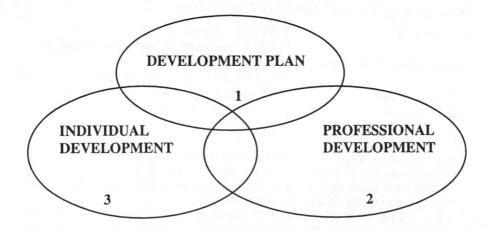

Figure 13.1   Priorities for staff development
Source: Ryan, 1991

offered. Career strategies identified by those involved in the research were subject/academic options or pastoral/administrative options. Within these options, subject hierarchies, with a clear distinction between academic and practical subjects, were seen to be significant factors in decision-making.

Definitions of career included an objective perspective that involved movement within a system, with increased status. Or alternatively a subjective notion which involved a person's own changing perspective. Three aspects to art teachers' careers were perceived as the low status of the subject, the subjective career orientations and attitudes of staff, and the nature of teacher training which emphasised the practical nature of the subject. Examples of art teachers' attitudes towards career development suggest an antipathy towards senior management posts:

> Art teachers don't want those sorts of jobs.
> It would restrict one's personality, one's social life, and would be an alien sort of life.
> The higher up you go, the greater the threat to your creativity.
> If the art teacher is worth his [or her] salt, he [or she] won't be interested in being a head or deputy. In my last school the head of art became the deputy head but that was only because he was a real smoothie and good talker.
>
> (Bennet, 1985, pp. 124–5)

Any provision of management-focused components of staff development would be received by people with these attitudes in a negative way, unless careful preparatory discussion occurred. A focus could be to attempt to change the teachers' perception of what management is or to change their attitudes towards their prospects of management posts or, of course, to omit this dimension from their own programme.

IMPLEMENTING AND MONITORING STAFF DEVELOPMENT

There are several different modes of staff development activities. Everard and Morris (1990, p. 92) highlight these as:

1. Counselling, coaching and consultancy
2. planned reading
3. self development
4. projects (eg. organising a school event)
5. change in responsibilities
6. sitting in on meetings
7. producing a research report
8. visits.

Oldroyd and Hall (1991) and Fidler and Cooper (1992) both stress the importance of monitoring staff development activities primarily to ensure that they are actually occurring, checking upon costs and identifying issues for the school or college as they arise. Fidler and Cooper, however, consider reviewing as an intrinsic part of formative evaluation, or monitoring, in which they include, *inter alia*, checking on satisfaction with the activity, suitability of the provider and the appropriateness of the design.

A model originated in the East Midlands project on Personal Development Planning (East Midlands Nine, 1992) can be used as a looser monitoring process. Since staff development should be seen as offering a balance of experiences, the model can be used, formally or informally, as an indicator of the extent to which a programme is meeting a range of needs (see Figure 13.2).

Since the institution must be concerned with supporting the development of the whole teacher (i.e. as a person, as a professional, as a teacher, as a member of the institution's community), all these opportunities should be available. Managers need to assess the balance between these opportunities. For example, there may be too much or too little emphasis in a current year's programme on those areas which only have immediate benefit to the institution. Any balance needs to be considered with reference to the proportion of resources (including time) allocated to each area.

EVALUATING STAFF DEVELOPMENT

Fidler and Cooper (1992, p. 361) describe the purpose of evaluation as 'to establish a correlation between the need, the activity and the outcome in terms of classroom and management practice' if we are to 'enhance teachers' capacities to manage the quality of learning'. Oldroyd and Hall (1991) suggest that summative evaluation – 'was the process and were the outcomes worth while and valuable?' – and review – 'should we change our assumptions, aims, priorities and approach?' – are the final two stages of an overall evaluation process. If the ultimate aim of staff development is to improve the quality of learning that takes place in the school or college, then its evaluation must be geared towards that, even allowing for the fact that some activities will be designed to have outcomes which may be more immediately reflected in teacher response (Kinder *et al.*, 1991). Middlewood (1996) suggests a hierarchy of the evaluation of the learning that may occur as a result of training/development activities. Evaluation of:.

1) reaction to learning event;
2) learning of trainees;
3) changes in trainee practice;
4) impact of these changes; and
5) impact upon the organisation.

The practical application of these stages could be expressed as a continuum of practice, ranging from the conventional immediate post-session

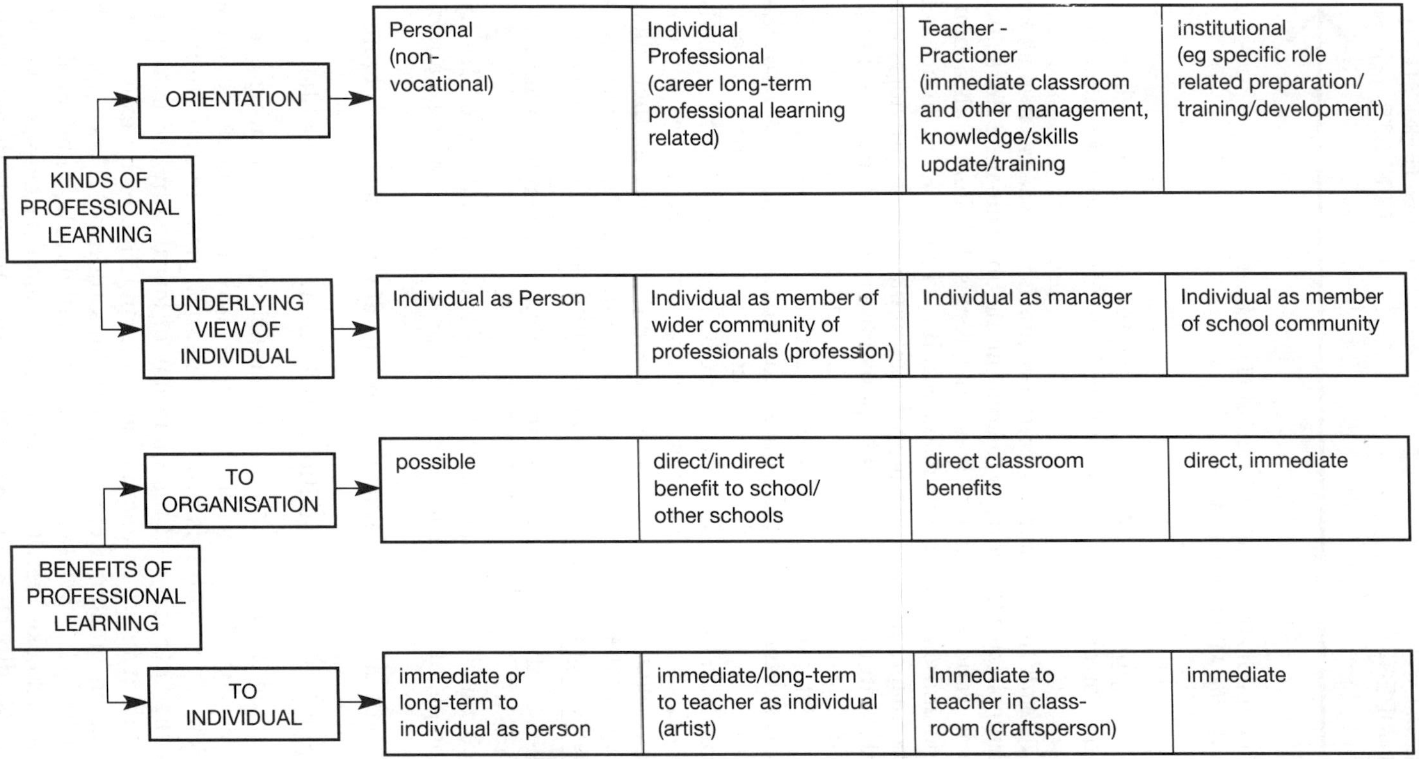

Figure 13.2 Kinds and benefits of planned learning opportunities
Source: Day *et al.*, 1993, p. 51, adapted from the Personal Development Planning project, East Midlands, Nine, 1992

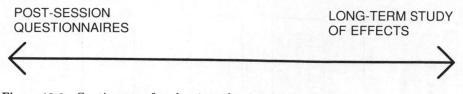

Figure 13.3   Continuum of evaluation of training practices
Source: Adapted from Middlewood, 1996

questionnaire ('happy hour' returns) to longitudinal studies related to the implications of changes for the institutional development plan (see Figure 13.3).

Evaluation of staff development is complex precisely because it is about people. The temptation, therefore, is to concentrate on evaluating the actual process. This is valid since it involves vital issues of client satisfaction, staff motivation and efficient use of resources. It also informs medium-term planning, since managers need to know, for example, which providers can or should be used in the future. Formal evaluation is not without cost but is necessary to provide a sound basis for improving and upgrading programmes.

Stake *et al.* (1987) argue that some goals for staff development may be hidden or even contradictory. They stress that the specific context of the programme is all important and this may limit the transferability of some evaluation tools from one context to another. Given the complexity of needs to be addressed, as discussed earlier, the evaluation questions for one 'subunit' (Bush, 1995) may not necessarily be appropriate for another. Stake *et al.* (1987) suggest that managers of staff development programmes should ask 'foreshadowing questions' as a means to planning the evaluations:

- With all the attention to change, is ample attention given to what needs to be preserved?
- Is there too much emphasis on staff development for those already qualified or persuaded and too little for those most needing help or persuasion?
- To what extent are there similar perceptions among teachers/lecturers as to changes needed?
- Will the opportunities for practitioner reflection/self-study be offered?

If staff development is planned as part of an institutional planning cycle, as suggested earlier, the manager's ultimate task is to evaluate on a timescale which aligns with this process. This may provide opportunities for evaluating the later stages of the hierarchy of learning by, for example, interviewing staff at intervals about changes in practice or by examining student work as an outcome related to previous training. This approach presupposes, above all, a *coherent* approach to staff development, enabling it to be regularly checked for its relation to the school or college's values or mission. As Griffin (1987, p. 32) pointed out, the staff development programme actually begins at the time of selection, because staff should be selected not just because they will be technically effective, 'but because it appears likely that they will interact positively with other colleagues and [this] is laying firm groundwork for effective staff development'.

DEVELOPING A CULTURE FOR EFFECTIVE STAFF DEVELOPMENT

However well structured and organised a staff development programme may be, its effectiveness will be limited unless it operates within a climate which enhances it. Hoyle and McCormick's (1976) model of extended professionality (see Figure 13.4) stresses the notion of collaboration and the limitations of the teacher in isolation.

A person operating under the restricted professionality mode is likely to focus upon teaching as essentially a craft, with an emphasis on practitioner

Restricted professionality	*Extended professionality*
Skills derived from experience	Skills derived from a mediation between experience and theory
Perspectives limited to the immediate in time and place	Perspective embracing the broader social context of education
Classroom events perceived in isolation	Classroom events perceived in relation to school policies and goals
Introspective with regard to methods	Methods compared with those of colleagues and with reports on practice
Value placed on autonomy	Value placed on professional collaboration
Limited involvement in non-teaching professional activities	High in involvement in non-teaching professional activities (esp. teachers' centres, subject associations, research)
Infrequent reading of professional literature	Regular reading of professional literature
Involvement in in-service work confined to practical courses	Involvement in in-service work considerable and includes courses of a theoretical nature
Teaching as an intuitive activity	Teaching as a rational activity

Figure 13.4 Restricted and extended professionality
Source: Hoyle and McCormick, 1976

skills. Predominantly, this person sees each individual lesson or session as separate and may do a reasonably competent job if one particular condition prevails – that things do not change. It is essentially a *maintenance* mode. Only the extended professionality mode is capable of enabling the practitioner to develop and respond to change, something which is critical in the world described by Tony Bush in Chapter 1.

As O'Neill (1994, p. 44) comments, 'a norm of extended professionality is more likely to promote development for individuals, and to rely on the very inter-team practice which is deemed essential for integration and development at whole school or college level'.

Nias *et al.* (1989) found that collaborative cultures were most effective in promoting genuine change, even where there was disagreement about specific plans or proposals. Where the conditions provided by the managers facilitate sharing, they should reinforce the integration of personal and institutional improvement, thus making it a two-way process. As Bradley (1987, p. 191) says: 'it will be an ineffectual institution which subordinates the former to the latter.'

Day *et al.* (1985) argue that development cannot be forced because it is the teacher who develops (active) and not the teacher who is developed (passive). The reliance of those responsible for development therefore should be on encouragement rather than authority and their role should be consultative. Unless there is teacher participation in decision-making and planning, only superficial change will occur. Hargreaves' model of cultures in educational institutions (Figure 13.5) reflects the issues for staff development.

An example of 'Balkanisation' would be subunits which are committed to their development as teams, use their resources on a shared basis within the team but are not interested in staff development which reflects the whole institution. 'Contrived collegiality' in this context refers to an institution where all the structures and mechanisms for whole institution staff development are in place, e.g. a staff development committee with representation from all areas, but there is no ownership by individuals of the training which is 'sent' to them. Only in a fully collaborative culture would the benefits of a staff development programme, as identified by Drucker (1988), be realised:

- Where development is holistic
- The organisation develops clear and explicit values.
- Development integrates theory and practice so as to inform action.
- There is a belief in the continuous improvement of the organisation, individuals, processes and outcomes.

Hargreaves (1994, pp. 180–3) adds a note of caution with regard to a culture of collaboration: 'Efforts to eliminate individualism should proceed cautiously, therefore, lest they also undermine individuality and the teacher's competence and effectiveness that goes with it . . . Vibrant

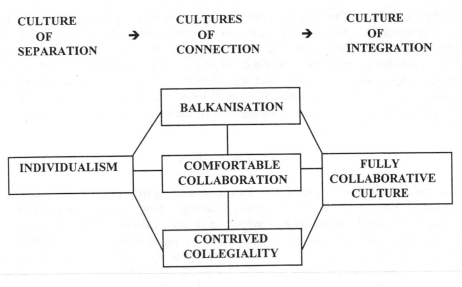

CULTURE OF SEPARATION ➔ CULTURES OF CONNECTION ➔ CULTURE OF INTEGRATION

BALKANISATION

INDIVIDUALISM

COMFORTABLE COLLABORATION

FULLY COLLABORATIVE CULTURE

CONTRIVED COLLEGIALITY

Figure 13.5
Source: Day *et al.*, 1993, p. 9) Adapted from Fullan and Hargreaves 1992

teacher cultures should be able to avoid the professional limitations of teacher individualism, while embracing the creative potential of teacher individuality.' The lesson for managers of staff development in developing an appropriate culture is that 'sharing' cannot be forced. As studies of effective schools in disadvantaged areas reveal, 'important as formal systems and pre-arranged meetings are in providing foundations . . ., it is the ongoing, informal personal relations among staff which provide the cement' (Maden and Hillman, 1996, p. 346). Thus, opportunities for collaborative developmental work may be critical such as observation of each other's teaching, teaching/lecturing each other's groups.

Hopkins *et al.* (1994) argue that classroom research is the key to school improvement while Fielding (1996, p. 11) claims that this should form part of a development culture:

> . . . the nurturing of a collaborative professional culture, the provision of staff-led workshops and focus groups to service the substantial classroom-focused action-research programme . . . small but important changes in organisational structure reflecting a commitment to teachers-as-researchers, the public articulation of a classroom-focused research culture, and the development of critical friendship pairings . . .

Critical friendships are also seen by Day (1996) as being at the heart of what he describes as 'developing critical communities'. He suggests that managers need to facilitate these by agreements ('written or at least explicit verbal contracts') and that personal development profiles should be designed to 'foster the development of teachers as whole persons throughout their careers . . . recognising that teachers are not technicians, but that teaching is bound up with their lives, their histories, the kind of persons they have been, and have become' (*ibid.*, p. 124). Perhaps a final word on climate would be to note that a common factor in schools succeeding 'against the odds' (NCE, 1996) is of staff being thanked and congratulated for particular achievements. Change and improvement *are* achievements!

CONCLUSION

The task of managers of staff development is to facilitate 'planned learning opportunities', whether by structured programmes, group research or a culture of development within which staff feel valued. This last is critical and difficult because of the complexity of individuals' perceptions. Bradley (1991) argues that learning takes place in a climate characterised by a consistency of philosophy, delegation and participation, searching for improvement, problem-solving, ideas and initiative, and trust; 'freedom to do it your way'. One theme of this chapter has been to explore factors that might aid the development of a 'stakeholding' institutional culture through the management of staff development. Central to this argument is the need for managers to have a clear understanding of how adults learn, reconceptualise and implement change. Staff development managed with inclusion in mind also has to resolve the tensions that can be apparent when considering individual, group and organisational perspectives. A resolution of this tension is a view of staff as stakeholders. Taking an individual or a collective stance is not the only option:

> My ideal, in terms of the traditional spectrum between collectivism and individualism, is different, forming the third point of a conceptual triangle:

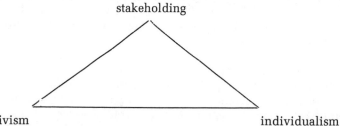

> This is different from, say, a classic compromise position . . . A stakeholder [institution] incorporates the social partnership and dialogue that you are trying to achieve.
>
> (Hutton, 1996, p. 305)

Stakeholding relies on an understanding of the individual. In the words of Woodward (1991, p. 120): '. . . we are essentially dealing with a very precious resource: people. Occasionally, amid the chaos and bustle we need to focus on this. FRAGILE – HANDLE WITH CARE labels are cheap to buy in any post office. The message, however, is priceless – think about it.'

REFERENCES

Association of Colleges of Further and Higher Education/Association of Principals of Technical Institutions (1973) *Staff Development in Further Education: report for joint working party 1973*, London.

Bennet, C. (1985) Paints, pots or promotion: art teachers' attitudes towards their careers, in Ball, S. and Goodson, I. (eds) *Teachers' Lives and Careers*, Lewes, Falmer Press.

Billing, D. (1982) *The Role of Staff Development*, Standing Conference on Educational Development Services in Polytechnics, SCEDSIP, *Occasional Paper 6*, Birmingham.

Bradley, H. (1987) Policy issues concerning staff development, in Wideen, M. and Andrews, I. (eds) *Staff Development for School Improvement*, Lewes, Falmer Press.

Bradley, H. (1991) *Staff Development*, Lewes, Falmer Press.

Brookfield, S. (1986) *Understanding and Facilitating Adult Learning*, Milton Keynes, Open University Press.

Bush, T. (1995) Developing management training in institutions, seminar for staff developers in polytechnics, Auckland, November.

Day, C. (1996) Leadership and professional development: developing reflective practice, in Busher, H. and Saran, R. (eds) *Managing Teachers as Professionals in Schools*, London, Kogan Page.

Day, C., Hall, C., Gammage, P. and Coles, M. (1993) *Leadership and Curriculum in the Primary School*, London, Paul Chapman.

Day, C., Johnston, D. and Whitaker, P. (1985) *Managing Primary Schools: A Professional Development Approach*, London, Paul Chapman.

Drucker, P. (1988) *Management*, London, Pan Books.

East Midlands Nine (1992) *Personal Development Planning in the Context of Whole School Management*, Nottingham, Nottingham University.

Esp, D. (1991) Staff Development, Local Management of Schools and Governors, in Bell, L. and Day, C. (eds) (1991) *Managing the Professional Development of Teachers*, Buckingham, Open University Press.

Everard, B. and Morris, G. (1990) *Effective School Management*, London, Paul Chapman.

Fidler, B. and Cooper, R. (1992) *Staff Appraisal and Staff Development in Schools and Colleges*, Harlow, Longman.

Fielding, M. (1996) Mapping change in schools: developing a new methodology, Paper presented at AERA annual conference, New York, April.

Foreman, K. (1996) Teacher professionality and the National Curriculum: management implications', in Busher, H. and Saran, R. (eds) *Managing Teachers as Professionals in Schools*, London, Kogan Page.

Fullan, M. and Hargreaves, A. (1992) *What's Worth Fighting For in Your School*, Buckingham, Open University Press.

Gough, B. and Hewett, K. (1995) *Staff Development Guidelines*, Camden, TRIN.

Griffin, G. (1987) The school in society: implications for staff development', in Wideen, M. and Andrews, I. (eds) *Staff Development for School Improvement*, Lewes, Falmer Press.

Hargreaves, A. (1994) *Changing Teachers, Changing Times*, London, Cassell.

Hewton, E. (1988) *School Focused Staff Development*, London, Falmer Press.

Honey, P. and Mumford, A. (1986) *The Manual of Learning Styles*, Maidenhead, Honey.

Hopkins, D., Ainscow, M. and West, M. (1994) *School Improvement in an Era of Change*, London, Cassell.

Hoyle, E. and McCormick, R. (1976) *Innovation and the Teacher*, Milton Keynes, Open University Press.

Hutton, W. (1996) The stakeholding society, in Marquand, D. and Seldon, B. (eds) *The Ideas that Shaped Post-War Britain*, London, Fontana Press.

Joyce, B. and Showers, B. (1980), Improving inservice training: the messages of research, *Educational Leadership*, Vol. 37, pp. 379–86.

Kinder, K., Harland, J. and Wootten, M. (1991) *The Impact of School Focused INSET on Classroom Practice*, Slough, NFER.

Kolb, D.A. (1993) The process of experiential learning, in Thorpe, M., Edwards, R. and Hanson, A. (eds) *Culture and Processes of Adult Learning*, London, Routledge.

Maden, M. and Hillman, J. (1996) Lessons in success, in National Commission of Education (ed.) *Success against the Odds*, London, Routledge.

Middlewood, D. (1996) *Hierarchy of Learning*, Supplement to Inset Evaluation – I, Northampton, Leicester University/Northamptonshire County Council.

National Commission on Education (1993) *Learning to Succeed*, London, Heineman.

Nias, J., Southworth, G. and Yeomans, R. (1989) *Staff Relationships in the Primary School*, London, Cassell.

Oldroyd, D. and Hall, V. (1991) *Managing Staff Development*, London, Paul Chapman.

O'Neill, J. (1994) Managing staff development, in Bush, T. and West-Burnham, J. (eds) *Principles of Educational Management*, Harlow, Longman.

Ryan, P. (1991) Teacher identity and its relationship to curriculum management in the context of the 1988 Education Act, unpublished MA dissertation, University of London.

Southworth, G. (1984) Development of Staff in Primary Schools, *British Journal of In-Service Education*, Vol. 10, No. 3, pp. 6–15.

Stake, R., Shapson, S. and Russell, L. (1987) Evaluation of staff development programs, in Wideen, M. and Andrews, I. (eds) *Staff Development for School Improvement*, Lewes, Falmer Press.

Taylor, D. and Bishop, S. (1994) *Ready Made Activities for Developing Your Staff*, London, Pitman.

Vaughan, J. (1983) Using research on teaching, schools and change to help staff development make a difference, *Journal of Staff Development*, Vol. 46, No. 1, pp. 7–23.

Warren-Piper, D. and Glatter, R. (1977) *The Changing University: A Report on Staff Development in Universities*, Windsor, NFER.

Wideen, M. (1987) Perspectives on staff development, in Wideen, M. and Andrews, I. (eds) *Staff Development for School Improvement*, Lewes, Falmer Press.

Williams, G. (1981) *Staff Development in Education*, Guidelines in Educational Management, *Series* 3, Sheffield, Pavic Publications.

Woodward, M. (1991) Staff development in further education, in Bell, L. and Day, C. (eds) *Managing the Professional Development of Teachers*, Milton Keynes, Open University Press.

14

MANAGING INDIVIDUAL PERFORMANCE

KEITH FOREMAN

INTRODUCTION

The challenge facing managers in educational organisations today is to reconcile concerns for the teacher as *professional* and the teacher as *person* with the increasing demands of the state for improved school and college performance. Growth targets, funding cuts, competition between institutions, prescribed curricula, performance-related funding formulae, detailed standards of performance and external evaluation drive management towards merit awards and penalties for failure. It is part of a paradigm shift from the paternalism and professionalism of the welfare state to a market, performance-driven model. It questions the notion that: 'incentives for effective performance are in the task or job itself or in the individual's relationship with members of the working team' (Vroom and Deci, 1989, p. 16), and suggests that organisational control is the means to improved performance.

Managers at every level – state, region, district, local authority, school, college – are under pressure to ensure that employee performance conforms with prescribed standards. These standards are not only applied to teachers and lecturers. Site managers, janitors, caretakers, cleaners, secretaries, registrars, bursars, caterers, technicians, librarians and all other support staff are faced with rising expectations of job performance.

This chapter focuses largely on teachers and the managers of teachers, and discusses three current issues related to the management of individuals:

• Assessing performance.

- Managing under-performance.
- Motivating performance.

Performance is here defined as 'the consistent ability to produce results over prolonged periods of time and in a variety of assignments' (Drucker, 1989, p. 156). It is important to note the emphasis on results or outcomes, a lengthy time frame and a range of tasks. Drucker, realistically, allows for failure: 'A performance record must include mistakes. It must include failures. It must reveal a person's limitations as well as strengths' (*ibid.*). But this is not a view which is universally accepted. Supporters of Total Quality Management (TQM) would argue: 'That "to err is human" becomes a universal let-out clause for poor performance. "Right first time" or "zero defects" are simply performance standards that fly in the face of conventional work practices that seem to have an anticipation of failure built into them' (Banks, 1992, p. 25).

ASSESSING PERFORMANCE: THE USE OF COMPETENCES AND STANDARDS FOR MANAGERS AND TEACHERS

The pressure of competition in the USA's industry and commerce gave rise in the late 1970s to a movement to develop competences based upon the leadership and management characteristics of managers who demonstrate *superior* performance. Work done there was developed and modified in the UK, though the emphasis was on the outcomes expected of managers performing at an *average* level. The motive, though, was identical: improved performance.

Competence-based approaches to performance management in education in England and Wales have their origins in the 1988 White Paper (DE, 1988, p. 156) which required 'recognised standards of competence, relevant to employment, drawn up by industry led organisations covering every sector and occupational group, and validated nationally'. The development of National Vocational Qualifications (NVQs) and the National Standards for Managers produced by the Management Charter Initiative (MCI) were a consequence. Competence was defined as 'the ability to perform in work roles or jobs to the standards required in employment' (National Council for Vocational Qualifications, 1989, p. 24).

The white paper gave rise to a number of initiatives to develop competences in educational management, some supported by the School Management Task Force (1990) which encouraged schools, LEAs and HE institutions to make management development in education a shared priority. Esp (1993) provides a useful summary of these pilot initiatives. They included assessment centres for practising and aspiring headteachers, and competence-based training and accreditation.

The most significant project was that of School Management South, a regional consortium of fourteen LEAs which analysed the *functions* of school management to create *standards* which define effective performance. School Management Standards, like MCI generic standards, were 'expressed as outcomes and *provide benchmarks or specifications against which school management performance can be assessed*' (Earley, 1993, p. 234, emphasis added). A process for the assessment and accreditation of performance using procedures for the collection of evidence (portfolios), mentors and assessors was also developed. Each School Management Standard was broken down into key purpose; key functions or roles; units of competence; elements of competence; performance criteria; and range statements.

The use of competences to measure the performance of senior managers in schools began in 1990 with the National Educational Assessment Centre (NEAC). It used twelve competences developed initially in the USA for secondary school principals (Green *et al.*, 1991). They are characteristic of *superior performers*. Assessors used a series of job-related exercises and interviews to grade clients' performance and identify needs. Follow-up development activities used trained mentors. Clients were initially experienced and aspirant headteachers, though processes have been developed for middle managers.

Lyons and Jirasinghe (1992) set up the Headteachers Assessment and Development Centre at the University of East London. The job of the headteacher was analysed to produce a list of managerial competences. The process involved self-assessment, centre-based exercises, interviews and assessors trained in psychometric testing.

Clients have responded warmly to these processes (see Esp, 1993, p. 46) but, in both cases the use of assessors has caused costs to be relatively high. Nevertheless, the idea of some form of assessment centre process which both measures performance and identifies needs for future development has gained ground. The framework for the National Professional Qualification for Headship (TTA, 1996) includes regional NPQH Assessment Centres.

Although regulations for the appraisal of teachers required them to be observed in the classroom, there were no prescribed competences as in, for example, the USA. Ofsted inspectors, however, used 'characteristics of good teaching' to judge classroom performance and then, from April 1996, began to grade teachers on the evidence of lessons observed. In 1996 the TTA made clear its intention to define standards of performance for experienced headteachers, middle managers in secondary schools, subject co-ordinators in primary schools and special needs co-ordinators. This topic is discussed in more detail in Chapter 13.

These developments raised a number of questions relating to competence-based performance assessment:

- The applicability and transferability of generic competences to individual contexts, circumstances and values.
- The apparent reduction of management, via behaviourist theories of learning, to long lists of elements or jobs. (Burgoyne (reported in Esp, 1993, p. 118) doubts the fit between competencies and management work which, in his judgement, creates and defines its own task. The same argument may be applied to teaching.)
- The place of individual needs assessment and how it can be done cost-effectively.
- The danger of focusing on an individual's weakness rather than the recognition and development of personal strengths, and the building of team strengths.
- The risk of concentration on trainable skills (i.e. functional competences) because of difficulties and doubts about developing 'high order' personal skills (e.g. forecasting, anticipating, creating change).
- Issues relating to the assessment and verification of evidence especially if accreditation is only obtainable through successful demonstration of a package of skills.
- The balance between functional and personal skills and abilities, and between them and knowledge and understanding.
- Uncertainties about differentiation between competences for managers and teachers at different levels of responsibility.
- The need for systematic review of competences in a period of rapid change.

The move towards competence-based assessment of managers and teachers is a feature of an international drive towards enhanced organisational performance in order to gain competitive advantage. But it raises a number of serious questions which have been highlighted above, not the least being the reliability and validity of the assessment instrument. It also raises the problem of how to handle underperformance, and it is to this topic which we now turn.

MANAGING UNDERPERFORMANCE

Underperformance of employees presents a challenge to every organisation and profession. Education is no exception. Bridges (1992, p. vii), reporting a visit to the People's Republic of China, stated that officials 'view teacher incompetence as a serious problem and estimate that there are three million such teachers in their country'. He also shows that American researchers estimate that at least 5 per cent of the teachers in USA public elementary and secondary schools are incompetent. This represents a figure of over 100,000 teachers with the total of students being taught (or 'short-changed') by them exceeding 2 million. However, as Fullan and Hargreaves (1992, p. 18) suggest:

If you open up classrooms to find excellence, you also risk exposing bad practice and incompetence. While this risk is real, the actual scale of the incompetence problem is smaller than the fears to which it gives rise. How many teachers do you think are irretrievably incompetent? It is likely no higher than 2 or 3 per cent.

The pressure for firm action

Responsibility for the employment of teachers and lecturers in England and Wales now lies with the governing bodies of schools and colleges. The pressure on them not to tolerate underperformance was demonstrated by HM Chief Inspector of Schools (Ofsted, 1995, p. 10, emphasis added) when he reported that

> Inspection . . . shows that the performance of a *small minority of teachers is consistently weak*. Such teachers damage the education of individual children and undermine the work of their colleagues. *The evidence is that it is rare for steps to be taken to resolve the problems they cause*. There appears to be an agreement in principle that *it is in nobody's interest for such teachers to remain in the profession*. That agreement must now be translated into *management action*.

The 'small minority' was identified as 15,000 failing teachers (about 4 per cent of the total teaching force). The new requirement was that, from April 1996, Ofsted inspectors would identify failing teachers as part of their four-yearly inspection procedure. The evidence of a minimum of two lessons graded 'poor' or 'very poor' would result in a confidential report to the headteacher based on:

* subject knowledge;
* expectation of pupils;
* classroom organisation;
* maintenance of discipline;
* marking effectiveness;
* the setting of homework;
* the use of time and resources; and
* the ability to plan.

Critics condemned both the basis of HMCI's calculation of the number involved and his methodology for dealing with the problem. The number of failing teachers was said to be based on the evidence of an incomplete sequence of Ofsted inspections, though the precise basis of the calculation was not published. The Director of Education for Northumberland (*The Times Educational Supplement*, 19 January 1996) wrote 'In medieval Europe it was witches. In late twentieth century Britain it looks like "failing" teachers. It is well known that highly centralised societies always need to seek out scapegoats for their weakness even if this now means professional expulsion rather than extermination'.

However, the union reactions to the new procedures (reported in *The Times Educational Supplement*, 22 March 1996) were more sympathetic. Nigel de Gruchy of the National Association of Schoolmasters/Union of Women Teachers is reported as saying that 'any head who did not know already that a teacher was good or bad should not be doing the job'. David Hart, General Secretary of the National Association of Headteachers said: 'I have absolutely no doubt that all heads will deal with this information in a thoroughly professional manner. There is absolutely no justification for suppressing such information.'

Managing the disciplinary process

The Education Reform Act 1988 required governing bodies in England and Wales to establish 'disciplinary rules and procedures' (Schedule 3, para. 6). Governors have the power to dismiss a teacher but arrangements must be made for an appeal against the decision. The role of senior management is to initiate action when the performance of a member of staff is causing concern.

Once action is initiated, managers must adhere closely to agreed procedures aimed at redeeming the identified failing. 'Both time and opportunity must be given for the staff member to respond to the disciplinary action. If they do respond, then any further progression up the disciplinary ladder stops. If they do not, then another rung is climbed' (Hume, 1990, p. 28) (Figure 14.1). Only in the case of gross misconduct may a member of staff be suspended, pending further investigation and allowing

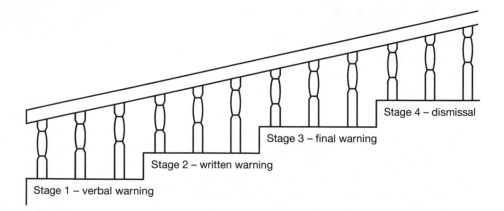

Figure 14.1   Steps on the disciplinary route
Source: adapted from Hume, 1990, p. 27

some reduction in the staging procedure. Appeals may be admitted at every stage.

Managers in FE must demonstrate that the main purpose of disciplinary action is to improve performance. The obligation on managers is to ensure that acceptable standards of behaviour or performance are made explicit. 'Setting expectations by personal example supported by an informal word in good time and on a consistent basis will form a foundation that will do much to set and raise standards. This, together with more formal advice and counselling will form the greater part of a college procedure' (Kedney and Saunders, 1993, p. 2).

It is difficult, but not impossible, to remove a teacher or lecturer from a permanent post on grounds of conduct or capability. *Conduct* usually refers to behaviour on (but sometimes outside) the job – drinking, drug-use, absenteeism, dishonesty and criminal activity. Dismissal on grounds of *incapability* (in the USA it is *incompetence*) is more complex and usually refers to work performance, the attitude of the member of staff, his or her ability or otherwise to sustain good working relations and his or her qualifications (Hume, 1990, p. 42). However, action is circumscribed by the existence of a legal framework which protects an employee against unfair dismissal. There are also severe constraints on governors and heads/principals: union involvement, the requirements of employment law and the practice of industrial tribunals. There is also the burden of *proof* where there are no clear standards of capability or unequivocal cut-off points. Bridges (1992, p. 4) states that, in the USA, 'incompetence is a concept without precise technical meaning' and that successful dismissal hangs on an administrator's ability to demonstrate incompetence to an impartial third party. The usual grounds are persistent failure in one or more of the following:

- To maintain discipline.
- To treat students properly.
- To impart subject-matter effectively.
- To accept guidance and advice from superiors.
- To demonstrate mastery of the subject-matter.
- To produce the intended or desired results in the classroom.

Because there are no clear-cut standards or yardsticks, supervisors need to collect numerous examples of shortcoming or demonstrate a pattern of failure. Methods of identification include (adapted from Bridges, 1992):

- supervisor ratings and observations;
- complaints from parents;
- complaints from other teachers;
- complaints from students; and
- poor test or examination results.

There are interesting comparisons to be made with the 1996 Ofsted criteria for the identification of the failing teacher.

In further education, Kedney and Saunders (1993) stress that the starting point for improving performance is the mission statement of the college which should set out basic values. Reference should be made to: 'quality, effectiveness, support for learning and caring . . . efficiency and setting high standards' (*ibid.*, p. 2). The authors recognise the difficulty of providing a precise definition of incapability or incompetence but suggest that the decision to take action must lie with senior managers. Failure to act against what staff and students regard as unacceptable standards is to neglect the interests of staff and students and may, in itself, be regarded as incompetence: 'Where competence is a serious concern . . . action should follow because incapability strikes at the heart of the contract of employment, whether *this is stated explicitly in writing or not*' (*ibid.*, p. 3, italics added).

The causes of incompetence

Bridges (1992, p. 10) found that unsatisfactory classroom performance may stem from three possible causes relating to the manager, the teacher and outside influences. He stresses their multifacetedness and their complexity.

Shortcomings of the manager
In his examination of the shortcomings of supervisors/managers, Bridges points to evidence from other professions, organisations and societies where the most common response to the problem of underperformance is to tolerate and protect. There is a general unwillingness to confront. The reasons were situational and personal resulting in double talk – a tendency to 'pussyfoot and equivocate'; inflated performance ratings; and 'escape hatches', e.g. transfer within or between schools, transfer to an administrative role, e.g. librarian, project officer (Bridges, 1992 pp. 19–48).

Shortcomings of the teacher
In seeking to define 'shortcomings', Kedney and Saunders (1993, p. 3) refer to wilful misbehaviour or misconduct – the failure to carry out simple administrative tasks or meet basic disciplinary rules: 'Poor time-keeping, incomplete registers, lax control of student work or the mishandling of cash or materials may be the preferred basis for management action, but may in reality be related to underlying incapability.' Ill-health or long-term absence may also be factors to be taken into account.

There may, of course, be personality factors which make some people difficult to work with and, as such, they are poor performers behaviourally. Fidler (1992) describes seven stereotypes, suggesting that such people have learned these behaviours, possibly unconsciously, as a means of

Hostiles	be assertive; do not show intimidation; deflect aggression; be ready to be friendly at the first opportunity
Complainers	adopt a problem-solving approach; listen attentively; acknowledge the complaint and then seek to reformulate it into a soluble problem
Silent and unresponsives	be prepared to listen attentively (even to silence!); ask helpful questions to try to get at the cause; adopt 'a quizzical, expectant expression'
Super-agreeable	try to get them to be honest; don't allow them to make unrealistic commitments; reassure; consider compromise; listen for hidden messages
Negativists	try positive and problem-solving approaches; look for solutions to issues which may then appear 'less dire than imagined'
Know-it-all experts	prepare your arguments in advance when dealing with bulldozers; counter those who seek admiration by presenting alternative points of view and facts
Indecisives	concentrate on the benefits of solutions to problems; follow up and support decisions; fix deadlines; don't allow postponement

Figure 14.2 Dealing with difficult people
Source: Adapted from Fidler, 1992, p. 297

manipulating others. He puts forward these 'coping' strategies (Figure 14.2) so that 'the business in hand can be accomplished' (*ibid.*, p. 298). The right-hand column relates to how management *might* respond to these stereotypes.

Outside influences

Job-related Jack Dunham (1992, p. 43) has highlighted the effects of the increasing pace of organisational and curricular changes in schools and colleges in England and Wales, resulting in major problems of role ambiguity and role conflict for staff:

'Some teachers are finding that the job they came into teaching to do is not the same job anymore . . . There are strong recommendations from Government, parents, school governors, media, industry and LEAs that the predominant values are those of market-place economics . . . Free-market competition between schools for pupils in an open enrolment situation is becoming more overt . . . These developments are anathema to teachers whose earlier experience was gained and enjoyed in a very different culture.

Reference has been made in the earlier chapter by Megan Crawford to problems of overcommitment, overload and burn-out.

Non job-related   For every manager dealing with underperformance there is a need to discover outside circumstances which may be a significant cause. Bridges (1992, p. 12), in his research on how Californian administrators dealt with incompetent teachers, reported that marital difficulties and financial problems 'were commonplace'. Several teachers had gone through arduous divorces. In some cases the data revealed that a teacher's problems preceded the decline in performance. In others, it was not clear if the problems, particularly marital, preceded or coincided with the difficulties at work. Perhaps, as he puts it, 'Problems at work and home fed on one another and created a downward spiral in both settings' (*ibid.*, p. 12).

What is clear from all the research data is that removing unsatisfactory, incompetent, underperforming or failing teachers is problematic in spite of the existence of legally binding conditions of service:

- Managers must work through governing or lay bodies which often lack essential knowledge and experience in handling such issues.
- Proof of misconduct is considerably easier than proof of incompetence.
- Managers may be inheriting the failure of predecessors to handle issues at an earlier, and probably easier, stage.
- Rapid changes in the management of schools and rising expectations from government and society – 'moving the goal posts' – have put some teachers under great occupational stress.
- The prime purpose in any disciplinary action must be improved performance with dismissal as the last resort.

It is, however, equally clear that 'a high concern for performance is as relevant to the health of service organisations as other organisations. It is essential that dealing with unsatisfactory performance . . . is perceived as a positive management action . . .' (O'Neill *et al.*, 1994, p. 87).

MOTIVATING PERFORMANCE

Everard and Morris (1990, p. 24) define 'motivation' as 'getting results through people' or 'getting the best out of people'. They prefer the second definition since 'the best which people can offer is not necessarily synonymous with the results which we might want from them though it should be in line with the overall goals and ethos of the school or college'.

Their analysis of the work of Maslow, Herzberg, McGregor and McClelland (*ibid.*, pp. 25–36) leads them to the conclusion that managers should remember that the prime motivators are people's need for achievement, recognition, responsibility, job interest, personal growth and advancement potential. They caution against jumping to conclusions about symptoms and causes which may be related to factors unconnected with work.

There are well tried techniques which may be used to encourage improved job performance. Stott and Walker (1992, p. 647) suggest that the main features of a delegated contract should be:

- a precisely defined task setting out what is expected;
- adequate resources to do the job;
- a clear statement of required outcomes;
- how success will be judged;
- how much time is allowed;
- the degree of authority delegated;
- how monitoring will be done.

Stott and Walker (*ibid.*, p. 428) use USA research evidence to list some common weaknesses of target-setting by managers leading to demotivation:

- targets set too low to challenge an individual's capabilities or too high to be reachable;
- targets reflecting an individual's perception of what the manager wants rather than what needs to be done;
- lack of clarity about who is responsible for what;
- unrealistic completion dates;
- lack of understanding as to why a target has been chosen;
- lack of specificity about outcomes;
- targets reflecting how to do something rather than what has to be done.

Fullan (1995, p. 9) argues for greater empowerment of teachers: 'New teacher roles, mentoring, curriculum leaders, staff developer, lead teacher . . . have been of great benefit to the individuals occupying the role.' With fewer opportunities for job advancement or promotion in schools and colleges a contentious issue is that of performance-related pay (in the USA the term 'merit pay' is used).

PERFORMANCE-RELATED OR MERIT PAY

The case for PRP in education was strongly stated by Tomlinson (1992). He argued (*ibid.*, p. 2) that PRP 'will give a clearer direction to schools, and will make them responsive and flexible enough to meet new challenges . . . Performance-related pay is part of a necessary change to school and college culture, if standards are to be raised significantly without a massive and possibly wasteful input of new resources'. He argues that the present pay system encourages teachers to leave the classroom and become administrators. Incentive pay would encourage them to stay. Target-setting and performance review would encourage superior performance and improve standards throughout the school. 'The present system of paying teachers for having a responsibility regardless of how successfully they carry it out . . . without evaluating whether it is leading to improved quality, and without any judgement as to the quality of performance is distinctly unprofessional, indeed arguably pretty amateurish' (*ibid.*, p. 206).

Central government support for merit or performance-related pay in public sector employments in the UK has been a feature of the 1990s. Its policy is two-fold:

- To move away from national pay scales for public employees.
- To encourage PRP in the public sector (teachers, NHS, police, civil service, etc.), in line with the aspirations underpinning the Citizen's Charter.

The 1995 School Teachers' Pay and Conditions of Employment circular (DfEE, 1995) provides guidance to employers/relevant bodies on the award of additional pay to teachers:

- *Recruitment and retention*: to teach subjects in which there is a shortage of teachers or 'in a post which is difficult to fill'.
- Teaching children with *special educational needs*.
- *Responsibilities*: 'The purpose of responsibility points is to reward teachers who undertake specified responsibilities beyond those common to the majority of teachers.'
- *Excellence*: 'up to 3 points may be awarded for excellent performance, having regard to all aspects of the teacher's professional duties but in particular to classroom teaching.'

Guidelines are also given for determining the salaries of headteachers and deputy headteachers. It is suggested that relevant bodies may use this framework:

- Setting at the outset of the school year the basis on which performance will be reviewed including *personal* and *school-based objectives*.
- *Reviewing progress towards objectives* during the school year taking account of any new factors which have arisen.
- Considering at the end of the school year *the performance achieved* over the year as a whole.

The review body proposed that the following *performance indicators* might be taken into account in setting objectives and considering headteachers' and deputy headteachers' performance in annual reviews:

- Examination/test results.
- Pupil attendance.
- Financial management.
- Where there has been an Ofsted inspection.
- Progress in implementing the proposed action plan.

Research into the impact of government policy was undertaken in Cambridgeshire among heads and chairs of governors of LEA and GM schools and representatives of unions/employers in 1995 by Curtis (*The Times Educational Supplement*, 19 January 1996). He reported:

> no significant use of local pay discretion;
> strong support for a national pay structure;
> schools were making much use of responsibility and SEN points and some use of recruitment/retention points;
> schools 'were not enthusiastically embracing points for excellence: only two teachers [in the sample] receive them'.

Salaries for heads and deputies, however, were affected by PRP – over 50 per cent of heads and 44.5 per cent of deputies had their salaries raised since 1991, though there were difficulties in measuring performance. He suggests that this mirrors other areas of employment where PRP is mainly confined to managers. The main reasons given for the limited use of PRP for teachers were inadequate funding, problems relating to criteria and opposition to the principle of PRP (Curtis, *ibid.*)

According to Simon Caulkin (*The Observer*, 12 December 1993), 'between half and two thirds of UK companies, and the vast majority of US firms use some form of individual performance pay'. Attempts have been made by the Department of Employment to introduce the principle into UK public sector organisations – NHS, local authorities, the police, the civil service as well as education. In every case there has been resistance. The opposition to PRP in education may be summarised thus as follows.

The historical legacy of 'payments by results'

The revised code of 1862 paid teachers according to the performance of children measured by attendance and performance on basic skills. The manifest unfairness of the scheme has become part of teacher folklore. The significant point is that performance payment, if introduced at all, must be related directly to teachers' personal efforts and to agreed criteria.

Lack of agreement about measures of performance and their assessment

Measures of superior or excellent performance in teaching are not universally agreed. Competence or classroom performance measures are intended for this purpose but there remains the problem of their appropriateness in all contexts, how the measures are taken and by whom. High grades awarded by Ofsted inspectors may be used by some teachers to argue for additional pay. Defining standards for use by schools is now a major element in the Teacher Training Agency's programme.

Lack of funding available to schools

Many governors in Cambridgeshire said that PRP would be acceptable if they had enough money to fund a scheme *or* if there were some form of specific grant. Most heads and governors felt that there would be opposition from teachers if only a tiny minority were rewarded bonuses, and that money used in this way could be more profitably used for 'books and materials'. A quarter of those responding wanted 'excellence' pay removed altogether.

Money is not a powerful motivator

Conventional wisdom is that money is a very powerful motivator. But both Maslow and Herzberg (Everard and Morris, 1990) came to the view that pay was a lower-order, or hygiene, factor. It was important and necessary, but it consistently rated well down the list of what mattered most to people at work. Overwhelmingly the important motivations were intrinsic to the work itself: achievement, recognition, job interest, responsibility, advancement. Dunham (1995), working with 164 teachers in 18 groups since 1987, confirmed these factors, though noting that there was considerable variety of response.

It is also suggested that extrinsic incentives may be demotivating in that such rewards are seen as controlling, manipulative and unsuitable for use in a service organisation. In a summary of the implications of PRP for schools and colleges, Fidler (1992, p. 314) concludes that 'without an earmarked budget for PRP . . . finding resources to implement PRP will be invidious'. He also suggests that a salary structure based on incremental scales is dysfunctional for cost-benefit purposes and questions whether it is sensible to try to graft on PRP 'bonus' payments to such a structure.

Finally, Cracknell (1992, p. 322), writing about the experience of PRP in local government, suggests ten requirements for organisations sympathetic to this approach:

- to be sure why PRP is being applied
- to be clear about every job in the organisation
- to get better at defining performance
- to defend stability in the organisation and continuity of purpose
- to continue to emphasise non-financial recognition
- to find a scheme which operates fairly and openly
- to minimise the diverse potential of PRP
- to maintain a strong staff development focus
- to communicate better and train more
- to see PRP in its wider context.

There is thus little current support for the views advanced by Tomlinson

(1992, p. 2). PRP does not appear to motivate and it can certainly damage organisational culture. Teachers react adversely to incentive measures which they see as inequitable, and dedicated funding is less likely to be set aside for this purpose as school and college budgets remain under pressure. But there seems little doubt that the impetus to measure individual performance and reward it accordingly will continue.

CONCLUSION

John Adair's model (Adair, 1983) of action-centred leadership argues that a leader must attach equal importance to achieving the task, building and maintaining the team and developing and motivating individuals (Figure 14.3).

Finding the balance between these three is elusive especially in a context in which there is external pressure for improved results. The task can then be seen as an over-riding aim. Whole staff development may be recognised as important but individuals may be neglected, their concerns given little attention during the course of an intensive school year. In the same way, an overconcentration on teamwork or collegiality may be counterproductive (*group-think* may be wrong) and lead to individuals being pushed aside and ignored.

There is also a danger in forgetting that if competence is one half of the equation, motivation is the other. While theories of motivation provide broad guidelines there is no substitute for finding time for one-to-one focused discussion with colleagues. In the end, it is the individuals'

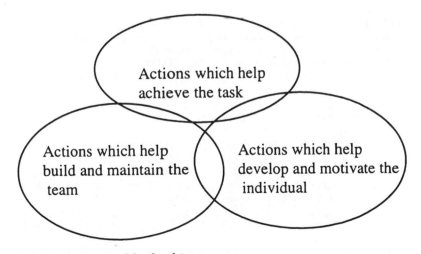

Figure 14.3   Action-centred leadership
Source: Adapted from Adair, 1983

perceptions of themselves and their organisation which managers need to try to understand.

Hunt (1992) describes the performance of an individual at work as a function of abilities, capacities, capabilities, experience, goals and values, energy or effort and rewards. He maintains that it is an individual's goals which are the most effective in predicting performance. It is as well to remember that teaching and managing are not just about being efficient, developing competences, having the required knowledge and mastering approved techniques. They are also about care, affection, creativity, feelings and emotions.

To get the best out of people in a rather hostile public sector climate may be to remember that participative theories of motivation suggest that collaborative systems provide opportunities for personal growth and improved performance and that 'the emphasis [must be] on creating conditions under which effective performance can be a goal rather than a means to the attainment of some other goal, and the philosophy is one of self-control or self-regulation rather than organisational control' (Vroom and Deci, 1989, p. 16).

This approach may provide the answer to the challenge facing educational managers posed at the beginning of this chapter: that of reconciling concerns for the teacher as *professional* and the teacher as *person* with the increasing demands of the state for improved school and college performance.

REFERENCES

Adair, J. (1983) *Effective Leadership*, London, Pan.

Banks, J. (1992) *The Essence of TQM*, Hemel Hempstead, Prentice-Hall.

Bridges, E.M. (1992) *The Incompetent Teacher. Managerial Responses*, Lewes, Falmer Press.

Cracknell, D. (1992) Experience of performance related pay in an education department, in Fidler, B. and Cooper, R. (eds) *Staff Appraisal and Staff Management in Schools and Colleges*, Harlow, Longman.

DE (1988) *Employment in the 1990s*, London, HMSO.

DfEE, (1995) *School Teachers' Pay and Conditions 1995* (Circular 5/95), London, DfEE.

Drucker, P.F. (1989) The spirit of performance, in Riches, C. and Morgan, C. (eds) *Human Resource Management in Education*, Milton Keynes, Open University Press.

Dunham, J. (1992) *Stress in Teaching*, London, Routledge.

Dunham, J. (1995) *Developing Effective School Management*, London, Routledge.

Earley, P. (1993) Developing Competence in Schools: a critique of standards-based approaches to management development, *Educational Management and Administration*, Vol. 21, No. 4, October, pp. 233–234.

Esp, D. (1993) *Competences for School Managers*, London, Kogan Page.

Everard, B. and Morris, G. (1990) *Effective School Management*, London, Paul Chapman.

Fidler, B. (1992) Performance related pay, in Fidler, B. and Cooper, R. (eds) *Staff Appraisal and Staff Management in Schools and Colleges*, Harlow, Longman.

Fullan, M. (1995) *Broadening the Concept of Teacher Leadership, New Directions*, Toronto, National Staff Development Council.

Fullan, M. and Hargreaves, A. (1992) *What's Worth Fighting For in Your School?* Milton Keynes, Open University Press.

Green, H., Holmes, G. and Shaw, M. (1991) *Assessment and Mentoring for Headship*, Oxford, Oxford Polytechnic.

Herzberg, F. (1966) *Work and the Nature of Man*, Cleveland, OH, World Publishing.

Hume, C. (1990) *Grievance and Discipline in Schools*, Harlow, Longman/AGIT.

Hunt, J.W. (1992) *Managing People at Work*, London, McGraw-Hill.

Kedney, B. and Saunders, B. (1993) *Coping with Incapability*, Bristol, The Staff College.

Lyons, G. and Jirasinghe, D. (1992) Headteacher assessment and development centres' *Educational Change and Development*, Vol. 13, No. 1, pp. 3–5.

Maslow, A.H. (1943) A theory of human motivation, *Psychological Review*, Vol. 50, pp. 370–96.

McClelland, D.C. (1961) *The Achieving Society*, Princeton, NJ, Van Nostrand.

McGregor, D. (1960) *The Human Side of Enterprise*, New York, McGraw-Hill.

National Council for Vocational Qualifications (1988) *The NVQ Criteria and Related Guidance*, London, NCVQ.

Ofsted, (1995) *The Annual Report of HM Chief Inspector of Schools (1995) Standards and Quality in Education, 1994–95*, London, HMSO.

O'Neill, J., Middlewood, D. and Glover, D. (1994) *Managing Human Resources in Schools and Colleges*, Harlow, Longman.

Stott, K. and Walker, A. (1992) *Making Management Work*, Singapore, Simon & Schuster.

Teacher Training Agency (1996) *The National Professional Qualification for Headship (NPQH)*, London, TTA.

Tomlinson, H. (ed.) (1992). *Performance Related Pay in Education*, London, Routledge.

Vroom, V.H. and Deci, E.L. (1989) *Management and Motivation, (selected readings)*, Harmondsworth, Penguin Books.

AUTHOR INDEX

Acker, S. 98, 107, 123, 128, 132
Adair, J. 80, 81, 217
Adams, J.S. 25
Adler, S., Laney, J. and Packer, M. 133
Alexander, R.J. 100
Al Khalifa, E. 72, 130, 134
Alimo-Metcalfe, B. 130
Anderson, R.A. 114
Argyris, C. 35, 37, 40
Argyris, C. and Schon, D.A. 32
Arkin, A. 58
Aspinwall, K. and Drummond, M. 128
Association of College of Further and Higher
    Education/Association of Colleges of Technical
    Institutions 187

Ball, L. 79, 83, 94, 145, 148
Ball, S. 76
Baltzell, C. and Dentler, R. 141
Banks, J. 204
Barber, M., Evans, A. and Johnson, M. 169–70, 173,
    175, 177, 178, 182
Bassey, M. 100
Beer, M. 170
Belbin, M. 73, 81, 145, 147
Bennet, C. 192, 193
Bennett, H., Grunter, H. and Reed, S. 180–1
Bennett, N. 54, 56, 65, 66, 71
Bennett, N., Andrae, J., Heggarty, P. and Wade, B.
    100
Bennis, W.G. 23
Berger, P. and Luckman, T. 61
Betts, P.W. 24
Billing, D. 187, 191
Black, H. and Wolf, A. 148
Bolam, R., McMahon, A., Pocklington, K. and
    Weindling, D. 55, 66, 79, 86, 88, 156, 164–5
Boud, D. 32
Boyatzis, R.E. 19
Bradley, H. 187, 198, 200
Brain, G. 69, 74
Bridges, E.M. 206, 209, 210, 212
Brierley, T. 141
Brookfield, S. 189
Brooks, V. 165
Brown, S. and McIntyre, D. 83, 85
Buchan, J. Pearson, R. and Pike, G. 143
Bush, T. 7, 45, 46, 47, 49, 50, 51–2, 55, 56, 58, 164,
    188, 196
Bush, T., Coleman, M. and Glover, D. 6, 10, 67, 156,
    159, 160, 161, 163–4, 165, 166
Busher, H. and Saran, R. 11
Butt, R., Raymond, D., McCue, G. and Yamagishi,
    L. 84–5

Caldwell, B. 83
Caldwell, B. and Spinks, J. 5, 6
Campbell, A. and Kane, I. 162
Campbell, R.J. 95, 107
Campbell, R. and St. J. Neill, S. 4, 11, 12, 13, 77,
    93, 100
Cantor, L., Robers, I. and Pratley, B. 161, 165
Carlson, R. 150
Carney, S. and Hagger, H. 162–3
Carter, R. and Kirkup, G. 127, 129
Carvel, J. and Macleod, D. 114
Cascio, W.F. 17
Caulkin, S. 215

Chadwick, V. 123
Clark, D. 31, 32
Clay, J., Cole, M. and George, R. 8, 9
Clement, M. and Staessens, K. 83–4
Coleman, M. 126, 127, 128, 129, 130, 131, 132
Coleman, M. and Bush, T. 76
Coleman, M., Low, G.T., Bush, T. and Chew, J.
    164, 165
Commission for Racial Equality 8
Convery, A. 83
Cook, R. 115, 120
Coopers and Lybrand Deloitte 97
Coulson, A. 55
Court, M. 83, 86
Cracknell, D. 179, 216
Crawford, M. 116
Cullen, D. and Luna, G. 129
Curtis, B. 215

Dalin, P. and Rolff, H.-G. 78
Daresh, J. and Playko, M. 164, 165
Darkin, L. 127
Day, C. 199–200
Day, C. Hall, C., Gammage, P. and Coles, M.
    195, 199
Day, C., Johnston, D. and Whitaker, P. 171, 198
Dearing, R. 5
Dennison, B. 20
Department of Education and Science (DES) 65,
    100, 108
Department of Employment (DE) 204
Department for Education (DfE) 125, 126, 159,
    162, 164
Department for Education and Employment (DfEE)
    57, 58, 108, 114, 124, 126, 177, 183
Dimmock, C. 83
Doe, B. 58
Donovan, B. 141
Drucker, P. 15, 16, 24, 139, 198, 204
Duffy, M. 108
Dunham, J. 113, 115, 121, 211–2, 216
Duthie, J.H. 109

Earley, P. 205
Earley, P. and Fletcher-Campbell, F. 64, 86
Earley, P. and Kinder, K. 156, 157, 158, 160,
    163, 167
East Midlands Nine 194
Eccles, R. 170
Elliott, B. and Calderhead, J. 162
Elliott, G. 68
Elliott, G. and Hall. V. 4, 10, 12, 20, 54
Emmerson, C. and Goddard, I. 159
Esp, D. 188, 204, 205, 206
Evans, L., Packwood, A., Neill, S.R. St. J. and
    Campbell, R.J. 93, 95, 105, 107, 110
Everard, B. and Morris, G. 33, 82, 193, 212, 216
Evetts, J. 47, 48, 49, 50, 51, 52, 56–7, 72, 111, 130,
    131, 132

Fagg, V. 143
Fidler, B. 143, 169, 175, 178, 179, 180, 210,
    211, 216
Fidler, B. and Cooper, R. 39, 193, 194
Field, M. 54
Fielding, M. 199
Fincham, D. 50, 51, 52
Fitzgibbon, C.T. 18

Forbes, R. 116

Foreman, K. 188
Fox, C. 172, 173, 182
Friedman, M. and Rosenman, R. 117
Frogatt, H. and Stamp, P. 118
Fullan, M. 104, 107, 213
Fullan, M. and Hargreaves, A. 199, 206–7
Funder, D.C. 150, 152
Further Education Development Agency (FEDA) 39
Further Education Unit (FEU) 85

Galloway, D., Panckhurst, F., Boswell, K., Boswell, C. and Green, K. 120
Galton, M. and Simon, B. 100
Gartside, P. 57–8
Gartside, P., Allan, J. and Munn, P. 156, 157, 158, 159
Gilchrist, H. 155
Gillborn, D. 87
Gilmore, D.C. 150
Glover, B. and Hewett, K. 191
Gold, A. 134
Goodyear, R. 109
Grace, G. 66, 68, 72, 76
Grant, R. 130
Gray, H. 46
Graystone, J. 15
Green, H. 148, 149
Green, H., Holmes, G. and Shaw, M. 205
Greenberg, S.F. 116
Greenberg, S.F. and Valletutti, P.J. 117
Griffin, G. 196–7
Gronn, P. 23
Gump, P.V. 101

Hackett, P. 150
Hall, V. 23, 66, 68, 71, 72, 73
Hall, V., Cromey-Hawke, N. and Oldroyd, D. 70
Hall, V., Mackay, H. and Morgan, C. 64, 66
Hammond, V. 133
Handy, C. 3, 33, 57, 70
Hargreaves, A. 62, 67, 94, 198–9
Harling, P. 49
Harris, I.M. 70
Harrison, B., Dobell, T. and Higgins, C. 79
Haslam, C., Bryman, A. and Webb, A. 182
HEADLAMP 149, 188
Health and Safety Commission 115
Hebb, D. 115
Helps, R. 55
Henry, T. 36, 38, 40, 176, 181
Her Majesty's Inspectorate 41
Hersey, P. and Blanchard, K. 24
Herzberg, F. 24, 213
Hewitt, P. and Crawford, M. 115
Hewton, E. 186
Hill, T. 139, 142, 147, 150
Hilsom, S. and Cane, B.S. 94, 96, 97, 98
Hilsum, S. and Strong, C. 94, 97, 98
Hinds, T. 144–5, 147
Hinton, P.R. 150, 152
Holbeche, L. 57, 58
Honey, P. 37, 38
Honey, P. and Mumford, A. 191
Hopkins, D. and Ainscow, M. 77
Hopkins, D. and West, M. 175, 176–7
Hopkins, D., Ainscow, M. and West, M. 199
Hosking, D.M. 23
Hoyle, E. 63, 98, 106
Hoyle, E. and Jones, K. 16, 22
Hoyle, E. and McCormick, R. 197
Hughes, J. 115
Hume, C. 208, 209

Hunt, J. 146, 169, 218
Hutton, W. 200

Inner London Education Authority (ILEA) 101
International Labour Office (ILO) 106

Janes, F., Gartside, P., Havad, B. and Kershaw, N. 45, 49, 53
Jenkins, H. 82
Jirasinghe, D. and Lyons, G. 64, 66, 149
Johnston, J. and Pickergill, S. 49, 50, 56
Joiner, D.A. 148
Jones, J. 181
Jones, A.M. and Hendry, C. 31, 33, 34
Joyce, B. and Showers, B. 190, 191

Keddy, N. 98
Kedney, B. and Brownlow, S. 10
Kedney, B. and Saunders, B. 169, 175, 209, 210
Kelly, M.J. 117
Kelly, M., Beck, T. and ap Thomas, J. 166
Kenny, D. and Albright, L. 150
Kinder, K., Harland, J. and Wootten, M. 190–1, 194
Knight, B. 78–9, 94
Kolb, D.A. 189
Kram, K. 160
Kydd, L. 16
Kyriacou, C. and Sutcliffe, J. 115

Laswell, H.D. 27
Launchberry, E. 67
Law, S. and Glover, D. 22
Lewis, S. 132
Levacic, R. 5, 10
Locke, E.A. and Latham, G.P. 25
Lofthouse, M. 4
Longenecker, G. 170
Longenecker, G. and Ludwig, D. 171
Lortie, D. 83, 99
Low, G.T. 165
Lowe, B. 97
Lumby, J. 53, 54
Lyons, G. 62
Lyons, G. and Jirasinghe, D. 205
Lyons, G., Jirasinghe, D., Ewers, C. and Edwards, S. 148, 149

Maden, M. and Hillman, J. 199
Maslow, A. 24, 213
McBurney, E. and Hough, J. 127
McCleary, L. and Ogawa, R. 148
McClelland, D.C. 213
McGregor, D. 24, 29, 213
McKellar, B. 127
McMullan, H. 125
Management Charter Initiative (MCI) 18, 19, 204
Marshall, J. 70
Matthews, E. 130
Maynard, T. 162
Maynard, T. and Furlong, J. 161–2
Meyer, J.W. 142
Meyer, J.W., Kamens, D.H. and Benavot, A. 100
Middlewood, D. 141, 146, 149, 173, 175, 177, 178, 180, 181, 182, 194, 196
Morgan, C. 141, 142
Morgan, C., Hall, V. and Mackay, A. 64, 130–150
Morgan, G. 38, 41, 148
Morris, B. 175
Mortimore, P. and Mortimore, J. 9
Mortimore, P. and Mortimore, J. (with Thomas, H.) 68, 116, 132, 143, 159, 176
Mortimore, P., Mortimore, J., Thomas, H. and Cairns, R. 9, 10
Mortimore, P., Sammons, P., Stoll, L., Lewis, D. and Ecob, R. 38

Mortimore, P., Sammons, P., Stoll, L., Ecob, R. and Taggart, B. 77
Moss, P. 124, 132, 133
Mullins, L. 46, 57

NAS/UWT 97
National Commission on Eduation 143, 163, 200
National Curriculum Council 100
NEAC 205
Neale, S. and Mindel, G. 110
Neider, L. 25
New Zealand Educational Institute/Te Riv Roa 77
Nias, J. 83, 99
Nias, J., Southworth, G. and Yeomans, R. 85, 109, 198
Nixon, J. 175
Norris, K. 139, 147, 150, 151

OECD 104, 106–7, 110
Ofsted 18, 100, 109, 110, 207
Oldroyd, D. 73
Oldroyd, D. and Hall, V. 26, 191, 193, 194
Oldroyd, D., Elsner, D. and Postner, C. 17
O'Neill, J. 5, 45, 46, 49, 50, 51, 52, 143, 198
O'Neill, J., Middlewood, D. and Glover, D. 7, 10, 12, 18, 145, 156, 170, 212
Osborn, M. 109
Ouston, J. 148

Packwood, T. 48
Paechter, C. 81, 86
Parker-Jenkins, M. 145–6
Pedlar, M. 32
Pedlar, M. and Boydell, T. 73
Pennington, M. 171, 178–9, 182
Phelps, L. 118
Pollard, A. and Tann, S. 19
Poppleton, P. and Riseborough, G. 99
POST 141, 148
Poster, C. and Poster, D. 26
Preston, D. 20
Purvis, J. and Dennison, W. 55

Ralph, M. 36–7
Rasberry, R.W. and Lemoine, L.F. 27
Rees, F. 117
Revens, R.W. 31, 32
Ribbins, P. and Marland, M. 66
Riches, C. 12, 13, 24, 26, 150
Riches, C. and Morgan, C. 22
Roach, M. 127
Rogers, L. and Badham, L. 18, 20
Ronan, W.W. and Prien, E.P. 17
Rowan, D. 176
Ryan, P. 192

Salaman, L. 178
Salaman, G. and Thompson, K. 150
Sallis, J. 67
Sammons, P., Hillman, J. and Mortimore, P. 32, 38, 41
Sampson, J. and Yeomans, R. 166
Schein, E.H. 35, 79, 156–7
Schon, D. 34
SCAA 101, 110
Schick-Case, S. 134
Schmuck, P.A. 126, 129, 133
School Management South 205
School Management Task Force 64–5
School Teachers' Review Body 97
Selye, H. 115, 116, 121
Senge, P. 33, 35, 41
Shakeshaft, C. 129, 130, 134
Sheen, L. 170
Silverman, D. 61
Sinclair, A. 77

Singh, R. 8
Smilansky, J. 114
Smith, P. 156
Smith, R. 172, 173, 183
Smith, T. 48, 57
Southworth, G. 33, 34, 35, 38–9, 40, 141, 142, 147, 189
Spence, B.V. 66
Stake, R., Shapson, S. and Russell, L. 196
Steers, R.M. and Porter, L.W. 25
Stephenson, T. 78, 79
Stewart, D. and Prebble, T. 85
Stott, K. and Walker, A. 213

Tann, J. 39, 40
Tansley, P. 76
Taylor, D. and Bishop, S. 190
Taylor, F. and Hemmingway, J. 144
Thomas, N. 109
Tibble, K. 89
Tickle, L. 157–8, 161, 166
Tizard, B., Blatchford, P., Burke, J., Farquhar, C. and Plewis, I. 100
Thody, A. 67, 71
Todd, M. 53
Toffler, A. 62, 73
Tofte, B. 27
Tomlinson, H. 13, 213, 214, 216–7
Thompson, M. 134
Torrington, D. and Weightman, J. 12, 13, 107–8
Trethowan, D. and Smith, D. 156, 159
Truch, S. 114
TTA 149, 175, 177, 181, 183, 188, 205, 215
Tuckman, B. 80
Turner, C. 38, 53
Turner, R. 63, 69

Universities' Statistical Record 126

Van Halen, B. 142, 146, 147
Vaughan, J. 187
Veniga, R.L. and Spradley, J.P. 120
Vroom, V.H. and Deci, E.L. 203, 218

Walker, A. and Stott, K. 76
Wallace, M. 48–9, 56
Wallace, M. and Hall, V. 9, 66, 68, 70–1, 72, 79, 82, 85, 86, 87
Ward, L. 127
Waring, S. 131
Warner, D. and Crosthwaite, E. 67
Warren, E. and Towl, C. 113
Warren-Piper, D. and Glatter, R. 187
Watts, M. and Cooper, S. 114, 116, 117
Webb, R. and Vulliamy, G. 65, 71
Webster, P. 120–1
Weightman, J. 125
Weindling, D. and Earley, P. 127, 131
West, P. 35
West-Burnham, J. 28, 32, 83, 171, 174, 180, 182
Whalley, C. and Watkins, C. 53
Whitaker, P. 26
Whitehead, S. 128
Wideen, M. 189
Wild, R. 128, 130
Wilkin, M. 166
Williams, E. 4
Williams, G. 187
Woods, P. 72
Woodward, M. 187, 201
Wragg, E., Wikeley, F. Wragg, C. and Haynes, G. 180, 182, 183

Yeomans, R. 81
Yinger, R. and Hendricks-Lee, M. 32

SUBJECT INDEX

Appraisal 169–183
  developments in management of 175–177
    as part of planning 176–177
    for all in organisation 176
    harder edge in 175
    visible outputs of 176
  dual function of 170–171
  effective management of 177
    establishing procedures for 180–181
    getting results from 182
    links with planning 182
    monitoring of 182–3
    setting climate 178–180
  introduction and implementation of 171–175
  purposes of 169–170

Curriculum, work related 4
Competencies 18–19

Equal opportunities **123–135**
  appraisal and selection and 134–135
  career breaks and 131–132
  changing context of 8–9
  changing ethos and 133–134
  extent of problems in 124–126
  gender and roles in 126–129
  implications for managers of 133–135
  mentoring and support in 129–130
  need for 123–124
  organisational factors and 133
  promotion and selection and 130–131
  role models and 134
  work and home and 132–133

Further education
  incorporation and 6

Human Resource Management **19–27**
  interpersonal relationships in 26–27
  leadership in 23–24
  motivation in 24–25
  schema for 19–22
  selection in 22–23
  staff appraisal in 25–26

Induction **156–160**
  characteristics of effective 160
  involvement in 158–159
  meaning of 156–158
  need for 159
Inspection, national system of 7

Leadership – see Human Resource Management
Learning organisation **31–41**
  creation of 34–39
    creating learning in 34–37
    creating structures for 37–39
  definitions of 33–34
  implications of 39–41
  origins of 31–33
Local Management of Schools 6
  and associate staff pay 9

Management
  of staff 9–13
  of performance 10, 17–19
    evaluation of 17–19

indicators (PIs) 17–18
individual performance, of **203–218**
  assessing performance 204–206
  managing underperformance 206–212
    disciplinary process in 208–210
    causes of incompetence 210–212
    firm action in 207–208
  merit pay – see performance related pay
  motivating performance 212–213
  performance related pay 213–217
    lack of funding for 216
    measures of performance 215
    money not motivator 216–217
    payment by results 215
organisational theory of 47
  bureaucracy 48
  collegiality 48–49
  culture and 49
  determinants of 50–51
  micropolitics in 49–50
  roles in **61–74**
    boundaries and 68–69
    definitions of 64–68
    positive aspects of 72–74
    taking and making of 63–64
    strain in 69–71
    theory of 69–72
staff development, and 12–13, **186–201**
  activities and outcomes 190–191
  adult learning in 189–190
  culture for 197–200
  evaluating 194–197
  identifying and prioritising needs 187–189
  implementing and monitoring 193–194
  planning of 191–193
staff morale, and 12
staff workload, and 11–12
structures
  academic/pastoral divide in 51–53
  determinants of 50–51
  in FE 53–54
  in primary schools 54–56
  meaning of 45–46
  objectives of 46–47
  salary structures and 56–57
  towards flatter 57–59
managerialism 16
market accountability 7
mentoring **160–167**
  headteachers, for 164–165
  in initial teacher education 161–162
  meaning of 160–161
  newly qualified teachers for 162–164
  training for 165–166
  whole-school impact of 166–167

national curriculum 7

open enrolment 6

recruitment and selection **139–153**
  contexts of 140–141
  evaluating effectiveness of 152
  importance of 139–140
  management of 143
    issues in 145–146
    job definition in 143–144

person specification in 144–145
selection 146–152
  assessment of candidates 147–148
  competency approaches in 148–149
  interviewing and 150–151
  people involved in 146–147
  structural approaches in 141–142

self-managing schools and colleges 5–7
  definition of 5–6
  in England and Wales 6
  reason for 6
staff
  appraisal and development of 25–26
  (see also: 'appraisal')
  interpersonal relationships and 26–27
  motivation of 24–25
  selection of 22–23
staffing
  needs-based 5
staff development, (see under Management)
stress,
  definition of 114–116
  implications for managers of 118–121
  individual and 116–118
  management of **113–121**

teachers
  use of time,
    classification of 93
    management issues arising 104–111
      conscientiousness and 104–107
      multiple demands and 107–111
    primary 100–102
    secondary 102–104
  work,
    changes in 98–99
    conceptualisation of 94–96
    main categories of 96–98
    structural changes in 98–99
teams **76–89**
  conflict in 77–80
  feminine management styles in 85–86
  limitations of 82–84
  Maori approach to 88–89
  teacher development and 84–85
  tensions in 86–87
  theories about 80–82
  towards effectiveness in 87–88

work, changing context of 3–5